Fundamentals for Self-Taught Programmers

Embark on your software engineering journey without exhaustive courses and bulky tutorials

Jasmine Greenaway

‹packt›

BIRMINGHAM—MUMBAI

Fundamentals for Self-Taught Programmers

Group Product Manager: Gebin George

Senior Editor: Rohit Singh

Technical Editor: Jubit Pincy

Copy Editor: Safis Editing

Project Coordinator: Deeksha Thakkar

Proofreader: Safis Editing

Indexer: Tejal Daruwale Soni

Production Designer: Prashant Ghare

Developer Relations Marketing Executives: Sonia Chauhan and Rayyan Khan

First published: May 2023

Production reference: 1070423

Published by Packt Publishing Ltd.
Livery Place
35 Livery Street
Birmingham
B3 2PB, UK.

ISBN 978-1-80181-211-5

www.packtpub.com

Thanks for listening to all my incessant begging about getting a computer many years ago, mom. I'm so glad you finally said yes. This is dedicated to you and Colleen for helping me get to where I am today.

– Jasmine Greenaway

Contributors

About the author

Jasmine Greenaway is a New York City-based technologist, software engineering instructor, speaker, and technical community organizer. Her background is in full-stack web development with experience across multiple industries. Jasmine graduated from Embry-Riddle Aeronautical University in Daytona Beach, Florida, with a BS in software engineering in 2011, and graduated with an MS in software engineering from the University of West Florida in 2016.

Jasmine has a passion for helping newcomers to tech, understanding the struggles of what it takes to get started and stay motivated. She is currently working at Microsoft and teaches programming and computer science fundamentals at local colleges in the New York City area.

About the reviewer

Dmitry Vostokov started as a self-taught developer in FORTRAN and PDP-11 assembly language during chemistry studies at Moscow State University and finally got an MSc in software engineering 20 years later. He is now an author with over 50 books on software diagnostics, anomaly detection and analysis, memory forensics, root cause analysis and problem-solving, memory dump analysis, debugging, software trace and log analysis, reverse engineering, and malware analysis. Vostokov also founded the pattern-oriented software diagnostics discipline and Software Diagnostics Institute. In addition, he has over 30 years of experience in various industries in software architecture, design, development, and maintenance. He lives in Dublin, Ireland.

Table of Contents

Part 1: Software Engineering Basics

1

Defining Software Engineering   **3**

2

The Software Engineering Life Cycle   **11**

3

Roles in Software Engineering 27

Part 2: Introduction to Programming

4

Programming Languages and Introduction to C# 39

5

Writing Your First C# Program   59

6

Data Types in C#   79

7

Flow Control in C#   97

8

Introduction to Data Structures, Algorithms, and Pseudocode   115

9

Applying Algorithms in C#   131

13

Tips and Tricks to Kickstart Your Software Engineering Career   201

Assessments   217

Preface

Welcome to the world of software development! In the years that I have taught technical courses that focus on programming, I have discovered that a lot of what we learn is focused on the *how* or *why* of software engineering, but not *what* it is exactly. If you're curious about the profession or about learning how to code, I have written this book for you. After completing this book, you'll be able to answer the question, "What does it mean to be a programmer?"

Many of my students are nervous on the first day of any of my courses. They think, "We'll be doing a lot of math!" or "I'm not smart enough for this." For those not pursuing a degree, there's this belief that it's a complex subject only for college-educated individuals. It comes off as an intimidating subject, but it's a skill that takes practice, just like any other.

I think about how these misconceptions have barred many brilliant minds from the potential of a promising career or creating something meaningful. If this has been something you have felt and experienced, it's not your fault. You can start here.

Here are a few things I hope you consider when reading this book:

- **Focus on the foundations, and you will continue to build your skills**. With so much information that is easily accessible to us today, it can feel like there's so much to learn. There is not one professional software engineer who knows everything about programming. What they *do* know are the basics, which enable them to learn and try new things.

- **Take all the time you need to build this new skill. Be patient with your progress**. Don't compare yourself to others. This is your own path.

- **Always stay inspired, stretching your imagination and creativity**. Draw inspiration from *Chapter 11, Stories from Prominent Job Roles in Software Development*, which has incredible stories from actual software engineers. I hope some of their thoughts and challenges resonate with you.

- **You can be a successful programmer without math or a computer science degree.**

Who this book is for

This book is for anyone interested in the topics of software development and software engineering, including those who want to turn it into a career. You do not need to know how to code to read this book.

What this book covers

Chapter 1, Defining Software Engineering, introduces the topics of computer science and software engineering at a high level. It will explain the relationship between the two, as well as describe the discipline of software engineering and the practices that it typically entails.

Chapter 2, The Software Engineering Life Cycle, takes a deeper dive into the practice of software engineering by splitting the practices into six pillars: planning, design, implementation, testing, deployment, and maintenance.

Chapter 3, Roles in Software Engineering, provides insight into common roles found in a software engineering team through a fictitious story about a team working on a project called Coder Bank.

Chapter 4, Programming Languages and Introduction to C#, offers an introduction to popular programming languages and the types of software they are typically used to build. The chapter then shifts focus to the .NET platform and the C# language.

Chapter 5, Writing Your First C# Program, introduces a hands-on approach to the C# language and writing a console application.

Chapter 6, Data Types in C#, explores variables, the various types of data that can be stored in them, and when and how they're used.

Chapter 7, Flow Control in C#, covers how to control which lines of code will run in your program with branching, method, and loop flow control statements.

Chapter 8, Introduction to Data Structures, Algorithms, and Pseudocode, introduces the basic concepts of data structures and algorithms and their common types, and how to implement them with pseudocode.

Chapter 9, Applying Algorithms in C#, teaches you how to write the algorithms from *Chapter 8* in C#, and then teaches you how to build your own.

Chapter 10, Object-Oriented Programming, covers why, when, and how to apply object-oriented programming to your C# programs.

Chapter 11, Stories from Prominent Job Roles in Software Development, presents a candid and transparent view of eight real software engineers who have been interviewed to share their backgrounds and what they do in their current roles.

Chapter 12, Coding Best Practices, includes practices and techniques that keep code readable and reusable.

Chapter 13, Tips and Tricks to Kickstart Your Software Engineering Career, explains what it takes to break into the industry and how to prepare.

To get the most out of this book

You will be getting started in the C# language in *Chapter 5, Writing Your First C# Program*. By then, you'll understand the purpose of the tools you'll be installing, which are listed in the following table. A laptop or desktop computer is recommended.

Software/hardware covered in the book	Operating system requirements
.NET 7 or higher	Windows, macOS, or Linux
Visual Studio Code	Windows, macOS, or Linux

If you are using the digital version of this book, we advise you to type the code yourself or access the code from the book's GitHub repository (a link is available in the next section). Doing so will help you avoid any potential errors related to the copying and pasting of code.

After reading this book, go to Microsoft's learning platform located at `https://docs.com` and continue to build on the C# foundations you have gained in this book through interactive tutorials and projects.

Download the example code files

You can download the example code files for this book from GitHub at `https://github.com/PacktPublishing/Fundamentals-for-Self-Taught-Programmers`. If there's an update to the code, it will be updated in the GitHub repository.

We also have other code bundles from our rich catalog of books and videos available at `https://github.com/PacktPublishing/`. Check them out!

Download the color images

We also provide a PDF file that has color images of the screenshots and diagrams used in this book. You can download it here: `https://packt.link/vxkKr`.

Conventions used

There are a number of text conventions used throughout this book.

`Code in text`: Indicates code words in text, database table names, folder names, filenames, file extensions, pathnames, dummy URLs, user input, and Twitter handles. Here is an example: "Nesting can be a useful tool in building algorithms and can be used with other statements, such as `if..else`. Let's use nesting here by adding another `for` loop."

A block of code is set as follows:

```
for (int i = 1; i <= 10; i++) {
    Console.WriteLine(i);
}
```

Any command-line input or output is written as follows:

```
dotnet new console -o MyFirstApp
```

Bold: Indicates a new term, an important word, or words that you see onscreen. For instance, words in menus or dialog boxes appear in **bold**. Here is an example: "When a programmer writes a program, they need to follow the **syntax**, which are the rules for how the software can be written."

> **Tips or important notes**
> Appear like this.

Get in touch

Feedback from our readers is always welcome.

General feedback: If you have questions about any aspect of this book, email us at customercare@packtpub.com and mention the book title in the subject of your message.

Errata: Although we have taken every care to ensure the accuracy of our content, mistakes do happen. If you have found a mistake in this book, we would be grateful if you would report this to us. Please visit www.packtpub.com/support/errata and fill in the form.

Piracy: If you come across any illegal copies of our works in any form on the internet, we would be grateful if you would provide us with the location address or website name. Please contact us at copyright@packt.com with a link to the material.

If you are interested in becoming an author: If there is a topic that you have expertise in and you are interested in either writing or contributing to a book, please visit authors.packtpub.com.

Share Your Thoughts

Once you've read *Fundamentals for Self-Taught Programmers*, we'd love to hear your thoughts! Scan the QR code below to go straight to the Amazon review page for this book and share your feedback.

https://packt.link/r/ 1-801-81211-X

Your review is important to us and the tech community and will help us make sure we're delivering excellent quality content.

Download a free PDF copy of this book

Thanks for purchasing this book!

Do you like to read on the go but are unable to carry your print books everywhere? Is your eBook purchase not compatible with the device of your choice?

Don't worry, now with every Packt book you get a DRM-free PDF version of that book at no cost.

Read anywhere, any place, on any device. Search, copy, and paste code from your favorite technical books directly into your application.

The perks don't stop there, you can get exclusive access to discounts, newsletters, and great free content in your inbox daily

Follow these simple steps to get the benefits:

1. Scan the QR code or visit the link below

https://packt.link/free-ebook/9781801812115

2. Submit your proof of purchase
3. That's it! We'll send your free PDF and other benefits to your email directly

Part 1:
Software Engineering Basics

This part introduces the discipline of software engineering as a subset of computer science and provides an overview of the common practices and roles in software engineering.

This part has the following chapters:

- *Chapter 1, Defining Software Engineering*
- *Chapter 2, The Software Engineering Life Cycle*
- *Chapter 3, Roles in Software Engineering*

1
Defining Software Engineering

Think of one of your favorite or one of the most memorable types of software that you have used or use often, something that runs on your mobile phone, computer, browser, or game console. Imagine the first day the team that created it got together to get started on it; how did they go from a blank slate on day 1 to creating something you enjoy using? The team could have started coding at the beginning, but how would they know what they were building? There are many questions to answer before a team can get started on a software project. Software that serves the purpose it was intended for, for a long time, and without failure can be defined as high-quality. Building high-quality software consists of thoughtful decisions to make sure these requirements are met. The creators of your favorite software probably didn't immediately put all their efforts into writing the code on that first day. Instead, they likely carefully planned how to create and deliver software that someone like you would enjoy. The effort that the team took to make quality software is a discipline within computer science called software engineering.

You may now be wondering how creating software relates to engineering. This chapter will answer this question by defining computer science and software engineering and exploring the relationship between the two. Next, we'll dive further into software engineering by exploring common practices within the discipline.

This chapter will cover the following topics:

- Learning what computer science is

- An introduction to software engineering

- Reviewing why software engineering is so named by comparing it to another engineering discipline

- The six phases of the software engineering process and the challenges faced by software engineers in each phase

By the end of this chapter, you will have an understanding of the difference between computer science and software engineering and you'll learn about the six phases of the software engineering process. You'll also understand why building software is an engineered process and how software engineers contribute to a project before, during, and after writing code.

Technical requirements

There are no technical requirements for this chapter.

What is computer science?

Computer science is the study of computational problem solving, where computation refers to systems built for the purpose of making a calculation to some effect. These systems could be computers, their internal and/or external hardware that interacts with them, the operating system and software that runs on them, the programming languages used to build them, and the mathematical equations and proofs used to make them efficient.

While computer science is a broad topic that mostly refers to theory, it also serves as an umbrella term for a vast number of practices that require computation, including the practice of writing code, also known as programming. One such practice is data science, which happens to branch out into multiple practices as well. Data science involves the use of scientific methods, such as statistics, to extract knowledge from and understand the hidden relationships within a given set of data. This practice includes building a model, which is a system typically comprised of mathematical computations that will take data as an input and produce a result as an output. This is usually an algorithm, which is a special set of instructions that achieves a certain goal and is typically a computer program that the data scientist may create or use. The output of a model is used to gain actionable insights from the data and is often used to "teach" the model how to produce a more precise output.

The use of models feeds into another practice called machine learning, which focuses on creating models to uncover meaningful information and patterns from data to support rational decisions. Machine learning is a subset of artificial intelligence, where acquired knowledge, such as data, is applied and used to make rational decisions without human interaction. A common example of this is using applications that adopt speech-to-text, where the application will improve and become accustomed to a voice over time, making the conversion to text even more accurate. Artificial intelligence converts your spoken words into text, whereas machine learning uses a model to confirm and improve on words it may have gotten wrong, and data science uses your voice as the data to make sense of.

As you can see, practices within computer science can produce their own set of specialized terms. It's common for professionals in the computer science field to have breadth in some of these areas and depth in others. For example, a data scientist may have experience building models and building AI applications. Computer science is a vast field of varied specializations but each path leads to computation for solving problems.

An introduction to software engineering

Building quality software is a process with a set of activities focused on creating software that works the way it is intended to. This process is defined as software engineering. If you look at the job description or listing for a software engineer role, you will find that the main requirements are that candidates have experience in a particular programming language, making it easy to assume that software engineering only involves writing code. The software engineering process can be boiled down to six phases: planning, design, implementation, testing, deployment, and maintenance. Software engineers are programmers who take an active role in all or most of the steps of the software engineering process. Making the justification for categorizing building software as engineering can sometimes be difficult to attempt when there's the belief that it only involves programming. So, let's make a parallel comparison to engineering a bridge.

Planning

The common phrase *"Rome wasn't built in a day"* rings especially true for any large project. Most successful projects take time, starting with careful planning. Planning is essential to ensure the team stays on task and that goals and milestones can be met. It is also important that goals are trackable enough to reach a defined state of "done", signaling when a project has been completed.

When planning a bridge, there are a few factors to consider before even beginning the design phase, one of the first being the cost. Constructing a bridge is an expensive multi-million dollar project and will need consistent and reliable sources of funding for building and maintenance. At first glance, this may seem to be non-essential information to an engineer, but costs can dictate how long they stay on the project as well as affecting their design choices. Something that a civil engineer may need to consider is the coating on a steel bridge, as it prevents corrosion from the elements, and they will need to make a decision on how to distribute the funds. They may have to choose whether or not to spend extra funding on a high-quality coating that extends the lifespan of the bridge and reduces maintenance costs in the future at the cost of limiting funding on other aspects of the project.

There are many factors to take into consideration when planning a software project: the technology used, the team, and the costs, just to name a few. Out of all things to consider in the planning phase, software projects heavily rely on requirements to guide the process. There are software engineering books that focus solely on requirements gathering because it is *that* big of a deal! In fact, it has its own field named requirements engineering. These requirements may come from various sources and have to be synthesized and communicated to whom it matters most. This includes the sources themselves in order to clarify that the requirements they ask for are actually the requirements that they want. Requirements are vital to a software project because they may dictate the team, resources, and technology that can be used, and murky requirements can slow down a project's progress. If a project must be built with a particular programming language, a software engineer may need to consider whether they will use resources or not and if so, how, specifically their time and funding for a project to get up to speed on the language and relevant tools to be able to contribute at an acceptable pace.

Design

Design is the confirmation and integration of project requirements. It's the first glance at what a finished product will look like and how it will work. The design stage breaks down the requirements into tangible problems, pairing them with practical solutions to create a vision for how it will all work together.

Designing a high-quality and safe bridge requires following a set of standards and specifications that engineers must adhere to. First, they need to design within their regional specifications, such as the **American Association of State Highway and Transportation Officials (AASHTO)** within the United States. Next are material-related design standards, which again may vary by regional location, such as the **American Society for Testing and Materials (ASTM)** within the United States. These standards also vary by material, such as steel and concrete, where various bridge components may be made of various materials. To be able to make some of these decisions, engineers need to know where they are building the bridge and will rely on inspections to guide their designs. If an engineer is building a bridge that is crossing a water channel, they will need a thorough inspection to investigate the risk of scour, or the washing away of naturally occurring materials in a body of water, posing a risk to the integrity of the bridge foundation. These and many other specific design considerations are collated into contract documents: a legally binding agreement on what the end result should look like.

Software design can be split into two categories: high-level and low-level design. High-level design focuses on the technologies and platforms that will be used, whereas low-level design focuses on how the decisions made for the high-level design will work. Because software engineers may specialize in a particular technology, the design stage is their first glance at where their skills will be used in the project. Here, they may own a particular piece of the project as the domain experts and be tasked with the design, delegating smaller tasks to other engineers, and communicating with other domain experts to design how their systems will all work together. This is common in web development projects, where software engineers may specialize in frontend development, or the visual and interactive pieces of a website, while backend development takes on the tasks focused on security and data management.

Implementation

The process of building the final product is one of the processes most of us can anecdotally recognize. If you have ever walked past, driven past, or lived near a structure that was built from the ground up, you will have witnessed an incremental change over time into its final state. What is truly being constructed in this step is the design that has been carefully planned and crafted, where it comes to life.

After careful planning of a design that has been thoroughly inspected and approved, bridge construction and construction engineering begin. Believe it or not, in the lifespan of a bridge, bridge failure is more likely to occur during construction than after its completion. Design engineers plan and calculate potential changes in stress on a bridge. For example, changes in traffic patterns will have an effect on a bridge's load. However, during construction, the components of a bridge will experience various stressors in tension, compression, and load that may be outside the range of normal use. Furthermore, temporary structures will need to be put in place to stabilize the bridge during construction. Bridge construction can be a constant cycle of strengthening and stabilization through decisions on what parts of the bridge to create first and how these parts all fit together to create the bridge to the standards and specifications that were designed.

Implementation in software engineering is programming, where software engineers build the software product as designed. It's the part of the process that software engineers will most likely spend most of their time on. The goal of implementation for software developers is not just focused on writing the code but also on taking the low-level design created in the design phase and converting them into code. It can be an arduous part of the process because coding takes time. Software engineers are in a constant cycle of coding and testing to ensure the code is working properly, efficiently, and as designed. It's an incremental and iterative team effort to accomplish building the end result with a minimal number of bugs and errors.

Testing

Testing challenges the fact that something is labeled high-quality or good for use and consumption. Here is where the implementation is confirmed to be working as designed. This cycle of quality control is a final pass at confirming two things: was the right thing built and was the thing built right?

Construction of a bridge involves building it to its designed specifications, where variables such as the external environment, load, and rate of fatigue are taken into consideration to make a sturdy and safe bridge. First, the components of a bridge go through a quality control process that starts with inspecting the raw materials that will be used to fabricate the components. This is to ensure that they don't contain any contamination in their overall chemistry that could lead to defects. When it comes to a completed project, the design may thoroughly explain how and why the bridge that has been built is in fact sturdy and safe, but is that really a fact when it hasn't been used yet? How do we really know it's safe? Bridges go through a critical period of evaluation to confirm these facts, where the goal is to assess all structural components and connections for possible points of failure at various loads. Methods for testing are categorized as destructive, such as drilling a piece of bridge material to examine its mechanical and chemical structure, and non-destructive where one approach uses a tool that sends ultrasonic waves to measure the thickness of the steel. These assessments produce ratings and measurements such as the safety margin that calculates the bridge's structural strength against its potential load to estimate the probability of failure.

The phrase "quality software" is a loaded term, because high-quality software really touches on multiple aspects of the software that has been built. **Software quality assurance (SQA)** is a set of activities that assess the requirements, design, and code, as well as the effectiveness of the quality process itself. While some of these aspects may be more of a priority than others, depending on the project and team, what this really alludes to is that quality assurance is a process that is visited at each step within the software engineering process. Yes, it's a process within a process! Quality happens at every stage in software engineering. Let's recall the examples we have seen so far: the requirements are checked for accuracy, domain experts work with each other to confirm that their designs will work together, and software engineers test their code for bugs and errors when they're coding. At this point, quality is quantified into particular metrics to measure and benchmark performance and efficiency. One common metric is test coverage, which is usually a set of additional code and tools used to test the code within the software to confirm its components are working as expected. This is then calculated and quantified into a percentage that signifies how much of the code has been tested for errors. The goal for most software teams is to reach 100% test coverage.

Deployment

Deployment, also known as delivery, focuses on delivering the finished product. Handing it over is not as simple as it seems; whether incremental or immediate, there may be additional steps to take before and after to ensure a smooth transition. Deployments may introduce a big change that has an effect on the people that will use it, or other things that may depend on it, and vice versa. With any large project, there can be multiple unexpected complications in the final delivery and the task may fall on the engineer to reduce these chances or resolve them when they occur.

Deployment considerations for a bridge begin in the planning phase. Restoring an existing bridge or erecting a new bridge will most likely cause disruptions in traffic, considerations that will be agreed upon in the design phase within the contract documents. This involves precautionary steps including mapping appropriate detours, carefully placing signs, warning travelers ahead of time when road closures are happening, redirecting traffic, as well as having a plan for opening or reopening the bridge. In the end, "completion" is an agreement that all parties involved have documented in a delivery and acceptance plan.

Deploying software begins with the tedious task of confirming every part is completed and has gone through sufficient testing. Although a team will design how it's built, how it's used, and where the software will run, they need to verify that the design matches the finished product and expectations on how users will interact with it. New or updated software can also involve changes in the systems that host it and the habits of users that consume it. Smartphone apps are a really great example of these changes; sometimes you need to update the operating system to use a new version, or even need a new phone that has the hardware to support it. Think about a phone app that you have used often in the past 5 years. The way it looks and the way you use it has probably changed significantly. Deployment is also the stage where consumers, users who are unaware of how the software was designed and built, may need training and documentation on how to use it. Not only do teams need to deliver the software but they also need to deliver information on how to use it and how to get support and report issues. Users sometimes discover new bugs that were not caught during testing, so providing information on how to be productive with the software helps manage user expectations and can uncover limitations in the software.

Maintenance

Many things that go through an engineering process will need some form of maintenance: airplanes, skyscrapers, space shuttles, or stoves, just to name a few. Built to "stand the test of time," maintenance makes sure they stay that way by keeping them safe, relevant, and robust. At times, this means starting the whole engineering process again from the beginning as maintenance can be a large undertaking that requires planning and moving through steps to get to delivery or deployment.

The lifespan of a bridge is determined mainly in the planning and some of the design phases, which affect how it's built and how long that will take. In the design phase, engineers make decisions based on cost, aesthetics, materials, and location, and will have to work these into regulated specifications. Sometimes, they don't have the financial incentive or enough data to support choices that will increase the durability of the bridge. An important step in assessing the maintenance requirements of a bridge begins with an inspection, using both destructive and non-destructive methods. Defects may be ranked from the most critical to least critical to assist with planning and costs, where some repairs may particular consideration depending on the design. Finally, any expected traffic disruptions may require scheduled shutdowns and signs.

Maintaining software is an expected part of the software engineering life cycle that expands to various activities, the most common being fixing bugs and errors. The goal of many software teams is to ensure the software is working well enough to not disrupt the goals of its users. This means that sometimes smaller bugs will remain until all the prioritized ones have been resolved. Adding new software features or improving existing ones include planning, design, testing, and deployment phases that make the code base larger and more complex to manage. While maintenance is the final step in the software engineering process, it is more of a strategy of how to preserve the quality of the software. Maintenance is a continuous set of practices that can range from collecting and addressing important bugs to rewriting the code of a particular feature. The software engineering process always ends with maintenance, which is an indefinite length of time focused on preserving the software.

Summary

We explored the field of software engineering, its relation to computer science, and how it expands beyond programming. Software engineering, like many applications of engineering, is a process that can be broken down into many phases. It's these interconnected steps that allow the software to serve its intended purpose for a long time.

Careful planning ensures the project will reach a final point of agreed completion, which enables a detailed and accurate design, makes implementation easier, provides clear testing strategies, and allows for deployment with minimal setbacks and maintenance. It all works together! So, while software engineers will code in a software project, they will also expand their awareness, apply their domain knowledge to all of these phases, and make a concerted team effort to deliver quality software.

In the next chapter, we'll leave behind the bridge analogy and focus solely on the software engineering process, diving deeper into the practices within these phases.

Questions

1. What differentiates computer science from software engineering?
2. Name the six phases of the software engineering process.

3. Identify the three problems that could arise in a software engineering project if a team skips the planning phase.

4. How can the deployment stage of a software engineering project get complicated?

5. This chapter drew similarities between civil engineering and bridge construction to software engineering. With this information, how can you justify that software engineering is engineering?

Further reading and references

- *Bridge Engineering Handbook: Construction and Maintenance (2nd edition)*, (2014), by W. Chen and L. Duan, CRC Press

- *Beginning Software Engineering (1st edition)*, (2015), by R. Stephens, Wrox

- *Bridge Engineering: Design, Rehabilitation, and Maintenance of Modern Highway Bridges, Fourth Edition (4th edition)*, (2017), J.J. Zhao and D.E. Tonias, McGraw Hill

- Microsoft. (2021, October 1). *Defining Data Science. Data Science for Beginners.* `https://github.com/microsoft/Data-Science-For-Beginners/tree/main/1-Introduction/01-defining-data-science`

2

The Software Engineering Life Cycle

The team that built your favorite application probably followed a process to deliver the first version of the software that was ready for someone like you to use. Have you ever sent a note to the development team, written in an open forum, or left a review asking for a particular thing to be added to an app? Imagine they saw what you wrote and decided that it was a good idea and should be added to the software. What happens when a team needs to deliver a second version of a software with more features?

As a start, most software teams hope to deliver software that achieves most of the main goals of its intended use, also known as the **minimal viable product** (**MVP**), as the first version of their software. Practices within software engineering are meant to produce quality software that can be used for a long time. Such software is adaptable to changes in technology, in staff, and, most importantly, over time. As a team approaches maintenance, the last step of the software engineering process, they may consider how the software will live on as there are many approaches to keeping a software maintained. This mostly depends on the team and its goals, the constraints of the software, and the available resources of a software project. Features add to the usability as well as the complexity of the software. Typically, they fall into the maintenance step because the software has already been delivered and is currently being used, which presents its own challenges.

Teams will typically plan, design, implement, and test new additions to the software to make sure changes integrate well with the entire product and enhance the experience for users. This is what makes the software engineering process a life cycle, where a team makes changes to the software to make it better. Believe it or not, your favorite apps and software all have bugs and improvements the team wants to work on! The software engineering process is only complete once the software is no longer being supported or maintained.

In this chapter, we will explore the steps of software engineering in further depth by detailing the goals, common practices, and indicators of success within the planning, design, implementation, testing, deployment, and maintenance steps.

This chapter will cover the following topics:

- Setting the scene for building software

- Planning and requirements gathering

- Creating a high-level and low-level design

- Developing software and implementation

- Software testing and quality assurance

- Software deployment and delivery

- Maintaining software after deployment

By the end of this chapter, you will be familiar with the common practices within the software engineering process. You'll also understand why building high-quality software can't only be centered around coding.

Technical requirements

There are no technical requirements for this chapter.

Setting the scene for building software

To illustrate the subject matter in this chapter, let's hear a story about a fictitious software application, an online bank for software engineers called Coder Bank. It was an idea created by a group of bankers who wanted to cater to the financial needs of programmers. These bankers, also known as stakeholders, have hired a large team to build Coder Bank. The software team of Coder Bank has some project managers who make sure the project is going smoothly. As well as this, they have software engineers to build Coder Bank who specialize in a variety of domains such as web development, mobile development, testing, and security.

Planning and requirements gathering

The planning phase is all about questions that can usually fit into these three buckets: what is needed and where can it be found, who is needed, and how many people are needed? Let's see an example of how the Coder Bank team approaches the planning phase. The team has their first kickoff meeting into the planning phase with stakeholders, project managers, and a representative from the software team, an engineer with the highest seniority. The team has arrived to gather information on what the stakeholders hope to accomplish. This information is crucial for the project managers to estimate how long it will take to build Coder Bank. The project managers, Betty and Charles, begin the meeting by asking the stakeholders to describe what they'd like to create. Betty asks, *"What is your vision for Coder Bank?"*

Raina, one of the stakeholders, speaks to the group. *"We imagine an app that coders can use and integrate into their daily lives. Our customer research suggests that programmers enjoy automating and customizing their software tools, and Coder Bank is an opportunity for them to do that with their finances."*

Betty and Charles exchange glances. Having worked together for a long time, they can read each other's expressions very well. They think it's a really strange concept but are not ones to judge. Charles types some loose notes on his laptop *"banking for programmers, automation, and customization."* In addition to taking notes, everyone in the room has agreed to record the audio in meetings for reference.

Betty replies, *"That's really interesting, Raina. What features do you imagine programmers will want to see in Coder Bank?"*

"Well, programmers want to see their balances in number systems other than decimal. Such as binary and hexadecimal." The engineer, Ada, is stunned at Raina's statement and can't imagine seeing her bank account in 1s and 0s. She quietly thinks to herself, *"Which programmers want that?"*

After some more discussion, the stakeholders require Coder Bank to have an online bank that is compatible with modern browsers, as well as a mobile app that is available on most modern mobile devices. While this requirement appears to be simple enough, Charles and Betty exchange glances again; they notice it is quite loaded with more questions that need clarification. Project managers have to be perceptive when meeting with stakeholders and they need to know what the customer is actually trying to say. They're tasked with gathering the requirements of a project and communicating them to the rest of the team; hence, they need clear and concise requirements so that everyone on the team understands what the stakeholders are saying. Usually, this leads to more questions.

Charles and Betty understand what they have to do: ask more questions to clarify what the stakeholders are asking for.

"What does "modern mobile devices" mean to you? How old can these devices be and what capabilities do they have?"

"Devices that have been released at least 5 years ago, have access to an app store, and have the ability to receive text messages and phone calls. It's not a priority for Coder Bank to work on devices older than 5 years old."

"5 years from when the app will be launched, is that correct?"

"Yes."

"What about modern browsers?"

"The top five most popular browsers used today will support the app."

"In the world? What about popular browsers used by programmers?"

"Oh yes, great catch. Ideally the top five most popular browsers used by programmers in North America, for now."

"Are your expectations that the web version and mobile app be launched at the same time?"

"Yes."

"OK, I think we have gotten a great start on gathering your needs, thank you. We'll need to discuss this with the team, but we will see you next week to talk through our progress and gather more information. We'll be in touch through email if we have any more questions."

Betty and Charles go through the list of requirements, then order them by priority:

1. Mobile and web versions launched at the same time.

2. Ability to use various number systems – Charles adds a note here: *"how many do they expect to see?"*

3. Mobile apps that are compatible with devices that have been released 5 years ago or less.

4. The web version works best with the top five browsers used by programmers in North America.

The list of requirements gets longer and becomes even more specific over time. Betty and Charles take these requirements to build estimates of how long it will take to achieve these requirements while continuing the conversation with stakeholders. During their meetings, the stakeholders ask whether they can launch within 1 year. They realize they'll need more engineers to achieve this and let the software engineering managers know so that they can hire more. It takes about 2 months before Betty and Charles build a definite timeline with the requirements. In the end, they have to negotiate a launch date of a year and 3 months with the stakeholders. During this time, the software engineers read the changing requirements, meet with the project managers, and build and design some minor examples of what they imagine the app to be. They don't commit to moving on to the design stage until all their questions are asked.

For many software projects, gathering requirements is a process of asking clarifying questions and understanding the customers' or stakeholders' wants and needs. It starts from a broad idea and turns into a continuous conversation that evolves with the project, such as in Betty and Charles' case. They were in constant communication with the bankers through weekly meetings and emails, and stayed aware of and cleared up any ambiguity in the requirements, which helped them prioritize the requirements in a way that would get their project launched closer to when the bankers wanted it.

Creating a high-level and low-level design

When a team has gathered enough requirements from the planning phase, they can then conceptualize how it all works together with a design that is used to help build the finished product. Having a good design makes it easier for teams to get started with coding in the implementation phase. Most complex problems are approached by breaking them down into smaller parts to solve them, and the same can be applied to software. When it comes to design, this process is typically split into two phases: high-level, which involves converting requirements into large functional parts of the software, and low-level, which involves breaking the larger parts into smaller pieces until they are manageable enough to describe how they work and will be solved.

After some back and forth, the Coder Bank team project managers and lead software engineers agree there is enough information to get started on the design phase. The project managers have decided to give them a month to get through the design so that they can present it to the stakeholders. The lead software engineers have particular specialties: the web, mobile apps, security, and data. The leaders of the team go through the requirements together and get started with the high-level design.

High-level design

The lead engineers have taken their pieces of the requirements and have made some decisions on how they will split up the responsibilities of building the software. In a meeting with the project managers, they illustrate these parts. The lead engineer, Ada, who has attended meetings with the stakeholders, depicts the details in the following diagram:

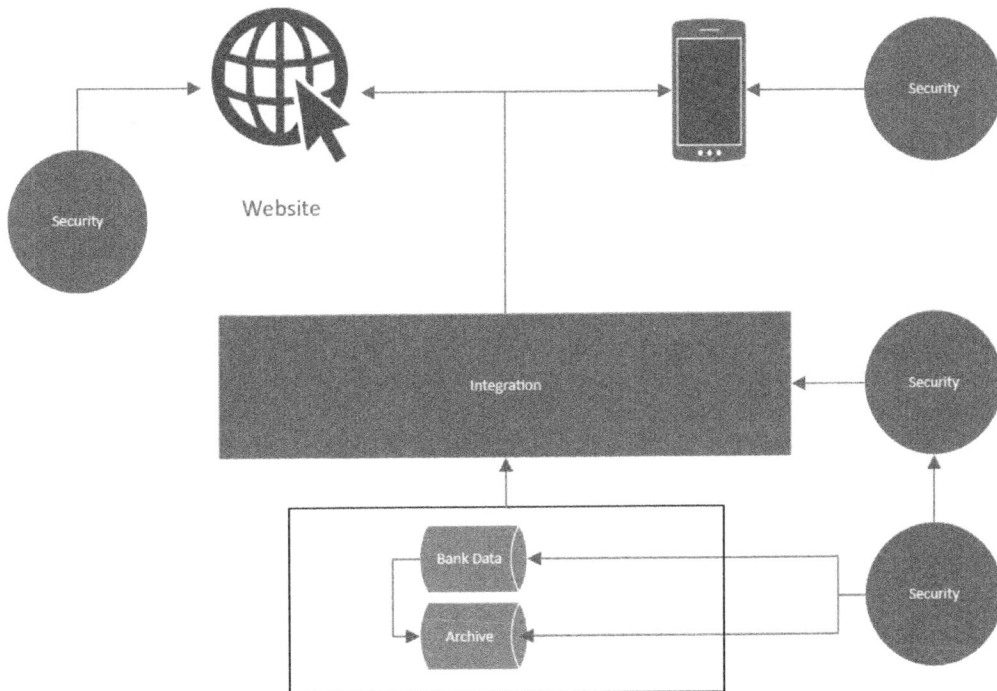

Figure 2.1 – High-level design of Coder Bank

"*Based on the requirements we were given, we were able to split up the project into five parts:*

- *Web, which will build the website*

- *Mobile, which will build apps for Android and iPhone*

- *Data, which will support databases for both web and mobile*

- *Security, which will work to make sure the apps, website, and data is protected from attackers and accidents*

- *Integrations, which will make sure the parts all work together where necessary"*

Betty asks, "*Why is the data connected to both the mobile and web versions, won't there be a need to have separation?*" The data lead engineer, Mary, answers, "*Having separate data would not be ideal for financial data, because we would want the user to have the same experience and have consistent information about their finances between app and mobile. Also, it's more manageable and easier to maintain one database than two.*" Betty also notices and comments on the security, "*But why does security have four separate parts for mobile, web, and data?*" The security lead, Larry, chimes in, "*Because each platform has different security targets to be aware of. This is financial information so we have to be very careful with how we manage keeping customers' information safe. We think it would be best to have coverage for Android, iPhone, the website, as well as the databases.*"

The team then decides to go around the room and talk through the parts of their high-level designs, starting with the web lead, Iris. "*On the frontend, the designers have begun drawing out what the website will look like and have provided us with the first version of a wireframe of what they're thinking about. Thanks to the project managers finding the top five browser software developers use, we were able to run some small tests to confirm some compatibility issues that may come up along the way that we will work out in the low-level design. On the backend, we have been thinking about the requirement to have the balances converted into different number systems. Since balances will come from the database, we decided to work with the integration team to think this through. We decided it's best that their team control converting the balances so that it happens in one place. This will reduce the number of errors that can occur from all of us having to convert it ourselves on various platforms.*"

Next is the mobile lead, Owen. "*We have decided to use a platform for building mobile applications using one code base. We decided to choose that to speed up the development time, and having one code base makes it easier to focus on the security of the application. We have also been sketching out a few designs for both iPhone and Android but they're the first version of the designs done yet. We have also been doing some testing on older devices to explore any compatibility issues, per the requirements, and we're happy to report that nothing has come up quite yet!*"

Next, data lead Mary describes the database. *"We'll build two databases: one that keeps current customer information for up to 1 year, and then an archive database, which keeps all historical data. We will build a script that will move any outdated data at the end of the day. We decided to have an archive because it's cheaper and will help keep the project budget low. The downside to this is that it will be slower, but not by much. With that said, customers will always be able to access their older data, but we have estimated it will take about 5 seconds longer for them to pull it up. Thanks to the requirements, we were able to generate 1 gigabyte of some sample data to discover what data the stakeholders expect to be stored."*

Larry describes the security pieces. *"We are thinking about how we want users to manage their login information. We definitely don't want them to only be able to log in with a username and password, so we will require two-factor authentication. Phone numbers are really popular as a way of providing that but we're unsure whether that's the safest option as phone numbers are often spoofed and stolen. We are also talking with the data team right now to walk through how we'll handle sensitive financial information. We're exploring whether it's worth having a third database that is just for storing personal information that has very limited access. However, this may be a challenge for customer service reps who are helping troubleshoot issues."*

Finally, the integration lead, Kofi, describes the interconnected parts. *"We're talking with all teams right now to stay in sync with the data team about what information customers will need to see on the page. We plan to build a central backend code base that each team will use to grab data. As Iris mentioned, we'll be handling the conversion from decimal into other number systems."*

Ada closes out the discussion with the project managers. *"We're all working through the high-level parts and should be done in about 2 more weeks. I will sign off on the internal pieces so we can move on to breaking those down into the low-level parts , and I will pass on finalized drafted visuals to discuss with the stakeholders. I don't expect them to have opinions about the internal pieces, but I will send over the high-level design we walked through today."*

2 weeks pass and Ada and the project managers present their designs to the stakeholders. They are happy with the way the visuals are designed but are adamant that they need a database just for sensitive customer information. Ada is grateful that she shared the designs with them early as, it would have been more work to resolve it if they had learned about it later! They redraw the design diagram and send it off to the stakeholders for final approval.

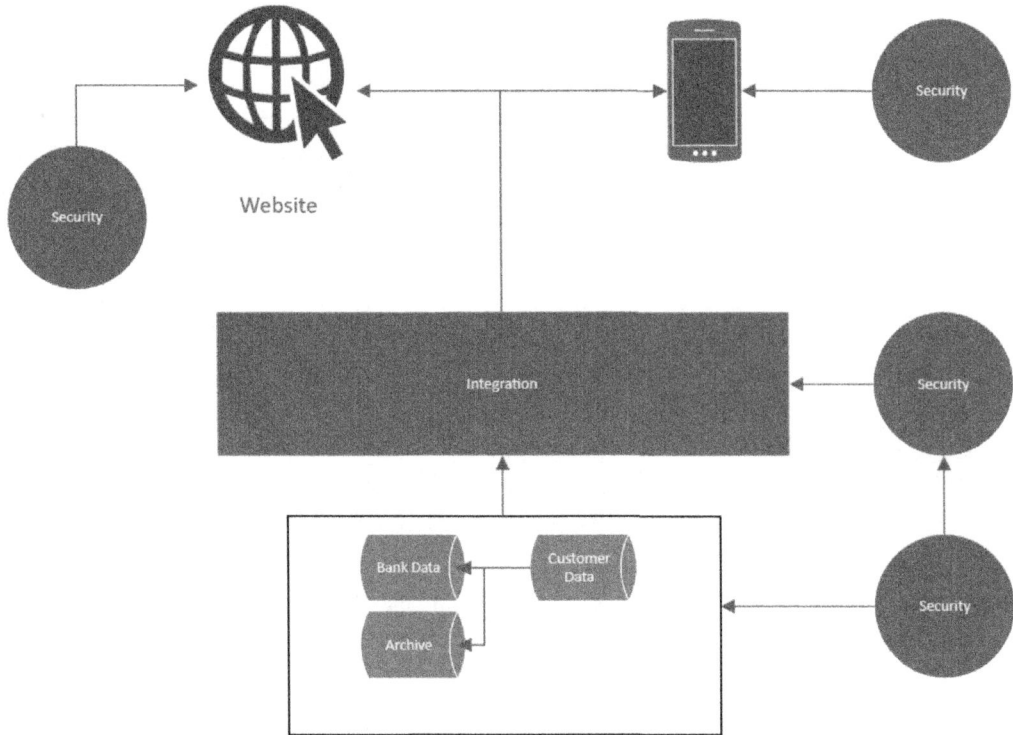

Figure 2.2 – The revised high-level design of Coder Bank

With the stakeholders happy with the high-level design, it's now time for the team to explore how these parts will work.

Low-level design

The lead engineers have broken down their respective parts into tasks and actionable items to build. They have decided to talk through some of the choices they have made with their engineers. Let's listen in on what the data and integration teams have decided to do for their low-level designs.

Mary has been working with the rest of the data team to review the requirements and the high-level design as well as make some final decisions on the technology used. They decided to choose a popular relational database for storing the customer data and have now built a diagram of what the customer tables in the customer database will look like.

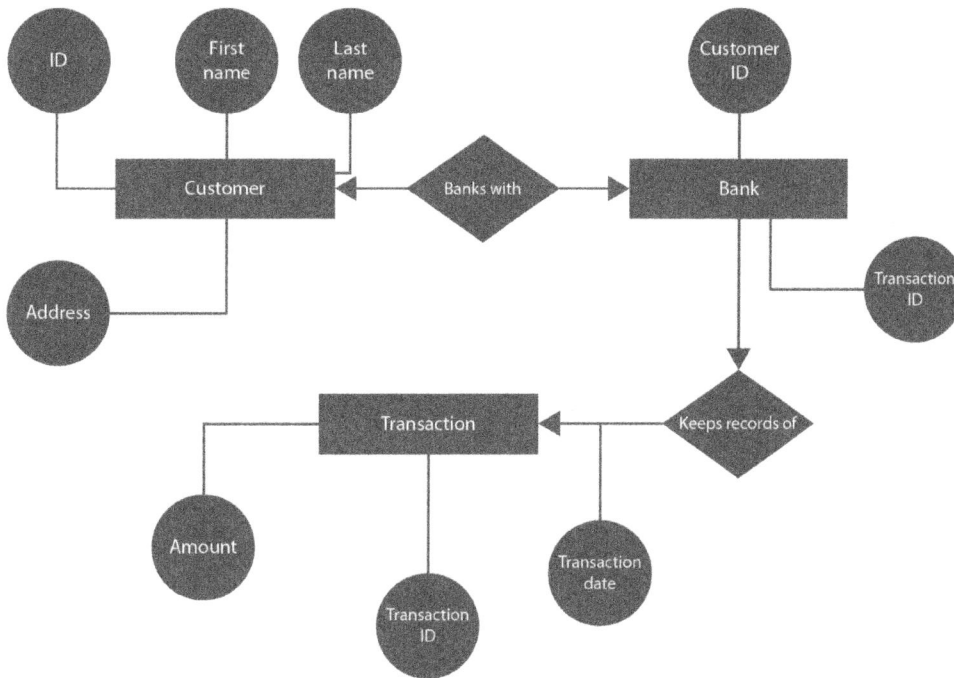

Figure 2.3 – An entity relationship diagram of Coder Bank's database

What Mary and her team have built is called an **entity relationship** (**ER**) diagram. The diagram visually details the tabular data that will be used in the software, and describes relationships the tables may have with each other. In the diagram, the squares are the entities or the tables in the database, and the circles are the attributes, which describe what type of data will be stored in the database. The diamonds are the relationships, which describe how the data in the tables is related. This diagram explains that a customer will have a unique ID, first name, last name, and address and will be associated with the bank that has their customer IDs linked to their transaction IDs. Each transaction will have a unique ID that also details the transaction amount and the date it was made on.

Mary is comfortable with the diagram and has decided to split up the three databases into tasks that the team will take on.

Kofi's team is tasked with writing code that will integrate with the data; their code will be how the web team and mobile teams work with the database to update, delete, read, or create new data. First, they have been working on defining classes, which are parts of the code that represent something or someone in the software application. In this case, it's the Customer class that they have been designing and refining. They have created some documentation to describe the Customer class:

```
Class Customer
Integer CustomerID;
```

```
String FirstName;
String LastName;
String Address;
getCustomerData();
createCustomerInfo();
updateCustomerInfo();
```

A class is composed of properties, which describe the class and methods and describe what the class can do. Here, in the `Customer` class, a customer has a first and last name, address, and a customer ID, and self-described methods that retrieve data with the `getCustomerData()` method data, create data with the `createCustomerData()` method, and update customer data with the `updateCustomerInfo()` method. Kofi is still thinking about what the process is for deleting customer data as it's normally complicated to close a bank account online. He thinks that he will have to add a method to do this but will need to limit its access to the internal tools used by customer service.

After more weeks of refinement and clarification with the project managers and the data team, Kofi and the rest of the integration team have designed all the classes they need and are ready to split up the tasks and start coding.

The design phase is used to identify *what* the key parts of the software at the high level are and *how* they work at the low level. As seen with the Coder Bank team, this is also a good time to ask clarifying questions and provide updates to the stakeholders who may have vital input despite not building the software themselves. This part of the process goes faster with clear requirements. This is also a great place to confirm requirements are being met and refined enough to move the project forward. As a bonus, design supports a faster implementation phase because the explicit details of how the software will be built have been planned.

Developing software and implementation

With enough information on how the software will work, it's now time for the part that everyone, developers included, are familiar with: implementation, also known as software development, programming, or coding. While low-level design documents how the software is built, it doesn't define the details of how. It's the job of the software developer to define those details according to the standards the team has set around the style of the code, which affects the readability and maintainability of the code. A common rule for software engineers working on a code base is to make sure it's built in a way that another engineer can continue the work on or fix any bugs that it might be contributing to. This means preparing clear documentation in addition to following the team's coding standards. Another phase that may take place while coding is testing, where it is common practice for software engineers to write additional code that tests their own code. A software engineer will often take advantage of tools to make their development process go faster and smoother. There are a variety of tools that they may use, which can differ between each team and even each developer. In this phase, we'll explore how developers working on the web, mobile, and integration parts work on their specific tasks.

The lead web engineer, Iris, has distributed tasks and has given Blair the responsibility of completing the login page. The web designers have completed the login pages with the textboxes and buttons, created with HTML and CSS. Blair has to implement the behavior of clicking a button, logging the user in, and completing the two-factor authentication process with JavaScript. Because the code to access the data is the responsibility of the integration team, Blair has received information from the team on how to integrate it into the login page, including a fake user account to use for testing. With everything needed to get started, Blair opens up their code editor and begins writing the code for pressing the button. After 3 hours, they successfully write the code for successfully logging in the user with two-factor authentication, as well as when the user logs in incorrectly. They submit their changes to source control, document their code, and write tests for it to make sure it's working as intended. When they run the tests, they notice a test is not passing. Blair checks and notices that the code for the login process has a bug, so they fix it, and after 10 more minutes of testing and fixes, the test finally passes. They submit their changes a final time into source control, plan for the next task, and end their day.

Owen, the mobile lead engineer, has tasked engineer Hari with displaying bank account transactions, a part of the application where the user must already be logged in. However, that part of the application has not been implemented yet, but Hari receives guidance from Owen on how to bypass that part of the application for now. The temporary workaround is for one specific test account and she'll need to come back and make it work for any account that is successfully logged in. The team also has a mobile designer that has built the visual parts of the mobile app. This is called the **user interface (UI)**. Hari will write the code that loads the transactional history onto the screen so that it loads with the provided UI. She'll need access to the database via the integration team, who has built documentation on how to use their API to load user data from their code base and load it into the mobile and web portions of the application. It takes her a few hours over the course of 2 days. She also writes tests to make sure her code is working properly and submits her changes to source control.

The project managers noted that one of the requirements the stakeholders wanted was to give customers the ability to update their own information. Because customer data is stored in the database, the integration team needs to provide a way to do this in the API. Kofi has tasked Opal with writing the code that allows customers to update their personal information. In the high-level design, it was stated that there would be a single separate database for storing identifiable customer information, and in the low-level design, it was designed in such a way that only specific engineers would gain access to it. Opal receives special permissions on her database access from the data team to access the database.

In the low-level design, the properties of the `Customer` class have the user's personal information and have already been written and are in the database. Opal's main goal will be to build a method that will load the data from the database, collect the updated data, and replace it with the older data in the database. She alters the `Customer` class to create a method called `updateCustomerInfo` and remembers that there is already a method called `getCustomerInfo`, saving her a little time in having to load the data herself. After using the existing method, she writes code to collect the new data and decides to submit her code to source control and write some tests to confirm the data she collected is from the correct user and is the correct data. One of her tests fails and she can't figure out why. She decides to take a break from it and come back to it the next day. She looks at it the next morning and notices her mistake, a typo!

After confirming her tests pass, she continues to build the code that updates the new data in the database, adds more tests that pass after some minor bug fixes, and submits her code to source control. She updates the API documentation and lets the mobile and web team know about the change to the API, as they will need to build the part of the website and app that will allow customers to make updates.

Out of all the steps in software engineering, writing code is one of the most common practices. Software engineers have different specialties, tools, approaches, and styles of coding to get the job done. In many cases, the job isn't complete until they have documented or tested their code. In team Coder Bank's case, we have seen that engineers write code to test as well as document their code, but different teams may take different approaches when building software.

Software testing and quality assurance

A bug is a failure in the way that software is intended to function and a common occurrence in a large code base. For every 1,000 lines of code, there may be an average of 15-50 bugs in it. They're impossible to avoid! Software engineers and users alike don't enjoy finding bugs in software. As seen in the previous steps, a team of software engineers will write code to test their software as a first attempt to catch any bugs. However, chances are that bugs will slip through and will sometimes be discovered through other methods of testing. Testing is also another point in the process to check whether the requirements are being met, which can be a test in itself. Doing this type of test for quality can be the job of a **quality assurance engineer** (**QA engineer**), another type of software engineer, who may be testing the code as it is being built and has a variety of other tests that they may run once code is submitted and considered completed. As bugs are very common in all popular software, it's impossible to get rid of them all. Your favorite software probably has bugs that you may or may not have noticed, that may or may not be resolved in its lifetime. The goal of testing is not to resolve all the bugs but rather to catch most of them and resolve the serious ones.

The project is nearly complete and team Coder Bank has a team of QA engineers who are working through the existing code base and checking the quality of the code. One QA engineer has been testing out the website, another has been testing the mobile app, while another has been tasked with testing security. With about 3 months left, their main goal is to find any major bugs that would provide a negative experience for the user or security flaws, which are always high-priority.

The web QA engineer, Jill, notices that the website is not accessible. The images on the site don't have alternative text or page titles, affecting users who cannot see them and use screen readers. Jill references the requirements documentation and is surprised that nobody noticed that it was not added as a requirement. She writes to the project managers and software developers that this needs to be addressed, "*Accessibility is, and has always been, an industry standard. We must never ignore all of our users and the way they interact with our software. This can have serious moral and legal consequences. This is a serious bug, we need to resolve this and add it to our requirements.*" Along with her message, she outlines the steps she took to find all the bugs. The web team uses tools to identify the bugs and resolves them within a few days. Jill takes another pass at the website and is pleased that it has been resolved. She finds some minor bugs but they will not get in the way of launching on time. The software team prioritizes the remaining bugs she has found and starts resolving them.

Mobile QA engineer Oscar has noticed some strange behavior on the login page: he clicks the button but it doesn't do anything, regardless of what he writes in the textbox. He doesn't think the code for the button has been implemented; someone must have forgotten to assign the task to an engineer. He checks the tracking tool the team uses to assign tasks and keep track of the project's progress and confirms that the task was not assigned! He sends a note to the team outlining the details and explains the steps he took to find the problem. The mobile team is able to resolve the issue the same day. Oscar tries again and confirms it's been resolved.

Meanwhile, security QA engineer Yari notices that while the login issue on the mobile apps has been resolved, when she adds symbols into the username textbox, she's able to bypass the authentication and log in as the username without the symbols, and it seems as if the password doesn't matter. She references the requirements to check whether symbols are allowed in usernames and confirms they're not. This is a serious security issue for all users. She lets the team know and mentions that the software cannot be launched without resolving the issue, in addition to a few other high-priority issues. It takes the team about a week to track them down. Some of the issues are due to bugs in the apps, the API, and the database, but they all get resolved and tested again with Yari's approval.

After about a month, all the major bugs are resolved. The team is now finally ready to launch and will now deliver the software to the bankers. The project management team excitedly lets them know that the project is slightly ahead of schedule and is nearly ready to be delivered and launched.

All engineers are aware that the more code they write, the more bugs they will introduce. Testing software is a valuable practice within the process because it's easier for engineers to resolve major bugs before it's released to users, making it a little less complicated to resolve. It's done in many different ways for software, where there are many more methods for assessing the quality of software outside of what these three engineers did. QA engineers provide a unique and valuable line of protection against serious bugs and work with software engineers to prioritize the severity of each bug and confirm when they're resolved.

Software deployment and delivery

Deployment is the stage where software is delivered and launched for use, but it's a little more complicated than that! Complex software, such as Coder Bank, will need additional details put in place to provide a positive experience for its users as well as a plan in case things go wrong.

Ava, the lead engineer, has been placed in charge of the deployment process and she has confirmed with the QA team that all security issues and major bugs have been resolved. She's also checked in with the project managers to make sure that all the requirements have been met. Things seem to be looking good so far, but she realizes that the documentation for the mobile application is missing information on how to update customer information. She checks with the documentation engineers, who are able to finish updating it by the next day. Now, things seem to be in place finally.

She knows that the first few days of deployment are going to be quite busy as they are deploying software that a bunch of programmers will use. She knows the number of bugs the users uncover will make the software better. However, she is also aware that she and the team will be staring at a large number of tasks to complete. She decides to shake the worry off for now and focus on strategizing deployment with the project managers Betty and Charles. She tells them, *"I think we should deploy one thing at a time. There are a lot of moving parts here and we want to be able to catch any serious issues before they get out of hand. Do you think I can explain my concerns to the bankers?"* Charles asks, *"What do you propose we deliver first?"* Ava responds, *"Let's start with the website."*

The three explain and propose the plan to the stakeholders, who seem disappointed but understanding. They ask whether they can deploy one of the apps first instead, *"Our customer research suggests that 80% of our users prefer apps over desktop or mobile web and that the majority will be Android users."* The team agrees to deploy the Android app first, the iPhone app the following week, and the website last. Before the meeting ends, Ava chimes in, *"I just had a thought, the code base for the apps is virtually the same; we outlined that in our design document. I believe we can launch both apps this week, and the website next week."* The stakeholders seem pleased with the adjustment and the team prepares to launch the next day.

While the mobile launch was successful, as expected, the app users found a lot of bugs. The busy team spent the next week prioritizing and fixing bugs, and they were able to resolve the issues and launch the website the next week. Unfortunately, the website had a few issues with its launch and had to be temporarily shut down while Ava and her team troubleshooted the issue. The issue was a solvable problem with the configuration of the cloud service they used to deploy the software but it took around 3 days to discover and fix. The team spent another week resolving the high-priority bugs.

Deployment can present its own number of checklists and challenges. When deploying a large code base, it may be beneficial to strategize how to provide a positive experience for the users and developers.

Maintaining software after deployment

The life cycle of the software engineering cycle remains in the maintenance stage until the software is no longer maintained by the team. Once the initial version of the software has been deployed, adding new features, despite them needing to go through the life cycle to be deployed, is considered maintenance. Maintenance is the phase that keeps the software relevant and useful to its users. Engineers keep it that way by prioritizing and fixing the issues that are discovered and planning for changes in the platforms where it's deployed. In addition to the software, engineers try to support the code base that is maintainable with clear documentation that is easy for all developers to understand and use.

In the case of Coder Bank, the forward-thinking planning of building a single code base for the mobile apps made maintaining the apps easier. This worked well when newer model of a phone came out and when there was a bad bug in the operating system of one of the mobile devices. After a few months of handling bugs, the team was able to take the time to make the website run faster and the code in the API a little more readable and better documented. They were initially deploying updates every week, which turned into every other month, and now is only four times a year.

Maintenance is a vital part of the cycle to keep the software usable and maintainable, until it's no longer used or needed. The Coder Bank team was able to resolve the influx of bugs that came with deploying a new app at a pace that wasn't too overwhelming and can probably attribute their success to the careful planning they decided to take to build quality software. They can now focus on new features and making the existing code base better.

Summary

The software engineering life cycle is a continuous and iterative process of planning and building quality software. Many teams adopt the process in their own ways and may give them specific names but they can be condensed into these six steps: planning, design, implementation, testing, deployment, and maintenance. Coder Bank's application of the software engineering process may differ from that of other software development teams, however, the practices within each step are some common scenarios that a team might face. Dedicating time to the steps prior to coding can produce a successful deployment and maintenance process; teams may sometimes need to compromise with stakeholders to keep it that way. To be a successful part of the team, software engineers will want to be active participants in all parts of the process to stay aware and active because building quality software starts with a good plan.

In this chapter, we have seen different parts of this project where the team had specialized experience that focused on certain parts of the project. In the next chapter, we'll explore these roles and talk about common responsibilities, practices, and tools within a team that builds software.

Questions

1. Why is it important for project managers to ask specific questions about expectations in requirements?

2. What is the difference between high-level and low-level design?

3. What are some common things that software engineers do when they complete a task while developing software?

4. Aside from catching bugs that were not caught in tests, what else can QA engineers do?

5. When does the software life cycle end?

Further reading

- *Practical Enterprise Software Development Techniques: Tools and Techniques for Large Scale Solutions*, Edward Crookshanks, Apress (2015)

3
Roles in Software Engineering

As seen in the previous chapter, large software projects will involve a lot of parts and will often require a team to complete them. Members of the team will need to take ownership over particular parts of the project, but how are they matched with these parts? The planning, design, implementation, testing, deployment, and maintenance phases have unique needs and problems to solve. Software engineers will spend most of their time in implementation, testing, and maintenance but may focus on specific parts within these steps based on their specialties. Software engineering has a vast number of roles and unique specializations that solve a particular problem in a project. Software engineers are able to take on various coding tasks but usually specialize in a particular type of coding. Building software also requires skill sets focused on technical planning and strategy, which are normally not the responsibility of a software engineer.

This chapter will examine some of the roles within software engineering that will typically be needed in a software project and define the specialties behind the roles. Because software engineering is such a large field, it would be impossible to list all the specialties. The roles that will be listed in this chapter are common, but will not reflect the vastness that is the software development industry. Furthermore, you may see the titles engineer, developer, and programmer used interchangeably. You will often see this switch in professional titles and job listings. It mostly depends on who is defining it but they mean the same thing: software engineers and software developers are programmers that develop software.

This chapter will cover the following job roles:

- The project manager
- The web developer
- The backend software engineer
- The mobile software engineer
- The quality assurance software engineer
- The DevOps engineer

By the end of this chapter, you will be familiar with the roles commonly seen on a software engineering team. You'll also be able to identify the responsibilities and specialties of these roles.

Technical requirements

There are no technical requirements for this chapter.

The project manager

The software engineering process, the path to building quality software, starts and ends with the **project manager** (**PM**). Project managers are sometimes referred to as product managers depending on the company. Generally, these terms can be used interchangeably. This chapter will use the title of PM. PMs get the project started, oversee its progress, and determine when it's complete. PMs are an integral part of any software team because of their technical, communication, and organizational skills. They'll typically have an active role in all the steps in the software engineering life cycle and may spend a lot of their time in one stage instead of others. For example, they may spend a lot of time defining requirements and understanding stakeholder needs in the planning stage, or they may spend some time meeting with key engineers during the implementation stage to get an idea of how long a particular task may take. The key goals of a PM are to determine why the team is working on the project, identify who is responsible for its success, and make a plan on how to get it done. Let's discuss each of these goals in detail.

Defining the purpose and requirements

When PMs meet with stakeholders, they'll need to get a good idea of what it is that they want to accomplish with the software. In short, PMs want to know why it needs to exist or what problem it will solve. This information helps them build out a list of requirements, which eventually turn into tasks and are taken to software engineers to build. Not only do PMs use this to identify tasks but also to define what would make the project successful, as well as what it will take to mark the project as completed. PMs will produce a document of requirements that can turn into an agreement between the team and the stakeholders that their needs are documented accurately. This will sometimes become a contract.

Identifying and connecting with key contributors

PMs are the bridge of communication between the stakeholders and the rest of the software team; they spend a lot of time interacting with different people. It's important that they build trust to encourage team morale and enthusiasm, as well as promote credibility and reliability to their stakeholders so that they feel confident that they have been heard and are capable of the task at hand. Working on a team brings a lot of personalities together in one place: there's always the potential for them to clash so PMs will be responsible for handling conflicts. Because they work with so many people, PMs will need to use their personal and social skills to move a project forward.

During the planning stage, PMs will typically be the first to connect with stakeholders. To understand their needs, PMs will spend a lot of their time actively listening to them and asking clarifying questions. This is a key responsibility for PMs as they are the voice of the stakeholders for the rest of the team. They're responsible for interpreting their needs into requirements, which are the desired outcomes of the stakeholders, as well as indicators of a successful project.

PMs communicate with software teams to interpret the requirements into action items. They will verify they're building the software as intended and that they're on track to build it in the agreed time frame. While they don't need to learn how to code to do their job, they'll need enough technical knowledge to communicate with software engineers, understand what they are doing, and understand the challenges the team experiences at a high level. When it comes to stakeholders, having some technical knowledge allows the PM to effectively communicate the progress of a project or be able to talk through how a prototype works.

Creating an adaptable plan

When PMs turn requirements into tasks for the rest of the team, they are also defining what it takes to get it done. The conversion of requirements into tasks may be recorded in task management software and shared with the team so that they can be assigned to engineers. While the PM tracks the progress of a task in this system, engineers in turn can record their progress on a task and mark when it's complete.

This action plan may reveal some additional needs and risks that need to be accounted for. For example, a PM may need to break the news to stakeholders that their large set of requirements requires more time. They also may be able to propose that the team hire more software engineers, which means that more money needs to be spent. They would also be able to identify whether there is a need for an engineer with a specific skill set to complete the project.

PMs also deal with a lot of change and it can come from many sources. Changes in staff, progress, requirements, and technology can alter the course or length of a project. For PMs, dealing with changes falls into two categories: change management, involving adapting to changes in staff or an organization, and change control, which is controlling the changes in requirements to the project itself. No matter the category, product managers need to track and evaluate the progress of these changes and confirm whether or not the proposed changes will have the intended results. Sometimes, it takes teams a few changes to get it right, which is a common process in software engineering and other engineering disciplines, such as bridge engineering, as seen in *Chapter 1, Defining Software Engineering*. Solving problems, big or small, may take some trial and error.

Let's use the earlier example that led to the PM proposing to hire more engineers or extend the project, and what would happen if the stakeholders decided to hire more engineers. The process of change management began when the PM evaluated that more engineers would be needed to deliver the project on time. Now that a decision has been made to expand the team, discussions will arise around the existing budget and involve asking stakeholders to define the salary range and job requirements of the new engineers to be hired. This change affects all aspects of the organization; whether the financial decision-makers adjusting the initial budget to include more salaries than expected and purchase equipment such as laptops, recruiters seeking potential candidates, or engineering leaders taking time out of their schedules to conduct interviews and onboard the new team members. As more engineers join the team, the PMs evaluate that the project will be on time by reprioritizing tasks and distributing them across the larger team. They also realize that despite the increase in staff, their timeline for delivery is very tight and that more requirements will cause the project to be delayed. They now need to apply some change control so that the stakeholders stick to the initial requirements. The PM may meet with them to agree to a prioritized list of requirements to meet their deadline and state that any new requirements can be added after the initial version of the project is released.

PMs spend a lot of time communicating, planning, and adapting to changes during a software project. Their responsibilities rely on a set of skills that convert requirements into technical tasks and navigate various interactions to move the project forward.

The web developer

Web developers are software engineers who focus on building websites or web apps. They usually rely on a browser to see the progress of their work and may use various browsers to test compatibility. The common programming languages they use, but are not limited to, are **Hypertext Markup Language (HTML)**, **Cascading Style Sheets (CSS)**, and **JavaScript (JS)**. Web developers may specialize in frontend, backend, or full stack development. These three focuses apply to various parts of a web application and come with varied responsibilities and tools. One of the main things that a web developer will need to understand is the difference between the server and the client. The server is a computer that stores the website, including its code, and the client is where the website is accessed, typically a browser. Frontend developers normally work on the code for the client, while backend developers work on the code for the server, and full stack developers do both.

Frontend developers

Frontend development focuses on how a website works in the browser. When you look at a website and press buttons on it, there's a chance that a frontend or full stack developer built it. Frontend developers work exclusively with languages that run in the browser such as HTML, CSS, and JS. Frontend developers make these languages all work together to build an interactive website. HTML is used to build the structure of the page as well as display its contents, such as text and images. CSS is used to change how the HTML looks on a page so that the text and links may display different colors and can also alter the structure of the page in ways that HTML can't. CSS does this by identifying parts of HTML and applying changes to the way it's displayed. Finally, JS has many uses but is primarily used to add interactivity to a page by identifying parts of the HTML and applying behaviors, also called events, to them. One common type is a form with a button at the end that submits information to a form, such as signing up for a newsletter or filling out medical information. A good analogy of how these languages work together is a house. HTML is the foundation and structure and focuses on how it's shaped, but it can look quite plain and doesn't stand out on its own. We can change how it looks with CSS and give it some color and dimension, but stills need a little more work to make it functional. Finally, JS is how everything inside the house works, such as the microwave or security system. Keep in mind that a frontend developer and web designer are two separate roles. Designers and frontend developers will use HTML and CSS to make a website look nice, but frontend developers also focus on website interactivity with JS.

Full stack developers

Full stack web developers focus on the frontend and backend of a website, the code that runs on the browser or the server. The next section focuses on backend development responsibilities. Full stack developers use HTML, CSS, JS, and a backend language such as C#, Java, or maybe even JS on the backend. Full stack developers may seem like they have a lot of tasks to do and a very busy day, but these responsibilities vary. Their wide range of skills can support various projects and sizes of teams in which there is more development support needed on the frontend or backend.

The backend software engineer

If a frontend developer is writing code for a browser, the backend software engineer writes code for the server. A backend engineer can write on many different platforms, but it's a common name for web developers who write code for the server or server-side code. Common languages that backend engineers write in are C#, Java, Python, and SQL. Unlike the frontend, you won't "see" what backend developers build. For example, a login page with textboxes and a clickable button will be built by a frontend engineer, but a backend engineer will be responsible for writing the code that checks whether your login information is correct. Backend software engineers focus on a variety of different specializations such as data, security, and deployments. Generally, a backend engineer will be focused on three things: data, building a way to share or use data, and optimizing the performance of the backend code. Let's discuss each of these focuses in greater depth.

Building the backend with data

In most software applications, information, also known as data, is stored and saved for later use. From calculators to social media, data is always being moved around and generated. Backend engineers focus on how to effectively **create, read, update, and delete** (CRUD) data. These four operations are common occurrences in data and are normally built into every software application. Backend developers will often need to build ways to do CRUD operations in a way that keeps the data safe and valid.

For example, if a backend developer is doing update operations with sensitive information, such as an address, they'll have a few options on how to handle this, some of which are required for the software to handle the information in a secure way. First, they need to think about who will access the data, which will most likely be the user to whom the data belongs. The engineer will need to verify that they are logged in as a user who can access this data. Next, the engineer will need to verify that the user has permission to update the data. For example, if this data belonged to a shared, joint, or family account, there would be specific users who should be able to update the address. Next, the backend engineer will need to write code that replaces the old address with the new address and verify that the data was successfully stored.

This is a shortened example of some of the things a backend engineer may do with data, but keep in mind that backend engineers can specialize exclusively in data itself. One of these examples is the data engineer, who will write code to make sure that the data is being stored efficiently. Handling data is a common occurrence for backend engineers, who often write code to share, use, and alter it.

Developing the application programming interface

Because backend engineers often work with data, they will often write code that allows the rest of the software team to access it as well. In some cases, they write code that benefits all programmers so that they can use the data in their own applications. The code they write is called an **application programming interface (API)**. An API is software that allows software engineers to perform CRUD operations on data. Software engineers use APIs by integrating them into their own code. They learn how to use them by reading the documentation on the APIs. Backend engineers build APIs as a way to share data with other developers because having multiple software engineers accessing data directly can be a security issue. It's generally a better practice to build a single way for multiple engineers to do the same thing instead of them building multiple ways individually. APIs can be found in a lot of software projects and there are many that are publicly shared. For example, the website Wikipedia has public APIs for articles. Normally, public APIs do not allow engineers to modify the data in any way, so they will normally only do read operations for public APIs.

Improving performance

Software that runs really slowly is not a good experience because it can slow down the user's productivity and can sometimes cause issues with the computer or device. Have you ever had too many tabs open on a browser or maybe had a lot of applications running and saw how much slower your device got? This observation can be measured as performance. Depending on how it's being used and the software that is being run, computers can use a lot of resources. Resources such as memory, which is how a computer retains short-term and long-term information, can affect how a computer performs based on how well the software on it runs and it needs to use computer resources wisely. Backend engineers will want to build software that runs efficiently and might end up spending a lot of their time exploring ways to make their code and, in turn, the software, run faster or use fewer computer resources. Backend engineers will sometimes measure the performance of the software with special tools that measure how long it takes the software to complete a specific task. Then, they use this to identify where in the code base to make improvements.

Backend engineers spend a lot of their time writing server-side code in a backend language where they will build ways to interact with data or make the software perform better. Backend engineering is a profession that has a wide range of specialties, platforms, and scenarios.

The mobile software engineer

Mobile software engineers write software for devices, most notably mobile phones. The most popular mobile platforms, iOS and Android, are separate software development environments that have some common themes between them. iOS engineers will often write in the Swift language, while Android engineers will often write in Java or Kotlin, all of which can be categorized as backend languages. There are also cross-platform options for mobile developers who want to be able to support multiple mobile platforms with one backend language. Mobile software engineers may also have specialties but can be categorized as full stack developers for mobile applications. The majority of them can handle all aspects of a mobile application from the **user interface** (**UI**) to the backend and serve the same purpose as other backend languages. While these responsibilities seem to mirror full stack software engineering by being able to work with the visual and backend parts, there are some aspects of mobile software development that differentiate it from writing software for other platforms and devices.

The UI

The average mobile app will usually have a set of views, or visual parts, that serve a particular purpose such as updating the settings. These visual elements will be part of the UI, which is the part of the application that the user interacts with. Mobile developers will be able to create the visual parts of an app with their tools. Most tools give them the option to use an editor that allows them to drag and drop the elements of a view or use code to place them, and sometimes these tools are a mixture of both. Next, they'll write code to set up the behavior of the view. For example, a mobile engineer who creates a login page view will then have to write additional code for verifying login information when the user presses the login button. Because mobile platforms come in various shapes and sizes that mobile engineers will need to account for, some tools are able to automatically change the shape of a view's layout to make it fit a particular device properly in various orientations.

Accessibility

There are about 15 billion mobile devices in use today worldwide, and it's a fair assumption that the people who use them have different needs for their devices. When it comes to accessibility, many features that support visual, hearing, motor, and learning customization are already built into the operating system of the device that will also be in the app. There are options for developers to enhance the experience for users. One such example in iOS is VoiceOver, a feature that helps those who are visually impaired navigate an app using their voice, where the engineer can write code to provide descriptions of the result of interacting with an element in a view. For example, for someone who forgets their password, a mobile engineer could add a description to a button that says "**goes to forgot password page**."

The quality assurance software engineer

Quality assurance (**QA**) engineers focus on testing the software to confirm its quality. They confirm the software is built to a particular standard and meets the intended requirements, as well as catching bugs and other unusual behaviors in the software. They will sometimes manually inspect the software or will write code that automatically verifies the behavior of the software. QA engineers build plans for testing, called test plans, that contain test cases, which are a list of conditions and inputs that should produce an expected result or output.

For example, if the software has a login page, the QA engineer must think about all the things that a user could do on the page. They could enter the username but not the password and vice versa, they could not enter anything, or even enter the wrong information. It's the job of the QA engineer to record and verify the behavior of the software and that it is doing what it was intended to do in each of these separate test cases.

Automating test cases

When a code base is very large, it can be difficult for QA engineers to be able to visit every test case manually, and they will rely on code and tools to do some of the work for them so they can prioritize other tasks and test cases. These automated tests run test cases for them and report the result automatically. These tests are normally common manual tasks that don't change often. If part of the software that is tested through automation is changed, the QA engineer will have to update the documented test case as well as the code to make sure that the test passes. These tests can span across all parts of the software, from the UI to the code, and the data. There are multiple programming languages and tools that can support automated testing so it will vary from team to team. Many teams will develop the software and test cases in the same language.

Logging and documentation

One important aspect of automated testing is the ability to report the outcome of the test. These logs are important for QA engineers to review to make sure that tests are passing. Sometimes tests that pass can be false positives, where a particular set of inputs appears to have the intended output but there seem to be some conditions that have changed the behavior. In the example of the login page, if an incorrect username and password were entered but the test passed, a QA engineer would inspect the test case to understand the issue. Having a history of the logs would be beneficial for a QA engineer to understand how long a false negative has been present in the test case.

QA engineers also spend a lot of time documenting the behavior of the software in their test plans and test cases. Between logs and other testing-related documentation, QA engineers generate a lot of information about the past and current state of the software. This history is beneficial in understanding how the software changes over time and provides the software team with a way to backtrack to the source of issues when things go wrong.

The DevOps engineer

Teams working on the same project are all working toward the same goal of delivering high-quality software. But with different roles and specialties in a software team, they all have different ways of achieving this goal. How do they all work together on separate parts with this in mind? A DevOps engineer, a title that describes a combination of development and operations, builds on a team's vision of delivering reliable software by building and maintaining tools that can be used in all parts of the software engineering life cycle. To describe the role, let's dive into the difference between development and operations.

Development focuses on building software, where a team will collaborate on writing code to add new features or fix bugs. Operations focus on keeping the software that is being built secure and reliable by making sure the requirements are met and that the software works as intended. In a team with multiple roles, it's normal for a software team to build iteratively, or gradually, the independent pieces of the software and put them together to see how it all works as one unit. This means that while the development team build, the operations team confirms the quality. As you can see, there are two separate focuses on the team, and while they both want the same thing, there's a lot of manual work to be able to do both.

For example, a critical bug that a software engineer has fixed needs to be manually checked by QA engineers before a new version is released. Because the server where the software is deployed is different from a software engineer's machine, it can't be assumed that if it works on their computer, it will work everywhere else. A common solution to this is known as a staging environment, or a server that is set up the same way as where it will be deployed, also known as production. What if the engineer forgot to tell the QA engineer that they fixed it? It might take a while to get the code into the staging environment, slowing down the process of resolving the bug. What if the engineer could notify QA that the bug was fixed by simply submitting their code and the new version could be automatically deployed to the staging environment and be ready for QA to test? A DevOps engineer could build something such as this, automating the process of getting new code into a staging environment and enabling the QA engineer to test in a similar environment before deploying to users, which they could automate too! They build tools such as these with many types of backend languages but some common ones are Go, Python, and Bash.

Another approach to DevOps is the practice of DevSecOps, where "Sec" stands for security and integrates security into DevOps practices. The reasoning behind this is that identifying vulnerabilities and verifying secure software can sometimes be an afterthought in projects. This can be a big problem in terms of time, money, and privacy, in the case of software consumers whose personal information may be leaked or exploited because the security vulnerabilities are not found until the software is already in use. This doesn't just apply to the software itself but also to the internal tools, equipment such as servers, internal passwords, data, and networks that software teams use and build with, as these can all be vulnerable to security attacks. DevSecOps provides ways to catch vulnerabilities early through automated tooling to catch security issues.

DevOps engineers build tools to ensure a team is delivering quality software, allowing them to focus on their independent goals while being productive by speeding up manual processes through automation. In some teams, this process can be defined as DevSecOps, where additional tools focus on keeping the software and the tools that build it secure to prevent security attacks on users and the team that builds the software.

Summary

There are many roles within the software engineering profession. It would take thousands of pages to capture them all and these roles are always evolving, such that their descriptions would quickly become outdated. In this chapter, we covered some common fields and their responsibilities. Let's recap what we learned about these popular software roles. Web development is where software is built for a browser and can range from interactive visual elements in the frontend to managing interactions with data on the backend, or a combination of both as a full stack developer. Backend software development can also be a role that is separate from web development because CRUD data operations are common in software applications. They also provide a way for other software engineers to do these operations by building APIs. Mobile developers focus on all aspects of software for mobile devices and will do similar work to a full stack web developer as they focus on visual and backend elements but within the context of a mobile app. QA engineers test software and also write software to automate testing to speed up manual processes. Finally, the DevOps engineer automates quality and productivity in a software team to reach the common goal of delivering quality software, which may also include keeping the team and software secure in the practice of DevSecOps .

These roles span across all steps of the software engineering life cycle and have a special set of unique specialties that create a software team capable of building high-quality software. You have now learned about some popular roles and responsibilities that can be found within a software team. The next part of this book will give you a hands-on approach to building software. In the next chapter, you will learn about various programming languages, their common uses, and get an introduction to the .NET platform and the C# language. This is the language that you will use to write your first program.

Questions

1. How do PMs work with software engineers?
2. What are the three languages that frontend engineers primarily work with?
3. What are some differences between a frontend and backend web developer?
4. Why would a backend engineer want to improve their code?
5. Why do QA engineers write code?

Further reading

- *The Complete Project Manager: Integrating People, Organizational, and Technical Skills* (2012) by Randall Englund and Alfonso Bucero, Berrett-Koehler Publishers

- *The Full Stack Developer: Your Essential Guide to the Everyday Skills Expected of a Modern Full Stack Web Developer* (2018) by Chris Northwood, Apress

- *Complete Guide to Test Automation: Techniques, Practices, and Patterns for Building and Maintaining Effective Software Projects* (2018) by Arnon Axelrod, Apress

- *Head First Android Development: A Learner's Guide to Building Android Apps with Kotlin* (Third edition, 2021) by Dawn Griffiths and David Griffiths, O'Reilly Media

- *iOS Programming: The Big Nerd Ranch Guide* by Christian Keur and Aaron Hillegass, Pearson Education

- *The DevOps Handbook: How to Create World-Class Agility, Reliability, and Security in Technology Organizations* (Illustrated edition, 2016) by Gene Kim, Jez Humble, Patrick Debois, and John Willis, IT Revolution Press

- *Hybrid Cloud Security Patterns* by Sreekanth Ayer, Packt Publishing

Part 2:
Introduction to Programming

This part focuses on the foundational pillars of programming. You will learn about various programming languages and algorithms and the basics of writing a computer program through a hands-on approach to the C# language.

This part has the following chapters:

- *Chapter 4, Programming Languages and Introduction to C#*
- *Chapter 5, Writing Your First C# Program*
- *Chapter 6, Data Types in C#*
- *Chapter 7, Flow Control in C#*
- *Chapter 8, Introduction to Data Structures, Algorithms, and Pseudocode*
- *Chapter 9, Applying Algorithms in C#*
- *Chapter 10, Object-Oriented Programming*

4

Programming Languages and Introduction to C#

You have probably guessed from the previous chapters that building software requires working with programming languages. We have already learned that software engineers are programmers and will work in a programming language based on the platform and the specialty of their specific role. However, there are many options for programming languages, so how does a software engineer decide which one to use? There are many reasons why they would choose one language over another, or sometimes know more than one. These choices may depend on their job, personal preferences, or the platform they use, but at the same time, some languages may be more popular than others for a particular task or platform. Some benefits of adopting a popular language of any platform are the level of support for troubleshooting common issues, documentation, and community support. If a software engineer uses a popular language, this increases their chances of finding other software engineers who use it, as well as finding what they need in an online search if they need some help. Sometimes, a software engineer may join a software project where a language has already been chosen and have a skill set that allows them to get started on it.

This chapter explores the need for popular programming languages and the platforms they're often used in. Like roles in software engineering, there are many programming languages out there and this chapter may not even cover all the popular ones out there. Next, this chapter will focus on one popular language, C# on the .NET platform, which is a multi-purpose language that exists on multiple platforms.

This chapter will cover the following topics:

- Learning the basics and purpose of programming languages
- Building browser-based software with web development languages
- Understanding multi-purpose backend languages
- Development environments for mobile and smartphone software development

- Building software with low-code/no-code platforms
- Learning about the .NET platform and C# programming language

By the end of this chapter, you will know some popular programming languages, why they are popular on the platforms they are used in, and some of the tools and terminology associated with them. Finally, you will learn what the .NET platform is as well as its connection to the C# language and popular uses.

Technical requirements

There are no technical requirements for this chapter.

Learning the purpose of programming languages

A programming language is a special language that is used to communicate with a device such as a computer. Computers accept information and instructions using the binary number system, which only consists of 0s and 1s, and programming languages are the way they receive these instructions. Today, most software engineers work with what is called a high-level language, a programming language that is closer to a language that humans can understand, such as English. In contrast, low-level languages are closer to machine instructions and the binary system.

The following example is a side-by-side comparison of a high-level language, C#, and a low-level assembly language. They both illustrate the common programming technique of declaring a variable and assigning a value, which is a way of storing information that will be used throughout the software program. In this example, they are declaring a variable called num and storing a value of 5:

Assembly	C#
num_five dq 5	var num_five = 5;

As you can see, creating a variable is a little more descriptive in a high-level language in comparison to a low-level language, which takes a bit more code and doesn't look like a high-level language. Aside from readability, developers often go for high-level languages because they tend to work on multiple platforms, such as web and desktop applications. Low-level languages are typically dependent on the machine that is being programmed.

So, how does a language get converted into 1s and 0s? This is done with an interpreter or compiler, which is a piece of computer software that converts the language into something that the machine or device can understand and carry out the instructions. There are many details behind how they work, but one main point to note about them is that compilers and interpreters are not the same. While both have the same goal of interpretation, compilers and interpreters have different ways of translating code, and how it's done will vary by programming language.

Defining common programming terminology

Now, let's define some terminology around programming and programming languages. These are common terms you'll hear as you learn more and begin to write your own **programs** and **software**. You may already have an idea of what programming is, which is the process of writing code or computer programs. A program is a sequential set of instructions and operations for a computing device, such as a computer or mobile phone, to perform. But what's the difference between software and a program? The main difference between the two is their purpose. Mainly, a computer program is the instructions for the device to carry out, while the software is a set of multiple tasks for the device and is normally for assisting a user through a task. In other words, software is a set of computer programs that carry out special tasks. A program is the instructions, while the software is the purpose of those instructions. Let's look at an example that differentiates the two: a computer program that multiplies the numbers 3 and 10. This can be calculated in a fraction of a second on an average laptop, but there's not much use for a computer program that only computes those two numbers. What if it was updated so that it does arithmetic with all numbers? It would still be able to do it quickly again but would not be of much use to an average user in its current state.

Most users will require a visual way to be able to calculate numbers, such as a calculator. To turn this computer program into a calculator, the programmer would need to build a visual way for the user to be able to enter any numbers they'd like to calculate. This is also known as a **user interface**, or **UI**, and is a common requirement for software that will be used by many people. This requires more code to create and that means more instructions. However, with a UI and a defined purpose of allowing the user to do math with the help of the laptop, this can now be defined as software. There are many different types of software; some may not require a user interface or may have multiple purposes. It all depends on its purpose and how it's used.

Writing a computer program requires a set of instructions provided by programming in a programming language. When a programmer writes a program, they need to follow the **syntax**, which are the rules for how the software can be written. Syntax is also something we observe in spoken languages with grammar rules that make it easier to communicate and comprehend what someone is saying. In programming languages, syntax rules are based on how symbols, punctuation, and characters can be used and combined to create programs. Failure to stick to a language's syntax rules means you won't be able to run the code and the program, which are called **errors**. For example, in C#, a line of code must end in a semicolon; otherwise, the program won't run because of a syntax error. Running a program means that a device performs the instructions written in a programming language. This is sometimes called **program execution**. Software that successfully runs does not necessarily mean that there aren't problems with it, just that the syntax rules have been met. Software is prone to human error, as computers only follow the instructions that we give them, and we often make mistakes. These mistakes can be defined as **bugs**, which are unintentional and unexpected problems in the software. When a software engineer is tasked with tracking down and resolving a bug, this is known as **debugging**.

Software engineers write and code by using a **code editor** or **integrated development environment** (**IDE**). The difference between the two is that an IDE installs additional software to be able to run and test a specific programming language and platform, while a code editor may require the programmer to install the programming language tools themselves to run it successfully. For example, Xcode is an IDE developed by Apple; their description of the IDE states "*Xcode 14 includes everything you need to develop, test, and distribute apps across all Apple platforms.*" This means that if you want to create an iPhone app, Xcode will provide you with all that you need to do it; you don't need to install any additional software. This is convenient for developers who are focused on a specific platform, but what about those who may be writing in different languages and for different platforms? Visual Studio Code is a great example of a code editor that allows programmers to switch between different languages. This is mainly done through **extensions**, which are additional software that a programmer can install to be able to run, test, debug, and check the syntax of the language of their choice.

Programming languages are tools for software engineers to build programs and software. Most will use high-level languages as their tool, for readability and the ability to be used on multiple platforms and devices. To run their code, they must use an interpreter or compiler to convert the code into something a machine can understand. For their code to run successfully, they'll need to follow the syntax rules of the language they're writing in to avoid errors. They'll need to do some debugging to find and fix unexpected behavior in their code.

Now that we have explored some terminology, the rest of this chapter will focus on programming languages, grouped by their popular usage based on developer surveys. We'll explore the topics of languages focused on web, backend, mobile, and no-code/low-code platforms.

Building browser-based software with web development languages

Web development primarily focuses on HTML, CSS, and JavaScript, where it's common that any website will have them, but may include other languages. The main platform for web development is the browser, where the user will interact with a website or web application software. **HyperText Markup Language**, or **HTML**, is used to create documents for the web and web browsers, where a document has a structure that allows someone to receive information. Using HTML alone on a website looks very plain, very similar to the text that you're reading; it's black and white and in a generic font. **Cascading Style Sheets**, or **CSS**, allows the document to have some styling so that an HTML document can have different colors, styles, and fonts that are easy to read and appealing to the user. HTML and CSS focus on the structural and visual elements of a web page, while JavaScript adds interactivity. If a page has a button that leads to a specific action, such as logging in or animation, there's a probable chance that this was achieved by JavaScript. It enables users to interact with the information that they're receiving in the browser.

As you learned in the previous chapter, web development can be full stack, frontend, or backend. Most frontend development uses HTML, CSS, and JavaScript, and involves developing the visual elements that someone will be interacting with in the browser. Backend development, which focuses on the server and is not directly seen by the user, might be JavaScript and another backend language. Full stack is a combination of the two, where the developer works on browser and server-based parts of a web application. Now, let's shift our focus to how other languages can be used in web applications.

Many programming languages have web development capabilities. Let's focus on two specific languages with support for web development: Python and C#. Python has a few options for web development. One is Django, a framework for building web applications with Python. A framework is a piece of software that has been built for a language to achieve a particular purpose, such as being able to make video games, make robots move, or build a website. A framework such as Django enables software engineers who write Python to be able to develop for the web. C# has a framework named **ASP.NET**, where **ASP** stands for **Active Server Pages**. Like Python, C# is a multipurpose language that enables C# software engineers to build web applications with C#. These languages all work together with the existing languages of the web and typically have a place in the multiple layers of web development. Let's visualize this by looking at an example of Django:

```
1   {% load static %}
2
3   <link rel="stylesheet" type="text/css" href="{% static 'polls/style.css' %}">
4
5   {% if latest_question_list %}
6       <ul>
7       {% for question in latest_question_list %}
8           <li><a href="{% url 'polls:detail' question.id %}">{{ question.question_text }}</a></li>
9       {% endfor %}
10      </ul>
11  {% else %}
12      <p>No polls are available.</p>
13  {% endif %}
```

Figure 4.1 – A template file containing code in Django

This example code from the Django documentation builds a small voting website. Django uses templates as the visual parts of the web page, which includes HTML and sometimes some CSS:

```
7   from .models import Choice, Question
8
9
10  class IndexView(generic.ListView):
11      template_name = 'polls/index.html'
12      context_object_name = 'latest_question_list'
13
14      def get_queryset(self):
15          """
16          Return the last five published questions (not including those set to be
17          published in the future).
18          """
19          return Question.objects.filter(
20              pub_date__lte=timezone.now()
21          ).order_by('-pub_date')[:5]
22
```

Figure 4.2 – A view file containing Python code in Django

The code in the `views.py` file is Python code that specifies which page should be displayed, as well as any data that should be displayed on the page. Notice that the `latest_question_list` value is in the `views.py` file and template document.

As you can see, these languages normally sit in a place that connects the interactivity with the data and backend capabilities of a language, sometimes using the same language as the backend part. This is where the framework comes in, using the language to create a connection between its capabilities and the web. This means that when developing for the web, sometimes, web developers will mix HTML, CSS, JavaScript, and languages such as Python or C# to develop a web application.

Web development is focused on browser-based software applications, where programmers will likely use HTML, CSS, and JavaScript to achieve this. Through the capabilities of frameworks, other languages can also be used to build web applications, where software engineers can use the language of their choice, combined with common web languages.

Understanding multi-purpose backend languages

Languages that are used for backend development are used for non-visual tasks such as managing data, improving performance to make the software run faster, working with hardware, making games, and much more. These languages are not normally used for interaction with users but will serve a purpose that will benefit them in some way. Some common backend languages include C#, Java, JavaScript, Python, SQL, and C++.

Backend languages are used to interact with data, by accessing the areas where it's stored and performing **create, read, update, and delete (CRUD)** operations on it. CRUD was briefly described in the previous chapter as common activities that are done with data. Backend languages are used to do CRUD operations and more with data. Before we get into an example of some backend languages that can do CRUD operations and more, let's talk about some defining characteristics of data. Data is a set of facts and information that are organized and formatted in a particular way. Consider a grocery store that has software that keeps track of the inventory of the store. The store manager is trying to find out how many eggs were sold in the past 3 days to see if they need to order more from the farm that supplies them. Let's walk through a backend language that could help the manager find this information.

Structured Query Language, or **SQL**, is a very popular language that is used to get data from a relational database, which stores data in a way that allows for parts of the data to be related to one another. Storing data in this way can be beneficial for situations where there's a lot of data to be stored; it makes it much faster to search for and collect generalized information about the data, such as sums and averages. Let's see what a software engineer could write to help the manager get this information from the database with SQL. First, let's look at the table of the egg inventory:

```
SELECT * FROM `sales`
```

id	product_name	product_sold	sell_date
1	eggs	3	2022-01-01
2	eggs	3	2022-01-02
3	eggs	4	2022-01-03
4	eggs	3	2022-01-04
5	eggs	10	2022-01-05
6	eggs	13	2022-01-06
7	eggs	9	2022-01-07
8	eggs	1	2022-01-08

Figure 4.3 – A SQL query retrieving all recorded egg sales from a table

This table contains data on egg sales, with the number of eggs sold in the **product_sold** column and when in the **sell_date** column. Each row contains information about how many eggs were sold on a particular day. So, because this table has eight rows, this information shows egg sales from the past 8 days, with January 8, 2022, being the most recent sale. The line of code above the table is called a **query**, which is code that is written to find data. This query displays all the contents of the table, but the manager only needs to see the past 3 days of sales. Let's refine the query to see what an engineer could write to show only the last 3 days of sales:

```
SELECT * FROM `sales` WHERE sell_date BETWEEN '2022-01-06' AND '2022-01-08'
```

id	product_name	product_sold	sell_date
6	eggs	13	2022-01-06
7	eggs	9	2022-01-07
8	eggs	1	2022-01-08

Figure 4.4 – A SQL query retrieving the last 3 days of egg sales from a table

This query is now only showing the past 3 days of data. It's common for other backend languages to use databases and SQL queries. This is how it could look with Python:

```python
my_database = mysql.connector.connect(
  host="localhost",
  user="myusername",
  password="mypassword",
  database="mydatabase"
)

mycursor = my_database.cursor()

mycursor.execute("SELECT * FROM `sales` WHERE sell_date BETWEEN '2022-01-06' AND '2022-01-08' ")

myresult = mycursor.fetchall()

for x in myresult:
  print(x)
```

Figure 4.5 – An example of a SQL query in Python

This is a small incomplete snippet of code that uses Python with SQL. Python is another popular language for data because it's great for managing repetitive tasks, such as running through a long list of information and doing CRUD operations. Because of this, Python also has many libraries, which are code that has been built to solve common problems that programmers can use in their software projects. This is beneficial because, as we have learned, a large software project is a set of large problems that have been broken down into smaller tasks. Some of these smaller tasks are common problems that software engineers face, and libraries help them solve them faster without having to write code from scratch to do it. The previous example would need a Python library to connect to the database to provide a way for the query to search within the inventory table.

Many backend languages are multi-purpose and can be used in various ways. You may have noticed that JavaScript is in the list of backend languages but is also common in web development. Node.js allows JavaScript to run outside of a browser, such as on a server as a backend language. JavaScript can also be used to make games, inside and outside of the browser. A popular library named **Phaser.js** allows someone to create 2D or 3D browser-based games with JavaScript. C# is another popular backend language for making games in Unity, a game engine that comes with a set of tools and libraries that allow developers to create 2D and 3D games or applications.

A unique type of backend language is scripting languages such as Bash and PowerShell. These programming languages build programs that run other programs, which is a powerful tool for programmers to have customized control over their computers and the systems where the software has been deployed. Scripting languages give programmers the unique ability to move files, run software programs, and interact with a computer or server. An example of this is a software engineer who is on call, where a dedicated engineer has been tasked with fixing any software or server issues that may occur during a software team's off hours, such as weekends. Typically, the person on call will receive some type of alert to a phone or device, informing them that something went wrong. In some cases, the issue could be resolved by running a script, where the engineer can log in to a computer and remotely access the server to fix it.

Backend languages have multiple purposes, though the user of the software may not be able to visually see what it's doing on the server. It provides ways for them to interact with data, interact with a computer or server, and efficiently use the full resources of their device so that it doesn't freeze or slow down when they're playing a game or have many tabs open in their browser. No matter what the purpose is, backend languages are essential in software development for carrying out a variety of tasks quickly by using the resources of the device or server.

Development environments for mobile and smartphone software development

Mobile developers, those who write code for mobile devices such as smartphones and tablets, usually use a multi-purpose language to create mobile apps. Common languages are Java, Kotlin, Swift, and C#. The difference between mobile development and something such as web and backend development is usually in the platform and tooling. Mobile developers often rely on an IDE to write and test their code. To recap from earlier in this chapter, IDEs provide all the software and tooling that a developer needs to write and test code on a platform. This is especially important for mobile developers as they're usually writing code on a platform different to where the software will be deployed. In other words, a mobile developer creates a mobile application on their computer that will eventually need to be run, tested, and deployed to a mobile device. Let's use the example of the Android Studio IDE to explain how this works.

Android Studio is for building Android applications, which can be built in Java or Kotlin. Both languages are used outside of mobile development, so the software and tools that are needed to successfully run a Java or Kotlin application need to be installed as well. The most important of these is the **Android Software Developer Kit**, also known as the **Android SDK**, which includes software to run, test, and compile the code. SDKs are a set of tools and software that enables a software engineer to write, run, and test a language or platform they are working on. The Android SDK includes the SDK tools, SDK build tools, SDK platform tools, and the SDK platform. SDK tools and build tools allow developers to write code and test it. Tools such as debuggers can be used to walk through the code line by line to find problems if there's a bug. SDK platform tools provide a way to run Android code on a computer, such as via a compiler, which will convert Java or Kotlin written by the developer into a format that the mobile device can understand and execute. Versioning is an important part of any platform, especially when it comes to Android devices. There are about 2 billion Android users worldwide with a variety of devices running different versions of the Android operating system. Some devices only work with certain versions of the Android operating system, and mobile developers need to be aware of which devices they are building for to ensure that the version is compatible. This means that, sometimes, they will need to install a particular platform version that is compatible with the version of the operating system. While this may sound complicated, there's documentation for the platform and tools that provides guidance on which platform will run successfully on a particular version.

Because these tools are all installed on a computer used for developing the software, and not the device itself, the developer will need a way to see what the application will look like on an Android device. They can either install a new version of the app on a device or use the Android Emulator, which allows them to view the app on a device of their choice, simulating what it would look like on a physical device. The following screenshot shows the Android Studio IDE, including the Android Emulator showing an app in development:

Figure 4.6 – An example of Android Studio, including the Android Emulator

(source: https://developer.android.com/studio/preview/features?hl=cs)

Note

This screenshot was reproduced from work created and shared by the Android Open Source Project (`https://developers.google.com/terms/site-policies?hl=cs`) and used according to the terms described in the Creative Commons 2.5 Attribution License (`https://creativecommons.org/licenses/by/2.5/`).

As you can see, different components go into building Android applications. These could all be installed separately, but that can become quite cumbersome and time-consuming. An IDE allows a developer to work with everything they need to develop for a particular application at once.

Other types of development environments allow mobile developers to develop for all mobile devices so that they can write code for both iOS and Android devices in one code base. Xamarin and the recent .NET MAUI use C#, while Flutter uses the Dart programming language to develop for multiple platforms, also known as **cross-platform**, with one code base. These platforms rely on an SDK to use the language and tools to create an app. You may be wondering, why would someone who writes code exclusively for iOS or Android, also known as native development, learn cross-platform development instead?

There are many reasons why a developer would choose a native platform instead of a cross-platform one and vice versa. There are too many to list, but it mainly comes down to performance and standards. Remember that code will need to be compiled for it to run on a device, and in a cross-platform environment, this can become quite complicated and take much longer to do because they are different. The cross-platform development experience can end up being slower in comparison to the native one. Another reason is that each platform has a set of standards focused on UI, **user experience (UX)**, accessibility, and more that can't be easily achieved in a cross-platform environment, where developing natively will have the advantage. Also, cross-platform development can get complicated because although there is one code base, that doesn't necessarily mean that the developer's job is done. They may need to pay close attention to the behavior of all platforms, including the platform versions they're developing on to make sure that it all works as intended, or write additional code to make sure it does.

Mobile development requires the use of special tools for developing apps on mobile devices. Sometimes, developing mobile software requires a variety of tools and components, where software such as SDKs, libraries, and IDEs make the process of getting started much easier. Cross-platform development enables developers to develop mobile applications with one code base, but it can also come with challenges in comparison to native mobile development.

Building software with low-code/no-code platforms

The concept of low code or no code is becoming quite popular among software teams. It's estimated that 70% of new software applications will be built by low-code/no-code platforms by 2025. One of the main motivators behind this technology is that software is often used to get something done and, sometimes, teams know what tools and software they would need to get something done but don't necessarily have the time to create the software to do it. This has created a unique type of software developer called the **citizen developer**, which is a software engineer who uses low-code/no-code platforms to create software. Building a software application as a citizen developer involves using a visual platform to create tools and software. A low-code/no-code platform can accomplish most things that any frontend or backend language can do, and sometimes, it's much faster. Some popular platforms are Microsoft Power Platform, Webflow, and Zapier. Let's briefly walk through some popular features of Microsoft Power Platform.

Microsoft Power Platform has cloud-based low-code/no-code tools and services for businesses of all sizes to build software. Power Platform is made up of PowerBI for data and analytics, Power Apps for building custom apps, Power Automate for automating manual workflow tasks, Power Pages for building websites, and Power Virtual Agents to create AI-powered chatbots. The following figure shows an example of automation in Power Automate. These are called flows. This flow is collecting email attachments from Outlook and automatically placing them in cloud storage with OneDrive, based on who the email is from. Manually downloading and storing email attachments can be a tedious task, especially in an example such as this where the user could be working with many clients. A flow like this in Power Automate enables those who are managing big projects or businesses to speed up their productivity without needing to build custom software to do so:

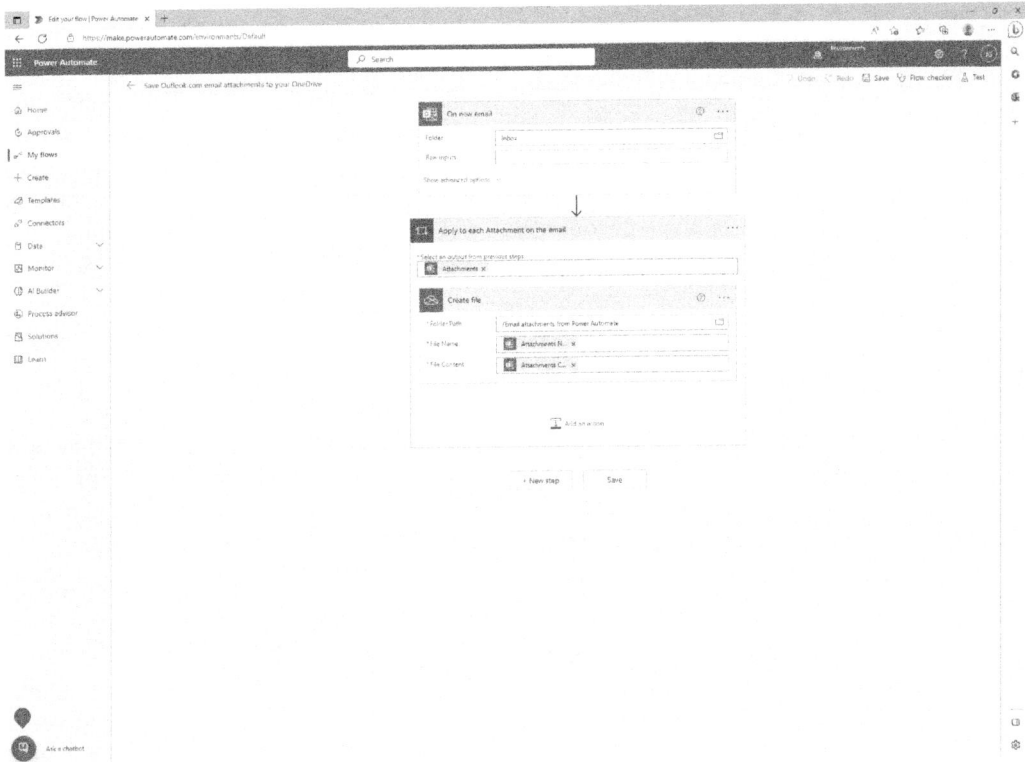

Figure 4.7 – An example of Power Automate, part of Microsoft Power Platform

The ability to build software with low-code/no-code tools does not mean that learning a programming language will be disadvantageous in the long run or that software engineers should worry about their jobs, but that programming languages have evolved. Earlier in this chapter, we explained the difference between high-level and low-level languages, where high-level languages allow us to write code that is much easier to read and work with. We also know that, sometimes, developers rely on libraries, SDKs, and tools to develop software. Low-code/no-code platforms can be seen as a combination of these technologies to build tools and increase productivity with software. Furthermore, these platforms are sometimes also used together with programming languages, depending on the scenario. It's also important to remember that these platforms are built with programming languages!

Whether it's a low-code/no-code platform or programming language, they're all tools that enable a software engineer to get a task done. They come with unique features and challenges, and can sometimes be integrated. Software engineers select the right tool for the job based on a variety of reasons and will specialize in one or more of these throughout their career to take on titles such as backend, web, or citizen developer. A beginner or junior software engineer will typically start with one language, except for web development, where the required HTML, CSS, and JavaScript technically count as three programming languages, and will continue to add more to their skill set and resume as they progress through their career. The rest of this chapter will focus on the C# programming language within the .NET platform.

Learning about .NET and C#

.NET is an open source platform free for any developer to use to build different types of applications. Let's define some of the important and relevant terms within this summary. You are familiar with the term *cross-platform* already, but what this means for .NET is that you can create applications for different devices and operating systems. Open source software is built in public and shared with the public, meaning that anyone can access it and use it for free. You have also seen the term *platform* a few times in this chapter, and it can have various meanings, where a software engineer's definition of the term will expand as they become more experienced. Here, it generally refers to where software and its tools can be used and found. A developer platform is a combination of software and tools that a software engineer or developer can use in their development environment, which is specialized software that is installed on a computer to create software. To sum this up, .NET is a free and open software platform that can be used to build many different types of software applications in various development environments.

As we have learned, the .NET platform enables software engineers to write applications in Visual Basic, F#, and C#. Out of the three, C# is the most popular, and you will see a lot of documentation and information on the language when you do an internet search about it. Stack Overflow, a popular website for seeking help with various programming problems, has over 1.5 million questions about C#. As mentioned in the introduction, popular languages have multiple community and documentation support options that help software engineers get unstuck from problems and will often have many libraries to speed up development time. Let's explore some popular uses of the language.

Popular uses for C#

C# is a multi-purpose language and can be found in many applications that span across different devices and operating systems. Web, mobile, backend, and gaming may be popular uses of the language but are not the only ones.

Full stack web development with ASP.NET

ASP.NET is a part of the .NET platform that focuses on web development and is part of the .NET SDK. Although web development can exclusively rely on HTML, JavaScript, and CSS, to make an interactive web page, ASP.NET allows web developers to use C# to build full stack web applications. ASP.NET includes Razor, which allows C# developers to write code that looks like C# with some minor differences as a frontend language and mix it with HTML to get data from the backend and display it on the page. C# can be used to build APIs, a backend task, with ASP.NET. Here's an example of a web page using Razor to display a list of pizzas in the browser:

```
1  @page
2  @using Pizza.Models
3  @model Pizza.Pages.PizzaModel
4
5
6  @{
7      ViewData["Title"] = "Pizza List";
8  }
9
10  <h1>Pizza List 🍕</h1>
11  <form method="post" class="card p-3">
12      <div class="row">
13          <div asp-validation-summary="All"></div>
14      </div>
15      <div class="form-group mb-0 align-middle">
16          <label asp-for="NewPizza.Name">Name</label>
17          <input type="text" asp-for="NewPizza.Name" class="mr-5">
18          <label asp-for="NewPizza.Size">Size</label>
19          <select asp-for="NewPizza.Size" asp-items="Html.GetEnumSelectList<PizzaSize>()" class="mr-5"></select>
20          <label asp-for="NewPizza.Price"></label>
21          <input asp-for="NewPizza.Price" class="mr-5" />
22          <label asp-for="NewPizza.IsGlutenFree">Gluten Free</label>
23          <input type="checkbox" asp-for="NewPizza.IsGlutenFree" class="mr-5">
24          <button class="btn btn-primary">Add</button>
25      </div>
26  </form>
27  <table class="table mt-5">
28      <thead>
29          <tr>
30              <th scope="col">Name</th>
31              <th scope="col">Price</th>
32              <th scope="col">Size</th>
33              <th scope="col">Gluten Free</th>
34              <th scope="col">Delete</th>
35          </tr>
36      </thead>
37      @foreach (var pizza in Model.pizzas)
38      {
39          <tr>
40              <td>@pizza.Name</td>
41              <td>@($"{pizza.Price:C}")</td>
42              <td>@pizza.Size</td>
43              <td>@Model.GlutenFreeText(pizza)</td>
44              <td>
45                  <form method="post" asp-page-handler="Delete" asp-route-id="@pizza.Id">
46                      <button class="btn btn-danger">Delete</button>
47                  </form>
48              </td>
49          </tr>
50      }
51  </table>
52
53  @section Scripts {
54  <partial name="_ValidationScriptsPartial" />
55  }
```

Figure 4.8 – An example of an ASP.NET Razor web page

The preceding code is a combination of HTML, CSS, Razor, and C#. Razor enables C# to be used with a frontend language such as HTML. The part of the code that starts with the @foreach statement shows the two languages working together to display every pizza with its specific details collected from the backend in C#, as well as an option to delete them individually.

Game development with Unity

Unity is a game engine that comes with a set of tools and libraries that allow developers to create 2D and 3D games or applications. In Unity, there's a visual tool that allows the game developer to test out the progress of their game and import assets such as images and characters into their game. They can write C# to define the behaviors of the assets, such as assigning keyboard commands to move characters, keeping scores, or calculating hit points. Let's see an example of a basic game in Unity:

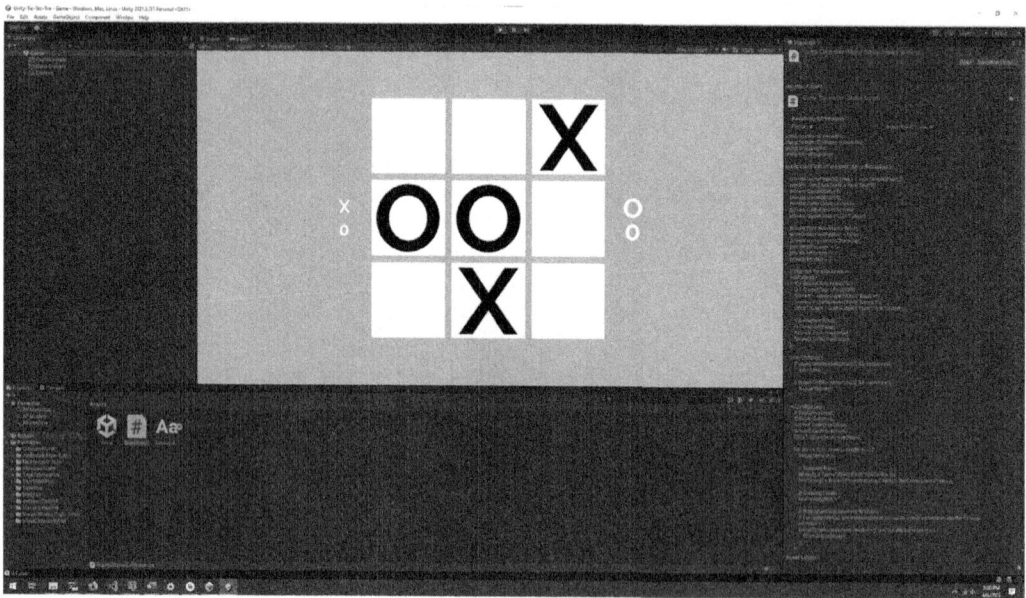

Figure 4.9 – Example of a basic tic-tac-toe board game in Unity

The Unity Editor has a few windows within it dedicated to building various parts of a game. In the center are the scene view and game view, where the developer can work on and see the visual parts of their game, as well as playtest it. At the bottom is the project window, where all the files needed to develop the game can be found, including the files containing C# code, which are called scripts.

Cross-platform development with .NET MAUI

.NET Multi-platform App UI, also known as .NET **MAUI**, is a new platform for building applications for multiple platforms in C#. C# developers can build iOS, Android, macOS, and Windows apps in one code base. .NET MAUI allows developers to configure the UI for each separate platform, which is beneficial for someone developing apps with this framework as different platforms have different standards in the UI and UX. As we learned within mobile development, there are benefits and drawbacks to using cross-platform frameworks, but a C# developer can quickly put together an app without having to learn a whole new language:

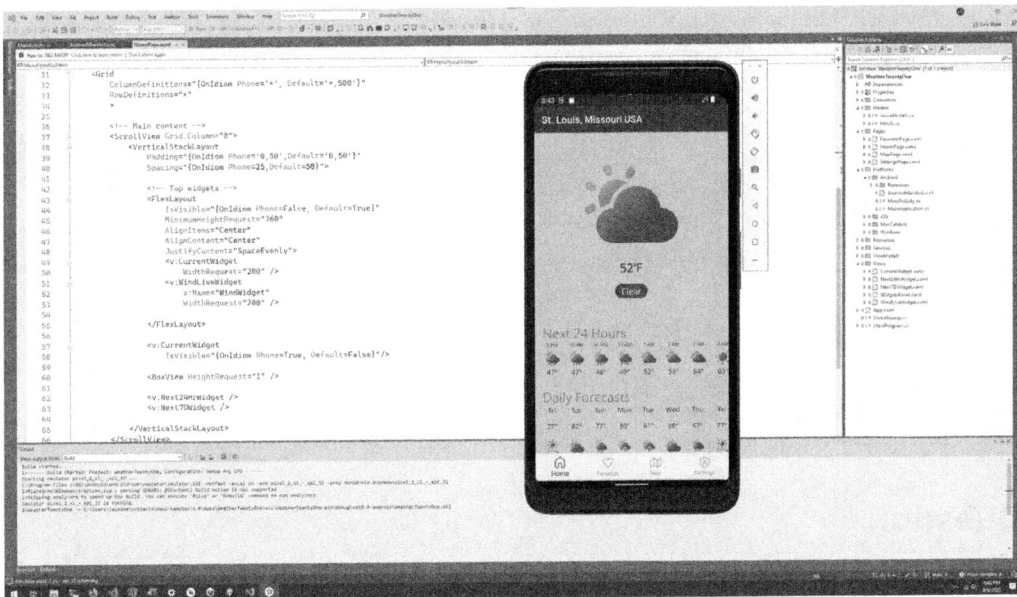

Figure 4.10 – A weather app demo of .NET MAUI

C# can be found in many platforms, applications, and devices, making it a popular multi-purpose language. It can be used to develop many software applications, such as websites, games, and mobile apps. The .NET platform enables developers to get started with building applications for free on any platform.

Summary

This chapter covered quite a lot of programming languages and there are more out there to discover. Whichever language a software engineer may reach for, it is primarily used as a tool to create something. First, we explored web development and learned that while HTML, CSS, and JavaScript are the most common, other languages can be used to develop for the web, such as Python.

Next, we moved on to backend languages, which focus on tasks that are not visible to the user, such as retrieving data from a database. We also learned that backend languages will often have multiple purposes, such as JavaScript, which can be used in any part of web development and to build games. We then learned that mobile languages also are sometimes backend languages that have a unique development environment on a computer to be able to build and test mobile applications. Depending on what platform and how it will be used, some languages may come with SDKs, libraries, and platforms that make developing software much faster and easier to do. There are many multi-purpose languages such as C# on the .NET platform, which has many uses, such as full stack web development, mobile, and gaming. Programming languages have evolved to the point where technology enables citizen developers who don't necessarily need to know a programming language to develop software, but that doesn't mean that programming languages are not a necessity anymore and over the years they will continue to evolve with new technologies. To that same effect, software engineers will continue to adapt and evolve to the new changes in their development environment and languages too.

You saw some small examples of programming languages in this chapter. The next chapter will focus more on the C# language and prepare your development environment with .NET so that you can create your first application in C#.

Questions

1. How does a programming language get converted into something that a computer can understand?

2. What are the three programming languages that a full stack web developer usually uses?

3. Name three multi-purpose programming languages named in this chapter. Multi-purpose programming languages can be used on two or more platforms, such as game development and the web.

4. Low-code and no-code platforms and tools can be used with programming languages – true or false?

5. What is the difference between .NET and C#?

Further reading

- *Concepts and Semantics of Programming Languages 1* (2021), by *Thérèse Hardin, Mathieu Jaume, François Pessaux, and Véronique Viguié Donzeau-Gouge*, Wiley

- *Data Science from Scratch, Second Edition* (2019), by *Joel Gruss,* O'Reilly Media

- *Create a web UI with ASP.NET Core* (2022), Microsoft Docs: `https://docs.microsoft.com/en-us/learn/modules/create-razor-pages-aspnet-core/`

- *Introduction to .NET* (2022), Microsoft Docs: `https://docs.microsoft.com/en-us/learn/modules/dotnet-introduction/`

- *Head First Android Development, Third Edition* (2021), by *Dawn Griffiths and David Griffiths,* O'Reilly Media

- *Low-Code and the Democratization of Programming* (2021), by *O'Reilly Editorial Team,* O'Reilly Media

5

Writing Your First C# Program

Now that we've gained a proper introduction to software engineering and programming, it's time that we try it out ourselves. You may now be wondering, with all these different languages and platforms, how do software engineers get started writing code on a computer? In the previous chapter, we learned about SDKs, libraries, and tools. Keep in mind that although they are how a software engineer would develop software, the tools software engineers use to build software are software themselves. That's right – software engineers use software to build software and, just like any software that you would add to a computer or phone, they will typically download and install the things they need to get the job done.

Now, you will get to experience how this is done. This chapter will guide you through setting up a development environment with .NET and C#, which includes installing the software runtime and SDK and a code editor. We'll also build a simple application called a console application in C#.

This chapter will cover the following topics:

- Introduction to software development tools
- Installing .NET and tools for .NET development
- Building a C# console application
- Editing a console application in Visual Studio

By the end of this chapter, you'll know how software engineers get their development environment set up to create software by doing it yourself. You will also be able to create and modify a small console program in C#.

Technical requirements

To complete the exercises in this chapter, you'll need a computer, either a laptop or a desktop with Windows, macOS, or Linux installed.

Introduction to software development tools

Many tools are available for building software and software engineers adopt a set of these to create applications, which may change over time and will often come down to personal preferences. These tools also differ based on the programming language and the platform that is being built on. As an example, in the previous chapter, you learned that Android developers need an Android device or a simulator to run and test the app they're building. However, a web developer will needs a browser to test out their web application. Despite the differences in tools and how the software is built, there are some common tools all software developers will need. These sets of tools can be described as development environments, the set of tools a software developer needs to write, build, run, and test software.

Writing code without configuring the development environment is like getting into a car without knowing how to reach your destination; you won't get very far. Without the development environment, the code can't run successfully, wouldn't be able to be tested for bugs and errors, and therefore wouldn't be suitable for distribution to users. Development environments are an important part of the software development toolset because they need to be configured to be able to properly build and run the software.

Let's look at some common components of a development environment.

Operating system

The operating system enables software such as browsers, games, and apps to run successfully on a computer. It's software that is built for the special purpose of managing the hardware resources available to a computer and maintaining and monitoring different software. When you're using a computer without any applications open, you're interacting with the operating system. So, when you are installing software on a computer, you're technically installing it on the operating system and not the computer directly. Common operating systems include Windows, macOS, Linux, Android, and iOS.

If you've ever installed software on a computer or a mobile device, you have probably noticed that there are different versions of that software that are compatible with different operating systems. That's because various types and versions of operating systems are only compatible with specific machines and devices. This is important to software engineers because the software they are building on may be dependent on the type or version of the operating system. For example, a Windows desktop application will most likely not work on Linux and vice versa, so the software engineer will most likely have Windows as their operating system. Remember that software is installed on the operating system, so the end users of the software will need the required operating system installed. Therefore, someone who wants to use a Windows desktop application will need a computer with Windows. Furthermore, software engineers will depend on it to install other compatible tools within their development environment. Because of this, the operating system can be seen as the foundation of the development environment.

There are a few exceptions where the operating system may not matter for the end user and the developer, due to the type of platform and the modernization of software development. The two common exceptions are web applications and cross-platform applications. Web applications rely on the browser, and popular browsers can be installed on different operating systems. The underlying technology of modern browsers and web development technology is standardized to provide a similar experience across all browsers and platforms, so the operating system may not matter as much.

In the past, developers who wanted to build software for different operating systems had to build two different versions. Due to various constraints in complexity, software team size, time, and even legal challenges, applications were built exclusively for just one operating system, ignoring the others. Today, cross-platform technologies allow developers to build software for multiple operating systems and devices, making it easier to maintain one application that can work for different users. However, this is still a challenge today for software teams with team members who have specialized in a particular platform and make the difficult choice to deprioritize other platforms. A great example of this is Microsoft 365, comprising multiple productivity tools such as Microsoft Word, Excel, and PowerPoint that can be used in the browser or on multiple operating systems on local computers, as well as on mobile devices. However, Microsoft Access is exclusive to Windows.

The operating system is a crucial component of a development environment because software is dependent on the operating system, where the tools are pieces of software as well. Because there are various versions of operating systems, software developers need to determine which ones will best fit their needs based on what they are building. There are some cases where the operating system may not matter as much, giving developers more flexibility in choosing the operating system of their choice for their development environment, where sometimes the choice may just be personal preference.

Browser

The browser is an important part of the development environment, especially for web developers. This is because the software they are building is dependent on the browser. Some common browsers are Google Chrome, Mozilla Firefox, Microsoft Edge, and Apple Safari. Most modern browsers have the same functionalities but will differ in layout and style, which will be the personal preference of each user. For software engineers who are not developing for the web, the browser is important for downloading tools, using browser-based tools, and looking up information.

No programmer of any skillset or experience can know everything about the language and platform they're developing for and will often have to look up information to work through complex problems. There's always something new to learn. A popular website that developers will use is Stack Overflow, which is an online forum for asking, answering, and finding programming questions. Chances are that if you search for a solution to a programming problem in your favorite search engine, it's likely Stack Overflow will show up in the results. Here's an example:

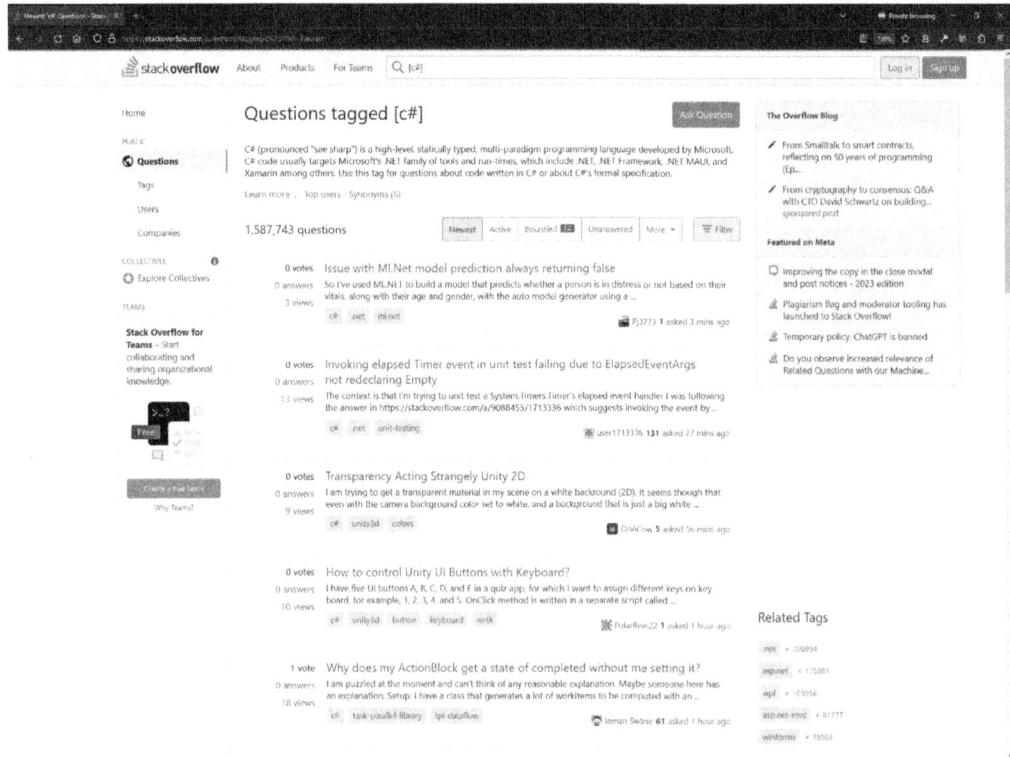

Figure 5.1 – A Firefox browser displaying the Stack Overflow website

Web developers will need to spend extra time in the browser, not only to search for help with their problems but also to test the software that they're building. While they will likely prefer a particular browser, chances are that their development environment will have multiple browsers installed. While web applications usually function and look the same as modern browsers, there are still some differences that arise during development, especially frontend web development, so web developers often use different browsers to test and confirm that everything still functions the same way. In cases where it does not, web developers have to either decide whether and how to support the difference in expected behavior, where they may decide it's not that big of a problem and ignore it, or write some extra code to support it.

Browsers are useful tools for any software engineer's development environments for getting information on tools and the software they are building. For web development, it's a crucial part of testing web applications, including checking for compatibility across multiple browsers.

Code editor

A code editor is a tool that software developers use to write code. Due to the variety in code editors, it's probably one of the tools that differs the most between software developers' environments. Most code editors can support multiple languages and can be important for any software that's dependent on more than one language. For example, web developers often work between HTML, CSS, and JavaScript in one day. Some benefits of a code editor are the language support features, built-in tools, and extensibility.

One of the biggest differences between programming languages is syntax, which is the rules for how the code is written. Different lines of code will do different things, and it can be hard to pinpoint where and what the code is doing without a marker or indicator of some sort that points out important information about the code. It's helpful for programmers to have a quick and obvious way to find things such as syntax errors, especially when the code base is quite large. Code editors can highlight these occurrences by changing the color of the text of the code, called syntax highlighting, or having line numbers to make the code easier to navigate. Earlier, we learned that building software includes installing tools to build it; with code editors, sometimes, the tools conveniently reside within them, saving time on extra installations and having to swap windows for multiple tools. Code editors can also be extensible, where developers can add extensions to use additional tools or can customize the editor to make it look and function the way that they prefer.

Code editors fall into two categories: text editors and **integrated development environments**, also known as **IDEs**. Text editors are code editors that support multiple languages and are usually very extensible and customizable. They are also likely to be cross-platform. They have the tools needed to write code but may require some extra tool installation to run the code. Some popular text editors are Visual Studio Code, Sublime, Vim, and Emacs.

IDEs are a combination of text editors and software that is used to run a language. Normally, a developer wouldn't need to install any additional software to successfully build, run, and test a software program with an IDE. In addition to this, the built-in tools tend to have more features, specialized for working with common platforms with the language. While this is a convenient combination, there are some cons to choosing an IDE that may constrain a developer into a few options. First, not all IDEs will support all languages and developers may be limited in the languages they can choose from when developing with the IDE. Second is the side of the IDE itself, as they tend to have a larger user interface in addition to installing everything needed to create and run the software. Typically, IDEs will need more computer resources, such as disk space and memory. Finally, some versions of IDEs will cost money, while most text editors are free. Popular IDEs include Visual Studio, Eclipse, and IntelliJ. Here's a sample Visual Studio UI:

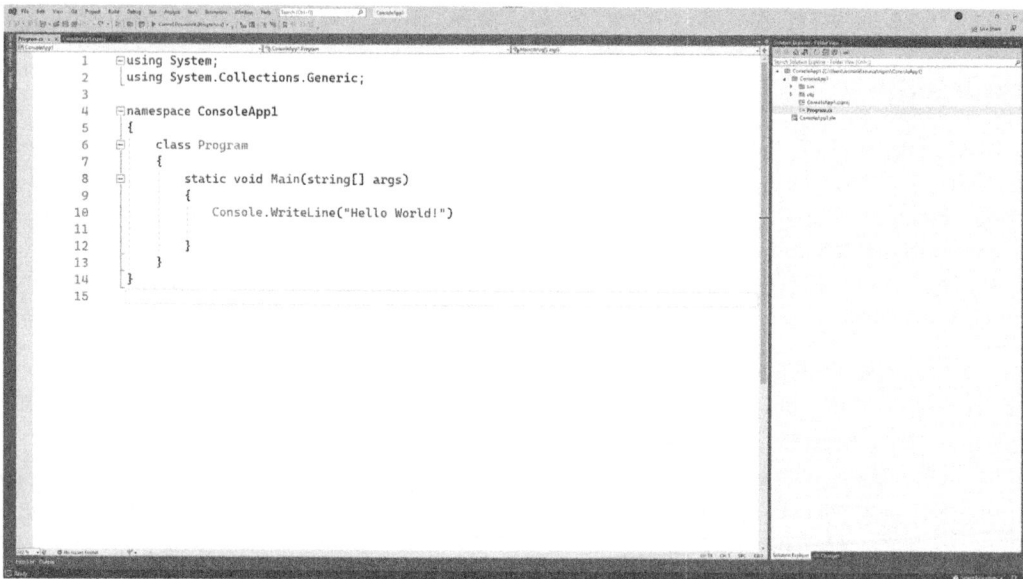

Figure 5.2 – The Visual Studio 2022 IDE

> **Note**
>
> Visual Studio and Visual Studio Code are separate tools, where Visual Studio is an IDE and Video Studio Code is an open source text editor. One rule of thumb to tell the difference between the two is that Visual Studio and the IDE will usually have a version associated with a year, so Visual Studio 2022 is the most current version of the IDE, while Visual Studio 2019 was the previous version.

Code editors can either be text editors or IDEs, where text editors provide flexibility in language support and extensibility but need additional tooling to run the software. In contrast, IDEs install everything needed to write, build, and run software but will be constrained to a limited number of languages and may be costly in terms of computer resources and money.

Software runtime and development kit

The software runtime allows for a language to be run successfully in the development environment. The runtime can be seen as the key to the computer resources needed to run the software successfully. In addition to the runtime, the **software development kit**, or **SDK**, is a set of tools that enable developers to build software with a programming language for a platform. The SDK has the compiler or interpreter, which translates the code into machine code instructions, and the debugger, which allows developers to track how the code is executed, line by line. While the runtime and SDK are a critical part of software development, they normally don't need extensive setup to use. Developers typically need to install the runtime and SDK to be able to run the software, and they are both often bundled together for a single one-time installation. Popular SDKs include the Android SDK, Xbox SDK, and **Amazon Web Services** (**AWS**) SDKs.

The runtime and SDKs of a programming language or platform roll up all software and tools necessary to build and run a software application into an installable package. It includes software that accesses computer resources and translates the code into machine instructions.

Command line

A command line is a tool that usually comes by default with the operating system. It's used for entering commands via a keyboard instead of a mouse. Many computer tasks can be done via the command line or **graphical user interface** or **GUI**, and it normally depends on the software engineers' preference. One of the benefits of the command line is that it can be quicker to complete tasks than manually clicking through multiple views with a mouse. For example, consider a file directory that contains 1,000 files, where 300 of them are images that need to be moved to another directory. With a mouse, you'll need to manually click each of them to move them to their new location, while the command line can select all the image file types at once and move them over in a few commands. Not only can command-based tasks prove to be quicker, but they can also be automated with scripts.

Imagine the same scenario regarding the file directory to which the images need to be moved. A developer could write a script that checks the directory for images and moves them automatically with the same commands. Additional tools can also be installed on the command line so that it can handle more tasks, such as accessing a remote server or computer, or managing code in the cloud. Common scenarios like these motivate developers to use the command line, where software development teams will rely on it for small to complex tasks that can range from moving files, testing new code, or deploying new versions of software to production. One of the downsides of the command line is that there are a lot of commands to use; because it's such a powerful tool, it's difficult to remember them all.

Software engineers who are comfortable with the command line have to actively use it to improve their skills. Here's an example of a Windows Terminal application that can run different command lines on separate tabs:

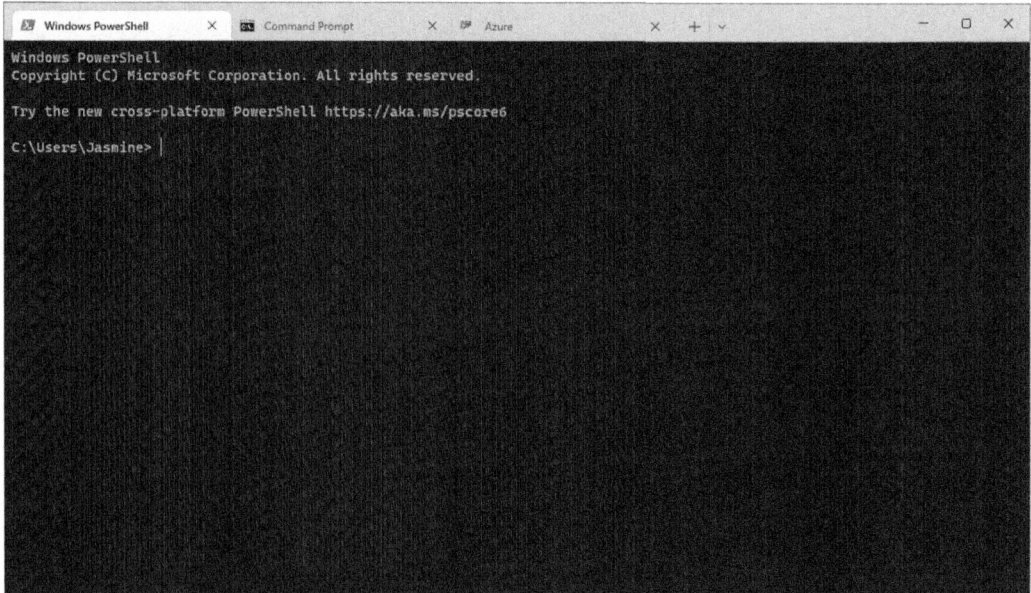

Figure 5.3 – Windows Terminal on the Windows operating system

The Command Prompt is the default command-line tool for Windows, but Windows Terminal and PowerShell are other popular tools. For Mac and Linux, Terminal is the default tool, but Hyper and iTerm are popular as well.

Source control

Software engineers, especially those that are part of a team, will have source control in their development environment. It's a tool that is used to save the progress of code and allows it to be integrated into the existing code base. Source control is vital to a team working on a large project because it is risky for each team member to only save their code locally on their machines. Have you ever dropped your phone in water and couldn't turn it back on? Imagine that a software engineer spent the day building a feature and accidentally did the same thing to their laptop. They would have lost a day's worth of work and will probably need to spend a day setting up their new laptop. Not only that, but if they were to save their code separately, it would technically be individual pieces of the software, so how are they able to make sure that they're building everything correctly? Putting it all together at the end would add different types of problems instead because, as seen with the integration team in *Chapter 2, The*

Software Engineering Life Cycle, sometimes, building software is dependent on others' software. It's much more efficient for software teams to build iteratively, or gradually build the independent pieces of the software and put them together to see how it all works as one unit.

Finally, source control saves a history of how the code has changed over time in a way that can be tracked. This is important for situations where there is an issue with the software. Source control provides a way to go "back in time" to find the problem. This can be crucial for resolving critical bugs, especially when the software has already been released and distributed to people who are actively using the software, also known as "in production." Source control can be beneficial for developers working alone as well, for the same reasons. Popular source control tools include Git, **Subversion** (**SVN**), and Perforce.

Now that you have learned about the common tools of the development environment, you'll be using some of them to write your first program with .NET and C#.

Installing .NET and tools for .NET development

In this section, you will be installing the most recent version of .NET, .NET 7. The installation and setup will be split into three steps:

1.   Installing the .NET SDK and runtime

2.   Installing Visual Studio Code

3.   Configuring Visual Studio Code for C# development

Let's start!

Installing the .NET SDK and runtime

The .NET SDK and runtime can be installed on Windows, macOS (including ARM64 for machines with M1 chips and higher), and Linux. Installing the SDK and runtime can be done in one installable step for all platforms. Visit the download page at `https://dotnet.microsoft.com/download`, select your operating system to get started, and follow the instructions. For Windows, be sure to select the SDK to install both the SDK and runtime.

Once the download has been completed, click on the file to install the SDK and runtime. Once the installation has been completed, you'll see a prompt confirming that the installation has been completed:

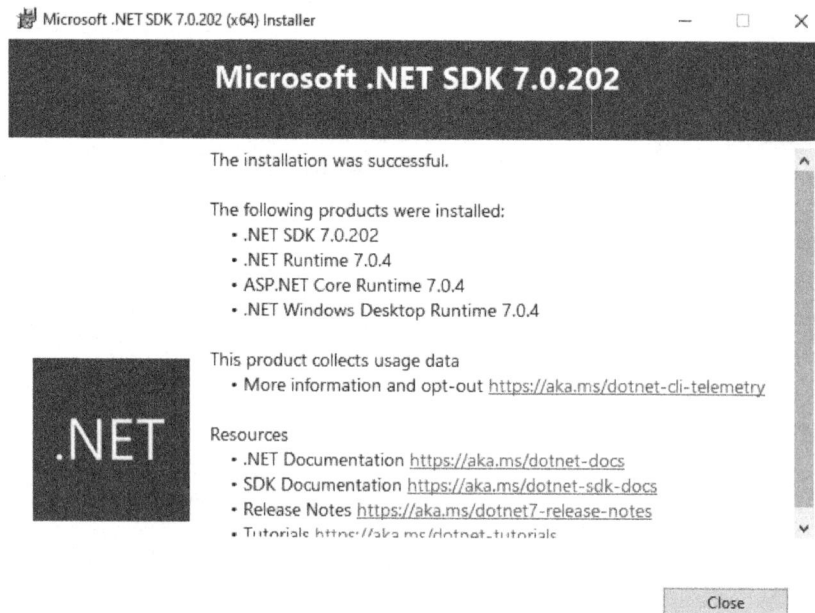

Figure 5.4 – Installation wizard of the .NET SDK on Windows

If successful, you will now be able to build and run .NET applications on your computer. You can test it out on the command line by opening the Command Prompt on Windows or Terminal on macOS and Linux and typing dotnet and pressing *Enter*. If you see the following display in your command-line tool, you have successfully installed .NET:

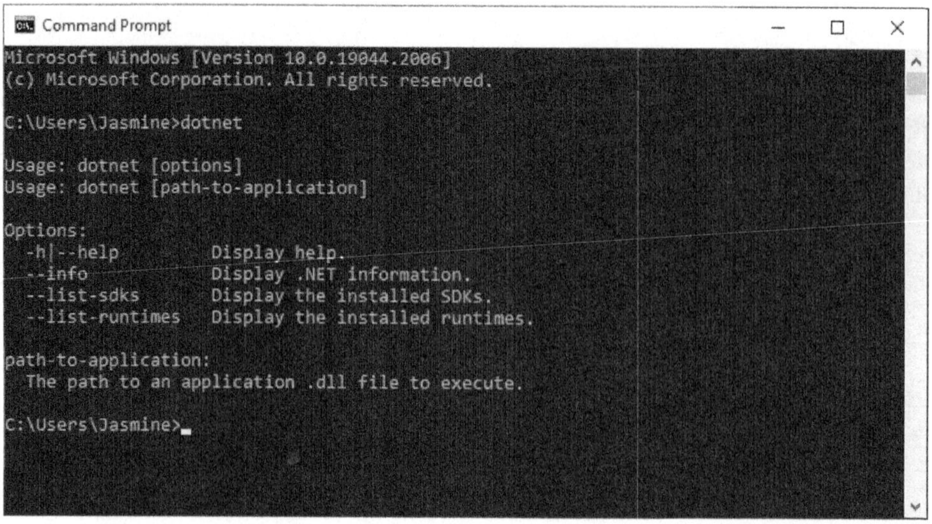

Figure 5.5 – Running the dotnet command in the Windows Command Prompt

With .NET successfully installed, you can move on to installing the code editor. We'll be using Visual Studio Code to create our application.

Installing Visual Studio Code

Like the .NET SDK and runtime, Visual Studio Code is also available for Windows, Mac, and Linux. You can get started by downloading it from `https://code.visualstudio.com/`. Next, click on the downloaded file to begin installing it.

During installation on Windows, you may see a few configuration options. It's up to you if you'd like to include them:

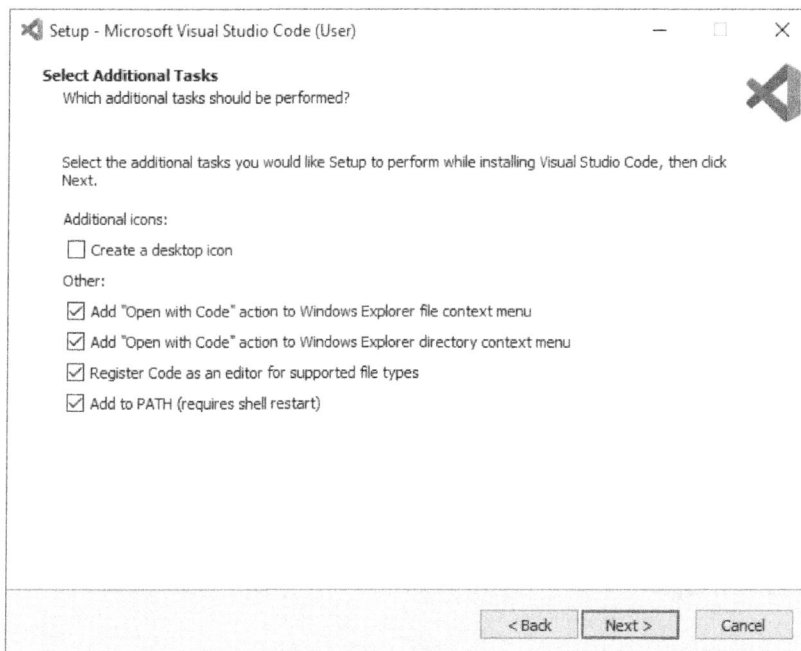

Figure 5.6 – Installation options for Visual Studio Code on Windows

Here's what they all do:

- Checking **Create a desktop icon** will make a shortcut icon on the desktop of your computer, where clicking on it will open the editor

- Checking **Open with code** in the file context menu will allow you to right-click on files and open them in the editor

- Checking **Open with code** in the directory context menu will allow you to right-click in file directories and open them all in the editor

- Checking **Register Code as an editor for supported file types** will open files, primarily files used for coding (`.html`, `.css`, `.cs`, and `.py`), to be opened in the editor without the need to right-click to do so

- Checking **Add to PATH** will allow you to open Visual Studio Code in the command line by typing `code` and pressing *Enter*

For more installation information, refer to the documentation for your operating system: `https://code.visualstudio.com/docs/setup/setup-overview`. Don't be concerned about any options that you forgot to select or missed during installation – you can always select them later in Visual Studio Code or on your computer by referencing the documentation.

Once the installation has been completed, you'll see a prompt confirming this. Keep the **Launch Visual Studio Code** box checked to open Visual Studio Code after you click on **Finish**:

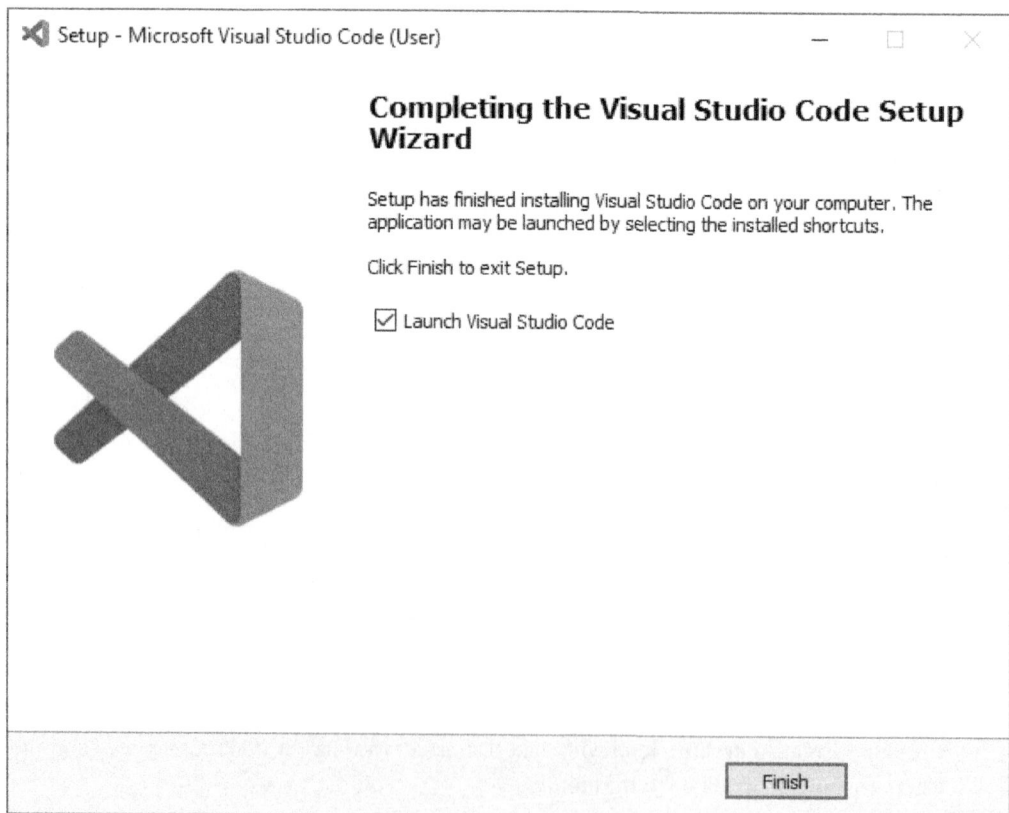

Figure 5.7 – Installation wizard of Visual Studio Code displaying a successful installation message

With .NET and an editor installed, you can now create and edit C# applications and files. However, adding C# support in Visual Studio Code will make working with C# a better experience. We'll do this by installing an extension.

Configuring Visual Studio Code for C# development

When you open Visual Studio Code, you should see a blank screen with some icons on the left-hand side. Select the icon with the four boxes to open the extension screen. In the search box that opens up on the left, type C# and press *Enter*. The first option that should show up in the list is the C# extension, as shown in the following screenshot. Click on it, then click on **Install** to install it:

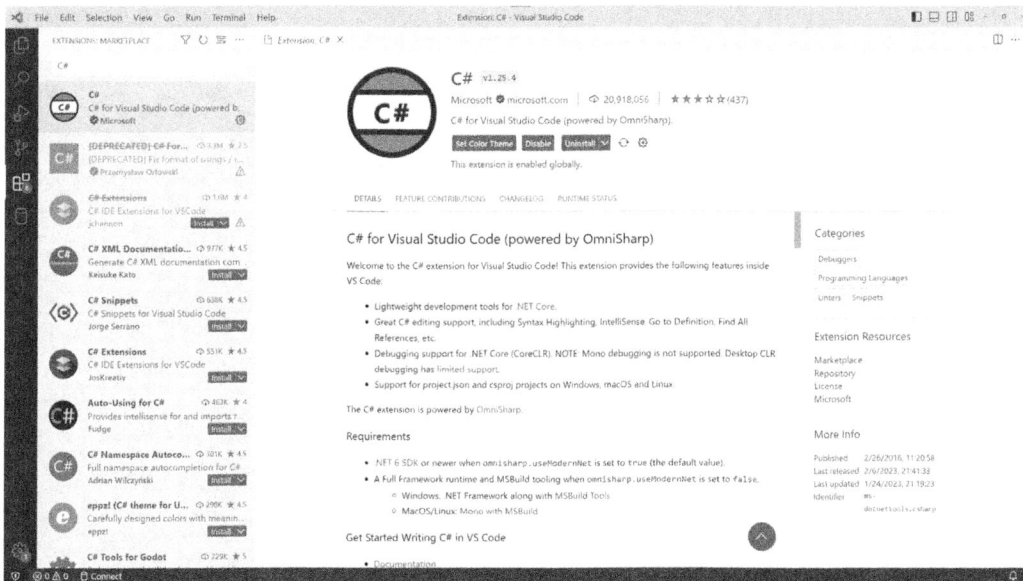

Figure 5.8 – The C# extension in Visual Studio Code

With that, we have set up our development environment with the .NET runtime, SDK, and an editor with language support for the C# programming language. Now, we will build our first application.

Building a C# console application

With the proper tools in place, you can now begin building your first .NET application with C#. In this walkthrough, you'll be creating a console application, which is an application that can be run in the command line. To get started, you must create and run the app in the command line, then make changes to it in Visual Studio Code.

Let's start with the following steps:

1. Open your default command line, which is Command Prompt on Windows or Terminal on macOS and Linux.

2. In the command line, type the following command:

    ```
    dotnet new console -o MyFirstApp
    ```

3. Press *Enter*.

    After pressing *Enter*, you may see some additional text if this is your first time working with .NET, but at the end, you should see a few status messages, ending with **Restore succeeded**:

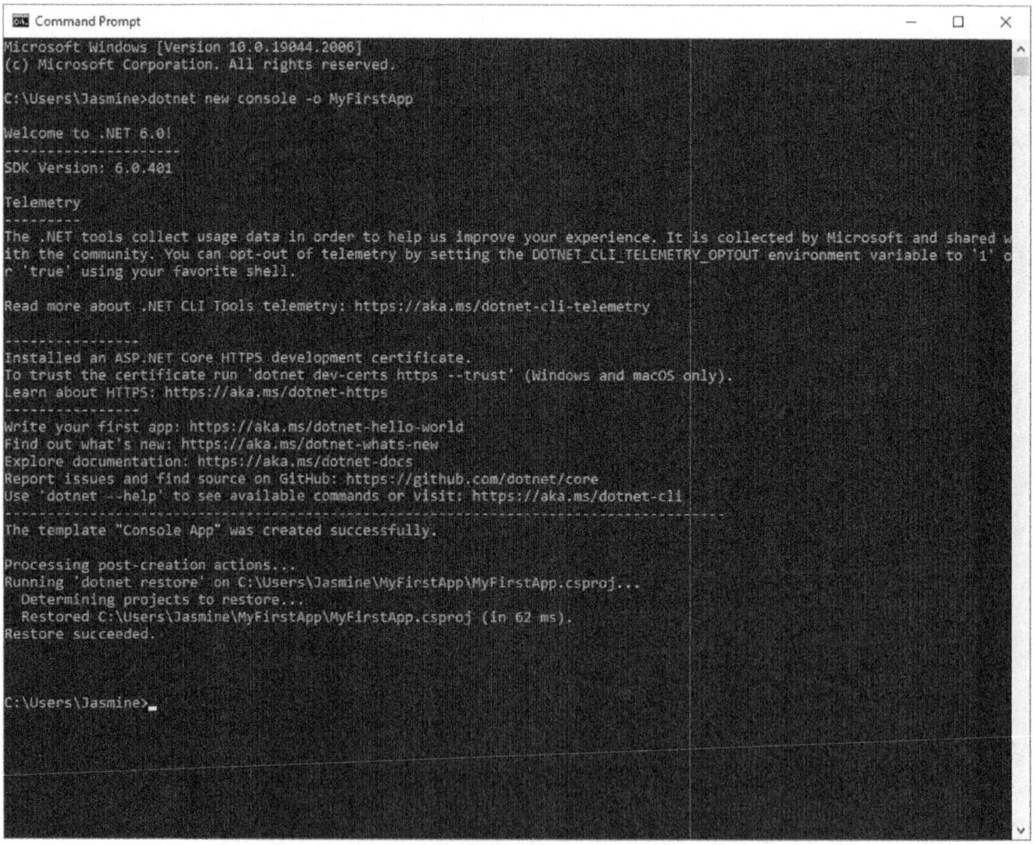

Figure 5.9 – Creating a console app in the Windows Command Prompt

4. Continue by typing the following command in the command line:

```
cd MyFirstApp
```

5. Run the application by typing the following:

```
dotnet run
```

You should see the message **Hello, World!** on the screen:

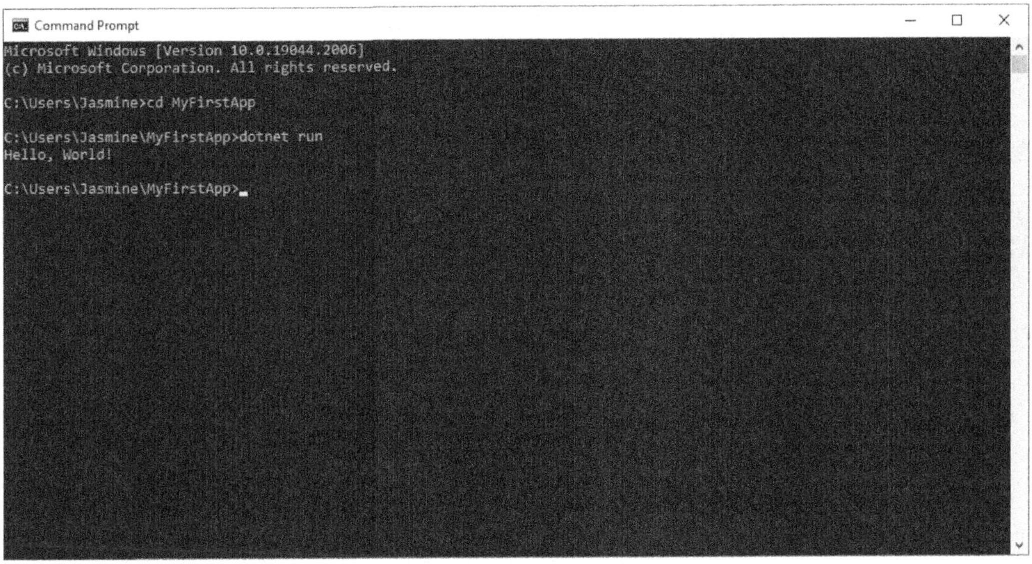

Figure 5.10 – Running a console application in Windows Command Prompt

Congratulations, you have just created and run your first .NET application!

Let's take a moment to understand the commands we used in this walkthrough. First is the command we used to create a new console application:

```
dotnet new console -o MyFirstApp
```

The dotnet new console command created a new console application. This command will work by itself, but to make your file directory more organized, we added an option to the command, which provides additional configuration steps for commands. The -o option stands for "output," which is the location of where we want the newly created application to be named and located, which is MyFirstApp in the MyFirstApp directory.

Because we made a new directory, we now have to navigate to it to run the application by using the following command:

```
cd MyFirstApp
```

The cd command stands for "change directory." This means we move our current directory location to where the app was created.

Finally, we can run the application with the dotnet run command.

Now that we have successfully created our first application, let's make a small change to it with Visual Studio Code.

Editing a console application in Visual Studio Code

The application we just created can now be changed and run again. You'll open it up in Visual Studio Code, make a small change, and then run it again. The steps are as follows:

1. Locate the MyFirstApp folder. If you still have the command line from the previous walkthrough open, you can find it by typing explorer . in Windows, open . in Mac, or xdg-open . in Linux.

2. Open Visual Studio Code, go to **File | Open Folder**, and find and open the folder named MyFirstApp.

3. You should now see a few files on the left-hand side of the editor. Click on Program.cs to open the C# file.

4. You may also notice a notification asking you to add assets to debug the application. Select **Not Now**.

5. Open up the terminal by selecting **Terminal | New Terminal**. When it loads, you will notice that the current directory is in MyFirstApp and that you can test it out by running dotnet run in it:

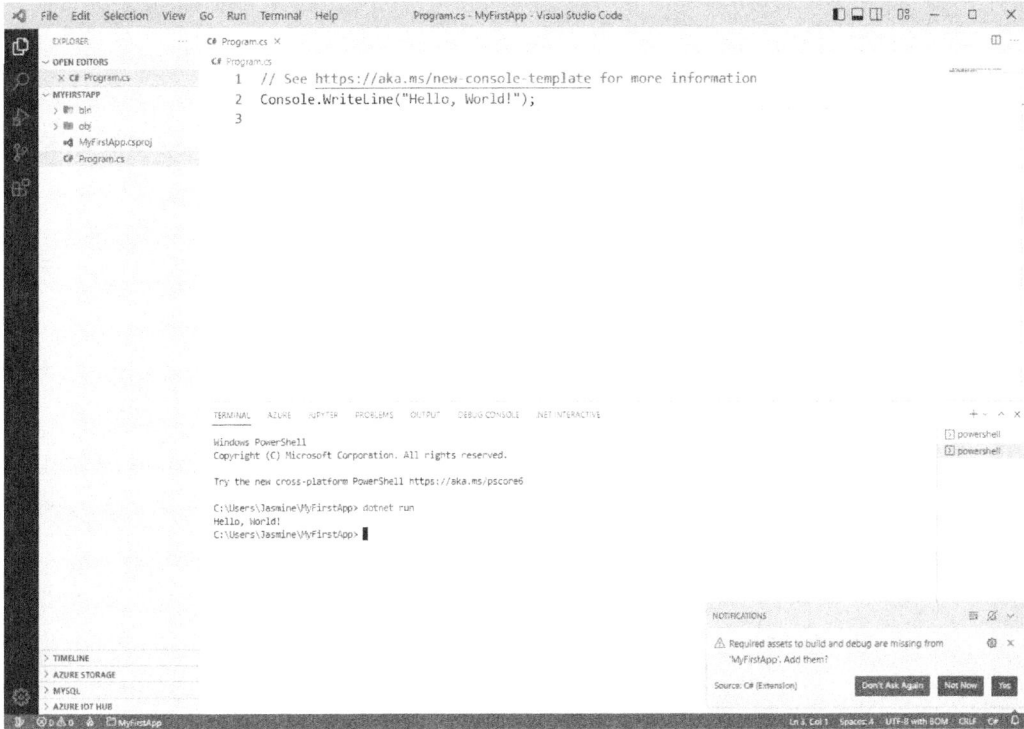

Figure 5.11 – Opening a console application in Visual Studio Code

6. In `Program.cs`, on line 2, replace `World` with something else. For example, in *Figure 5.12*, it has been replaced with my name (`Jasmine`).

7. In the terminal, run the `dotnet run` command.

You should now see your new message in the terminal:

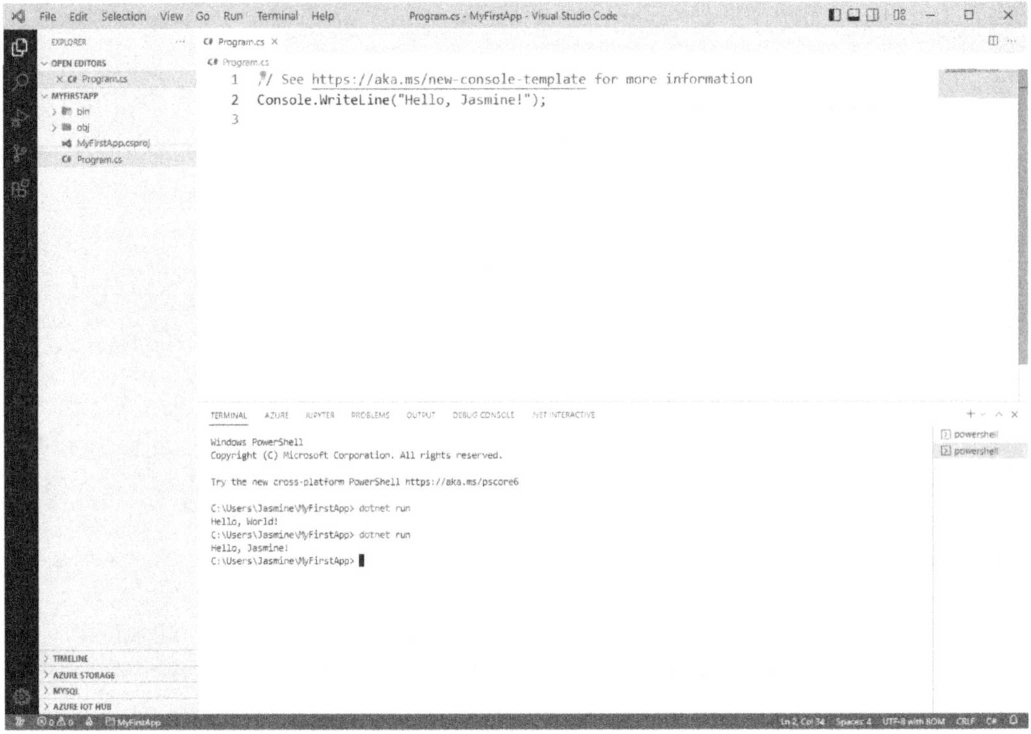

Figure 5.12 – Running a console application in the terminal of Visual Studio Code

You can try a few other things to change your code, including changing the message again and copying and pasting the line to include a new message on another line. See the following example of modifications you can make:

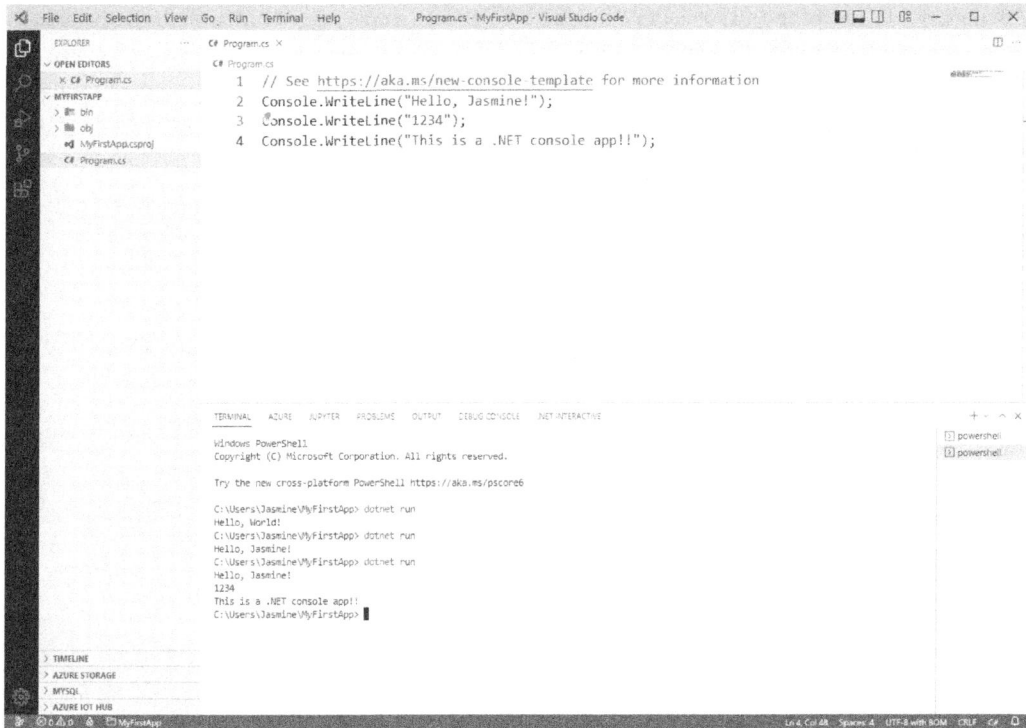

Figure 5.13 – Running a modified console application in the terminal of Visual Studio Code

With that, you have installed an SDK and runtime on your computer, used the default command line on your operating system to make and run a new .NET application, and modified it in a code editor. That brings us to the end of this chapter.

Summary

In this chapter, you learned about and tried out some of the many tools that a software engineer will use to create software, which will be contained within their development environment. The most common tools you learned about are the operating system, which is where all the software and tools are installed, the browser for information and tasks, and a key tool for web development, the code editor, for editing and running code. We also learned about the software runtime and SDK needed to run and build software on a platform, the command line for computer operation, and source control to maintain versions of software.

You then tried some of these tools yourself with .NET by installing the runtime and SDK, installing a code editor, and making and running a console application in the command line. You then continued working on it in Visual Studio Code. Again, congratulations on your first hands-on step into software development. Now that you have a basic development environment, you can keep practicing by reading the C# documentation and tutorials and learning even more!

In the next chapter, we will explore more about the C# language by exploring variables and data types.

Questions

1. What options do software engineering teams have when they are faced with the choice to make software for different operating systems?

2. Why would a software engineer who does not do web development use a browser?

3. Name one difference and one similarity between a text editor and an IDE.

4. Operating systems come with a default command line. True or false?

5. What is the command to run a .NET application?

Further reading

*   Visit the Microsoft documentation page on C# to learn more about the language and find new tutorials to try: `https://dotnet.microsoft.com/learn/csharp`

6
Data Types in C#

In the previous chapter, we learned how to get started with building software and configuring our development environment for .NET and C#. Now, we will learn a little more about the C# language. Software is often used to share and use information, which we usually define as data. Data can be represented in a variety of sizes and formats, and the end users of any software will want to see it represented in a way that helps them be productive by providing information or assisting them in completing a task. As creators and maintainers of software, software engineers need to be able to work with data efficiently and securely so that users can quickly access and work with their data and only see the relevant data. In *Chapter 2, The Software Engineering Life Cycle*, and *Chapter 3, Roles in Software Engineering*, we learned that software engineers have common interactions with data, where they will often be creating new data or creating, reading, updating, or deleting existing data, known as CRUD operations. Because of this, we can consider data to be part of the software that needs to be maintained. But how can that all be done with a programming language?

In this chapter, we will explore the foundations of storing and representing data in C#, starting with variables. Next, you will learn about different basic types of data or data types. String, number (also known as integer), and Boolean are common data types used in C# and other languages. So, if you decide to explore other languages after this book, you will have enough knowledge about variables and common data types to be able to get started building in those languages. Finally, we'll end this chapter with a special data type called the array, which stores multiple data values.

This chapter will cover the following topics:

- Introduction to variables
- Introduction to the string data type
- Introduction to numerical data types
- Introduction to the Boolean data type
- Introduction to the array data type

By the end of this chapter, you'll learn about the purpose of variables, how to create and work with various data types, and how to store more than one data value with arrays in C#.

Technical requirements

To complete the exercises in this chapter, you'll need a computer, such as a laptop or a desktop computer, that has Visual Studio Code and .NET installed. Refer to the previous chapter for information on how to install them.

You can find the code files for this chapter on GitHub at `https://github.com/PacktPublishing/Fundamentals-for-Self-Taught-Programmers/tree/main/Chapter6`.

Introduction to variables

Variables are a vital part of programming because that's the way data is stored. Imagine you are trying to keep track of how much cash you have in your pocket, and you plan to do some grocery shopping. You decide you'd like to grab a cup of tea after shopping, so you'll need to budget your money wisely to make sure you have enough to enjoy some tea. You can most likely do some quick calculations in your head to get a rough estimate of how much you can spend on groceries that day. To double-check your math, you decide to use the calculator app on your phone, and you realize you should have enough to buy the book that you wanted. Let's try this out on a calculator app with a starting total of $75 as an example. You estimated that the cost of groceries will be $40 and that the tea will be $5, which has been calculated in the Windows Calculator app, as shown here:

Figure 6.1 – Windows Calculator app

Computers and the software that runs on them are great at tasks like this because they can do them quickly and accurately. Basic math, such as subtraction, which would be needed to calculate your remaining balance, is a common programming task that happens to be similar to what you would do on pen and paper. Creating a calculator app like this one would require taking the user inputs and using the subtraction operator to make a calculation.

We're not quite ready to make a calculator yet, but we can make a small sample console application that subtracts the grocery fee from the cash you have at hand. Let's create a new .NET console app named `MyBudget`:

```
dotnet new console -o MyBudget
```

Open the app in Visual Studio Code and replace the default `Hello World` text with the calculation for groceries and tea so that the line looks like this:

```
Console.WriteLine(75 - 40 - 5);
```

If you open the terminal and run the application with `dotnet run`, you will see **30** printed in the terminal:

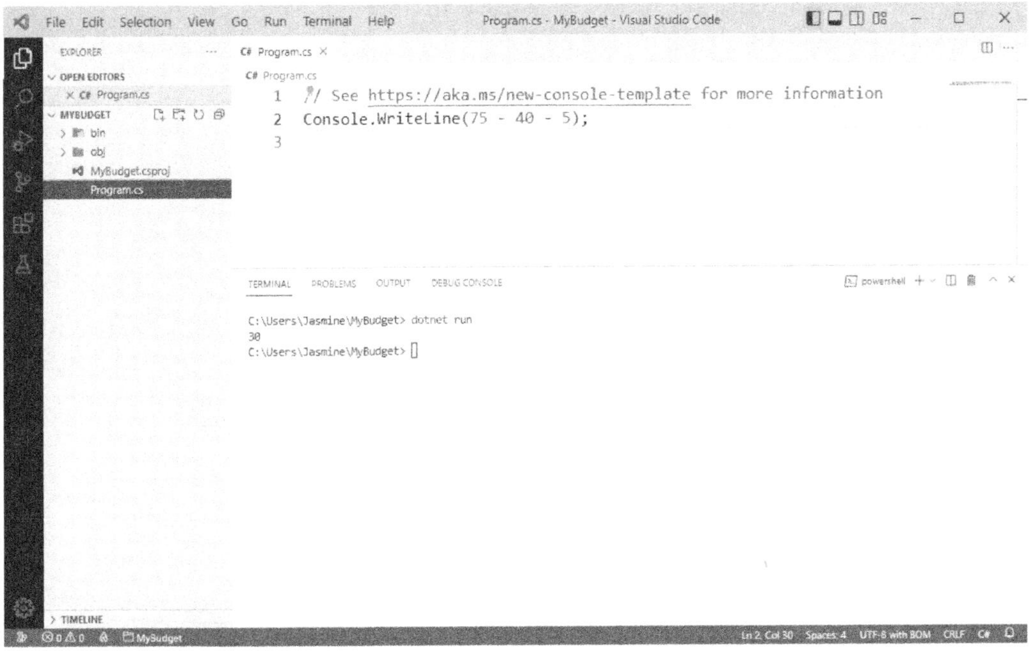

Figure 6.2 – Subtracting three numbers in a console application

We managed to calculate the grocery expenses and now have an estimate of the remaining funds. We can see that it's consistent with the estimate we saw in the calculator. While this is an accurate calculation, these costs are only an estimate, where the final cost of the groceries and tea might be more or less than expected. Remember that you decided to buy a book after tea and estimated that you should have enough left for it. How much money will you have after getting your book? How can we account for this in our application?

Variables, as the name implies, are data that can change in value over time in a software application. Creating variables makes it much easier to manage values that will change. Let's have a look at that.

Creating a variable

All these numbers could be considered variables in the application, but let's focus on keeping track of the cash you have by converting it into a variable by updating the application code by replacing what we have written so far with the following new lines of code:

```
int balance;
Console.WriteLine(75 - 40 - 5);
```

We have now created or declared a `balance` variable. In C#, a variable declaration consists of the data type of the variable, which is `int`, a type used for numbers, and the name of the variable, which is `balance`.

Running the code as-is should produce the same result from last time, but now, we can store the value of `balance` to keep track of how much is left for the book by updating the variable with the initial value:

```
int balance = 75;
Console.WriteLine(75 - 40 - 5);
```

This process of assigning the initial value of a defined variable is defined as initialization, where `balance` has now been initialized to 75. The following figure notes the declaration and initialization of the `balance` variable by adding the assignment operator and assigning a value:

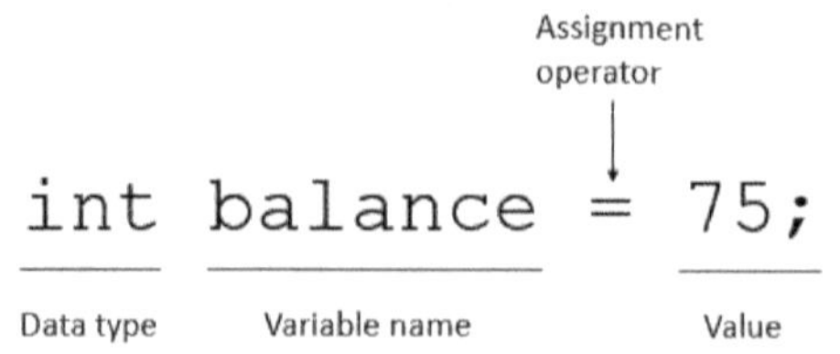

Figure 6.3 – Identifying the parts of a variable that has been assigned a value

Now that `balance` has been initialized, we can use it in the calculation, and the application will print the same value when run:

```
int balance = 75;
Console.WriteLine(balance - 40 - 5);
```

The benefit of variables is reuse, where the value of the variable can be referenced by a known name without us having to keep track of the value that's stored, which is now the responsibility of the programming language and the computer. We'll work more with this example later in this chapter, but this is a start to understanding the need for variables. Now that you know how to create a variable and assign a value to it, we will explore the different data types for variables, starting with strings.

Introduction to the string data type

A string is a sequence of characters, made up of letters, numbers, symbols, and spaces. You can think of strings as text. You already worked with strings in the previous chapter when you changed the `Hello World` message. Strings are enclosed in double quotations and can also be saved as variables.

Let's update our existing balance application so that it prints some text to the console:

```
int balance = 75;
string balanceMessage = "The current balance is:";
Console.WriteLine(balanceMessage);
Console.WriteLine(balance - 40 - 5);
```

The second line of code has introduced a new variable called `balanceMessage`, where the type is defined as a string and the value is enclosed in double quotation marks. It is then printed to the console. Here's a graphical notation:

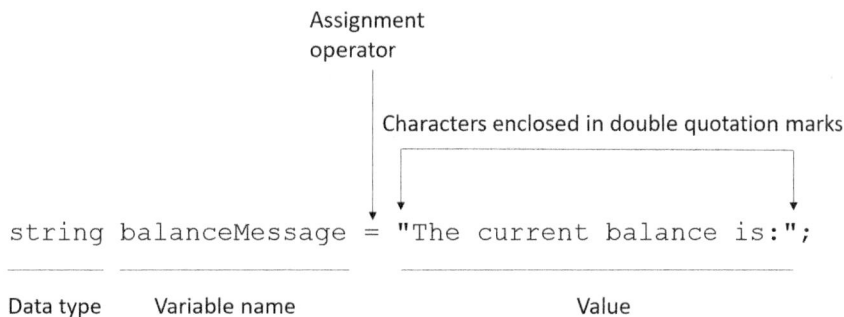

Figure 6.4 – Identifying the parts of a string variable that has been assigned a value

Now that you know how to create a string, let's explore common operations we can perform with the data type, starting with concatenation.

String concatenation

A common operation in strings is concatenation, which combines two or more strings to form a new string. One way to concatenate strings is to use the + operator between the strings you'd like to combine.

Here's an example you can try:

```
string hello = "Hello";
string world = "World!";
Console.WriteLine(hello + world);
```

When you run these lines of code, you'll notice that the console will print HelloWorld! instead of separating the two words. Because strings can be any combination of characters in various languages, sometimes, the string can be something that's not meant to be read or printed on a screen, such as a customer ID. However, C# cannot understand the context of the string and will not make assumptions about how it will be used, and will leave the task of separating the words up to you. You can add empty spaces, known as whitespace, to the string to add spacing between characters or at the beginning or end of the string, or even create a string that only contains whitespace. Let's try this out in our earlier example:

```
string hello = "Hello ";
string world = "World!";
Console.WriteLine(hello + world);
```

The hello variable now has a space at the end of it, which will add separation between the two words when the application is run. Here's another example of adding space:

```
string hello = "Hello";
string world = "World!";
Console.WriteLine(hello + " " + world);
```

Because concatenation can combine two or more strings, you could also concatenate three strings together with an empty string in the middle to separate two words.

You can also concatenate strings to other values, such as numbers. Let's try this out on the MyBudget console application:

```
int balance = 75;
string balanceMessage = "The current balance is: $";
Console.WriteLine(balanceMessage + balance);
Console.WriteLine(balance - 40 - 5);
```

The balanceMessage string variable has a space at the end to separate the text from the balance value with currency at the end and is then concatenated with the balance value. It will print The current balance is: $75.

Operators and type safety

Now that you know how to make strings, you can try to experiment with MyBudget to concatenate balanceMessage on line 4, as shown here:

```
Console.WriteLine(balanceMessage + balance - 40 - 5);
```

If you try to run this, you will see an error like the following in the console:

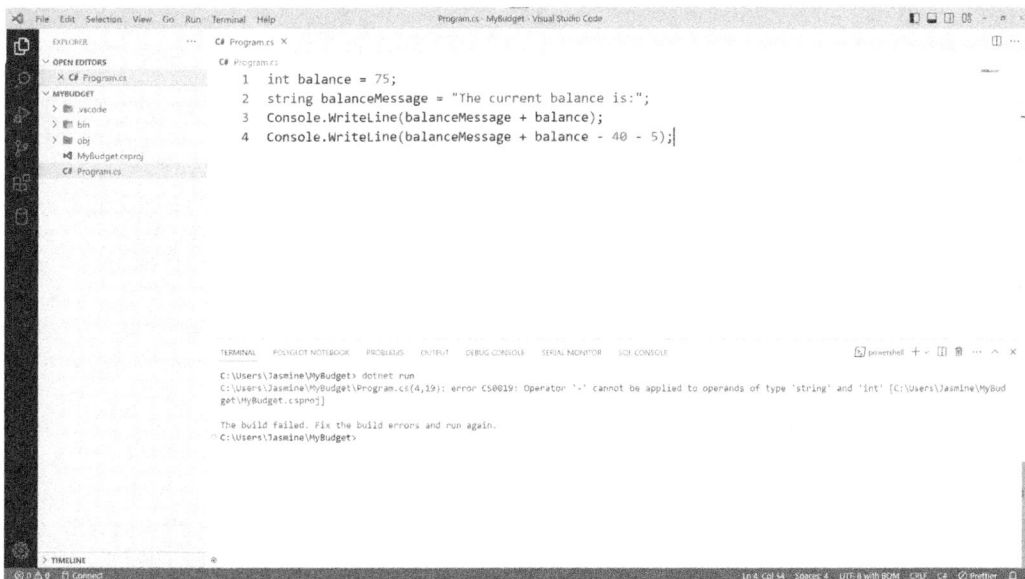

Figure 6.5 – Error in the MyBudget app

Note the error:

```
error CS0019: Operator '-' cannot be applied to operands of
type 'string' and 'int'
```

This error means that the - operator cannot be used with the int and string data types. Operators are symbols that are used to modify values in a computer program, and many operators can only be used with a particular type. We have worked with three operators so far: the - operator for subtracting numeric values, the = symbol for assigning a value to a variable, and the + symbol for concatenating strings. As the - operator is only for numeric data types, we can't use it with a string.

This is a key feature of the C# language, called **type safety**, where operations on types are validated to ensure that they are being used on the correct types. This is a way to prevent errors and incorrect values. This defines C# as a strongly typed language or a language that enforces type safety. Some languages do not enforce type safety in the same way that C# does, but this does not mean that other languages are unsafe to use; it's simply a choice of language design.

Let's focus on the error. Is there a way to print the calculated value of the subtracted balance on one line? Yes, we can do it with ToString, which can convert values into strings.

Let's update the line with ToString and get rid of the error:

```
Console.WriteLine(balanceMessage + (balance - 40 -
5).ToString());
```

The balanceMessage variable is already a string, but the calculation with the balance variable includes numbers, so we can use ToString to convert it into a string data type. ToString is a built-in method in C#, which are reusable lines of code that do common tasks such as converting strings. We will look at methods in more depth in the next chapter, but for now, we have a program that is free of errors.

There are many more things you can do with strings in C#, but we have learned some basics to continue building our console app. Can we update the balance variable so that it shows how much you have left over after groceries and tea? Yes, we can! Let's learn how by building on our knowledge to reuse the balance variable with arithmetic.

Introduction to numerical data types

Numerical data types are values that can be used for arithmetic operations such as addition, subtraction, multiplication, division, and more. The integer data type is used for whole numbers, while the decimal data type is used for numbers with decimals, also known as floating-point numbers. In the introduction to variables, you learned how to create an integer, so let's explore a use case for the double data type.

You find 45 cents in your pocket, increasing your balance to $75.45. Let's update the value of `balance` on line 1 of the `MyBudget` app to see what happens:

```
int balance = 75.45;
```

You will see a new error. This time, it focuses on the data type of the variable:

```
error CS0266: Cannot implicitly convert type 'double' to 'int'.
An explicit conversion exists (are you missing a cast?)
```

This error occurs because integer data types only are whole numbers, but we have converted our value into a floating-point number. How can we fix this?

Type casting

The previous error suggests that we might be missing a cast in the code. Casting is the process of converting a type into a different type. For example, we could convert the floating-point value into an integer, as shown here. Let's also print the value to the console:

```
int balance = (int)75.45;
Console.WriteLine(balance);
```

The console output is missing the 45 cents from the initial value: it has been truncated, which means it has been "cut out or off" from the value. A value within a variable is stored on the computer that is running the program, and a programming language directs the computer to allocate or make space for the variable. Space is a special resource on any computer, so variables have limits on how much space they can take and will vary by data type. Because the integer data type does not allocate space for floating-point numbers, the number must be truncated to make it a whole number.

Since the double data type supports floating-point numbers, could we possibly change it to a double? Let's give it a try:

```
int balance = (double)75.45;
```

Again, we received the error we saw earlier. This is because we are trying to change the defined variable type that has been allocated to another type that does not have the space to store it. In other words, this variable has already been defined as `int` on the left-hand side of the assignment operator (the = symbol), where variable declaration begins, but the value does not match the data type.

Here, we can see that casting doesn't help us in this current scenario because it's not an accurate representation of your balance. However, casting can be a powerful tool for developing software. Let's look at a small example where casting could be beneficial.

Imagine that you have been tasked with creating a small program for a restaurant to divide the cost of a meal between guests evenly and ignore change. Here's a small console program that does this calculation:

```
double bill = 53.40;
int guests = 7;
Console.WriteLine("The price per guest is: ");
Console.WriteLine((int)bill/guests);
```

In this example, the bill includes change and the number of guests that will not divide the bill evenly. The amount per guest is roughly $7.63, but if the requirement from the restaurant is to ignore the change, the balance can be cast into an int type, the numerical data type for whole numbers.

With what we know so far about numbers and casting, the least complicated option in MyBudget is to convert balance into a double data type in our application:

```
double balance = 75.45;
```

MyBudget should now be error-free and print the entire value without any truncation. This will help keep the balance accurate if the grocery or tea costs include change. Let's build a way to update the balance.

Updating variable values

Variables allow you to reuse the values stored within them, but what if you want to update the value? This is certainly the case for the balance variable in the MyBudget application, where we want to find out if the remaining balance is enough for the book.

Let's revisit the application code to find the current balance:

```
double balance = 75.45;
string balanceMessage = "The current balance is: $";
Console.WriteLine(balanceMessage + balance);
Console.WriteLine(balanceMessage + (balance - 40 -
5).ToString());
```

The console prints that the current balance is $30.450000000000003, which equates to $30.45. How did this happen? This is due to how storage is allocated for the double data type, which is a bit of a complicated subject for this chapter, but there are ways to make this a bit more accurate. Another type of floating-point number data type is the decimal, which is great for accuracy in situations such as money. Let's convert it into a decimal by updating the type and adding an M character to the end of the number:

```
decimal balance = 75.45M;
```

While adding a text character may seem like a strange way to maintain number accuracy, this is a way to control the precision of a floating-point number and maintain accuracy. If you run the code again, you'll notice the value that prints is now $30.45.

Let's move on to updating the value. You can reference a declared variable by name and use the assignment operator to update the value to the right of it. Here's an example of the balance being updated to 0. Notice that once the variable has been declared, there is no need to include the data type:

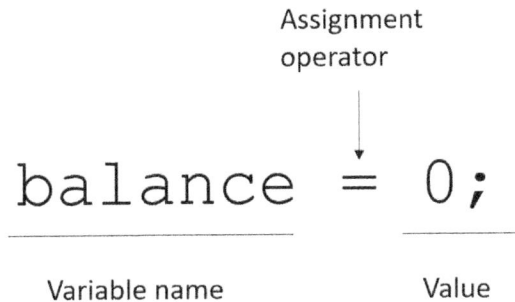

Figure 6.6 – Updating the value of a variable

We know that the ending balance is $30.45, so could we update it by adding a line to the end of the program like this?

```
balance = 30.45M;
```

While this looks like it would work, what happens if the price of the groceries changes or you find even more money? It would throw off the accuracy of the balance. This is called hardcoding, which involves inserting values into a program instead of letting the program do the work of calculating and generating the values. As you can see, this can cause issues and can sometimes create errors or bugs in the code. Let's look at a way to update the value by changing the last two lines:

```
balance = balance - 40 - 5;
Console.WriteLine(balanceMessage + balance);
```

In the prior version of this code, we did the calculation in `Console.WriteLine` but have now moved it to update the value of balance. To change the value of `balance`, we need to know what it is first, which is why the calculation includes subtracting from the balance. Notice that we no longer need `ToString` since we moved the complex calculation to the previous line. Run the code; you will see that the value of `balance` remains at $30.45.

This is a verbose way to update a numeric variable, and it's ok to let it remain as such, but let's update it with a shorthand way to update the balance and print the value after each purchase:

```
decimal balance = 75.45M;
string balanceMessage = "The current balance is: $";
Console.WriteLine(balanceMessage + balance);
balance -= 40;
Console.WriteLine(balanceMessage + balance);
balance -= 5;
Console.WriteLine(balanceMessage + balance);
```

The console now prints the following:

```
The current balance is: $75.45
The current balance is: $35.45
The current balance is: $30.45
```

The lines of code that change the value of the balance are called compound assignments, which calculate the new value and assign it to the variable. Let's take a closer look at the compound assignment:

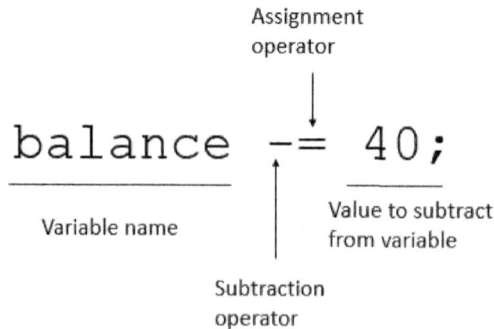

Figure 6.7 – Updating the value of a variable with a compound assignment

To the left is the variable to update, but before the assignment operator is the subtraction operator, which will subtract the value to the right from the variable's current value and assign the difference as the new value. This also works with addition, multiplication, division, and other mathematical operators.

Numerical data types come in many forms and sizes, but they can all handle arithmetic calculations, as well as various degrees of precision. Sometimes, numbers, as well as other data types, will need to be changed to other types with casting. When it comes to numbers, it's better to let the computer calculate the updated values to keep them accurate instead of hardcoding; this is because variables are reusable and can be changed often. Now that we have learned about numbers and have updated `MyBudget` with some accuracy and reusable variables, let's find out if you can afford the book you wanted.

Introduction to the Boolean data type

A Boolean is a data type that can have a value of either `true` or `false`, but most Boolean variables will have a bit more to them than just `true` or `false`. They are usually used with comparison operators or equality operators that compare values, including the value of other variables.

The comparison operators are as follows:

Operator	Symbol
Greater than	>
Less than	<
Greater than or equal to	>=
Less than or equal to	<=

Comparison operators are read from right to left, so in the following figure, the statement can be read as *value1 is less than or equal to value2*:

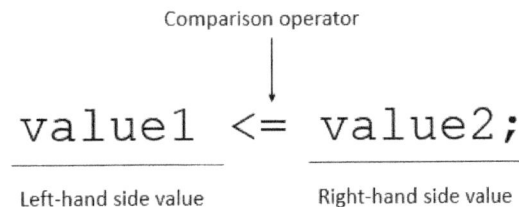

Comparison operator

value1 <= value2;

Left-hand side value   Right-hand side value

Figure 6.8 – Comparing two values with a comparison operator

Equality operators compare two values to evaluate whether they are equal. They are as follows:

Operator	Symbol
Equal	==
Not equal	=!

In the following figure, the statement can be read as *value1 is not equal to value2*:

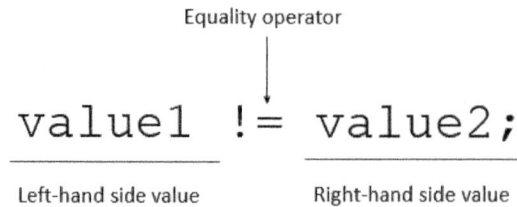

Figure 6.9 – Comparing two values with an equality operator

In these examples, we do not know the values, so we can't know whether the values will be true or false. Now, let's try it in our app.

Now that we have the current balance of your remaining cash, let's try a few comparisons with the estimated price of the book, which is $25. We'll save this to another decimal variable and print five comparisons to the console:

```
decimal bookPrice = 25;
Console.WriteLine(balance == bookPrice);
Console.WriteLine(balance != bookPrice);
Console.WriteLine(balance <= bookPrice);
Console.WriteLine(balance >= bookPrice);
Console.WriteLine(balance > bookPrice);
```

The console now prints the following:

```
The current balance is: $75.45
The current balance is: $35.45
The current balance is: $30.45
False
True
False
True
True
```

We can now see a few examples of the comparisons, but the one that we are most interested in is the last comparison, which we can use to find out if we have enough money to purchase the book. Let's change the last line and save it to a Boolean variable named `canAffordBook`:

```
bool canAffordBook = balance > bookPrice;
```

Because the value is true, it seems that you can afford to buy the book too. While there only are two values that a Boolean can ever be, they are an important part of comparing values in a program and are vital to developing software. There are more things that Booleans can do in a program, as we will explore in the next chapter.

Introduction to the array data type

So far, we have created variables that can only have one value, but what if there was a way to get multiple values from one variable? This can be done with arrays. Arrays are special types that can hold multiple values of the same type. The following figure shows how they are defined:

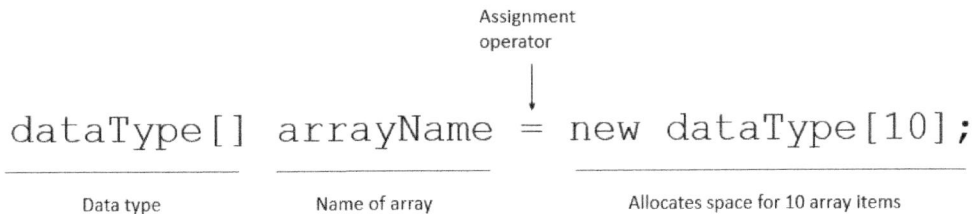

Figure 6.10 – Defining an array

Getting started with arrays is easier when you declare and initialize the number of items in the array, also known as the size. The size can only be a whole number. Follow along with the examples by creating a new console application and trying them out for yourself.

If you wanted to make an array of five integers, you would define it the following way:

```
int[] numberArray = new int[5];
```

Let's try another way to make an array, but this time, we will initialize it with values:

```
string[] primaryColors = {"red", "yellow", "blue"};
```

In this example, we created an array of strings with three values, avoiding using the `new` keyword and defining the size. The values within the `primaryColors` array can now be retrieved and read.

To access the contents of the array, you can use an index, which is a numerical representation of the position of the array element. The following figure shows how to access values in an array:

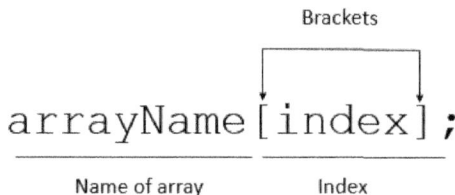

Figure 6.11 – Accessing data in an array

The index always starts at 0, so to read the first element in the `primaryColors` array, you would insert 0 in between the brackets:

```
primaryColors[0];
```

If you print the line to the console with `Console.WriteLine`, it will print a value of `red`, while if you increase the value by 1, it will print the next value, which is `yellow`. Try to print the following line:

```
primaryColors[3];
```

You should see the following error:

Unhandled exception. System.IndexOutOfRangeException: Index was outside the bounds of the array.

This error appears when an index that does not exist in the array is accessed. The `primaryColors` array only contains three items, which are at indexes 0, 1, and 2. Trying to access the array outside of these items will produce an error.

To add items to an array, you can insert values via the index. Let's try to add a number to the `numberArray` array we created earlier:

```
numberArray[0] = 100;
Console.WriteLine(numberArray[0]);
```

This will print the number `100` to the console. If you try to insert a value that is outside the allocated space of this array, which would be an index of 6 or higher, you will receive an error similar to the earlier one.

Arrays are an important part of working with large sets of data because they can store multiple values. Because arrays have a finite number of allocated spaces for values in them, it's important to work with an index that is within the range of the array. There's much more to learn about arrays, but that would take up an entire chapter, and with what you have learned so far, you can make your own arrays and experiment on your own. This brings us to the end of this chapter on the various ways of storing data.

Summary

In this chapter, you learned about the importance of data in a software program and how to store various types of data in C#, starting with a variable. This variable can hold different types of values, called data types. In a strongly typed language such as C#, data types must be used consistently with appropriate operators; otherwise, it could cause errors in the software. You then created your first variable in C#, worked with various data types, and updated the values in a variable.

You learned that string data types can be used to make textual values, such as sentences and messages, and can be combined through concatenation. Numbers can be whole or fractional with decimal points and can do all mathematical operations and be customized for precision. Booleans can be used to compare values that equate to true or false. Arrays contain multiple values of the same data type. Keep practicing with the MyBudget app, explore the documentation in the *Further reading* section, and experiment with what you learn.

In the next chapter, you'll learn more about C# and make more complex programs by building what you have learned so far to branch out to different parts of the code by making decisions and controlling the flow of the code with functions and loops.

Questions

1. What is the benefit of variables?
2. What is string concatenation?
3. What is the difference between an integer and a double data type?
4. How should you read comparison operators?
5. What is the index of the first item in an array?

Further reading

- Learn more about strings: `https://learn.microsoft.com/en-us/dotnet/csharp/programming-guide/strings/`

- Learn more about floating-point numbers: `https://learn.microsoft.com/en-us/dotnet/csharp/language-reference/builtin-types/floating-point-numeric-types`

- Experiment with numbers in this interactive tutorial: `https://learn.microsoft.com/en-us/dotnet/csharp/tour-of-csharp/tutorials/numbers-in-csharp`

- Learn more about arithmetic operators: `https://learn.microsoft.com/en-us/dotnet/csharp/language-reference/operators/arithmetic-operators`

- Learn more about comparison operators: `https://learn.microsoft.com/en-us/dotnet/csharp/language-reference/operators/comparison-operators`

- Learn more about equality operators: `https://learn.microsoft.com/en-us/dotnet/csharp/language-reference/operators/equality-operators`

7
Flow Control in C#

As the code base – the code being used to build the software – grows, it tends to become more complex. A company is a great example of the complexities of a business. Depending on the company rules or the industry regulations, there are certain processes and practices a company must adopt to make it successful. For example, a financial company will want to follow rules and regulations regarding how to handle sensitive customer information. How can software engineers approach problems like these in their language of choice?

In this chapter, we will learn how to create decisions and choices in how a software application works. Flow control enables programmers to change the behavior of the software based on certain criteria so that it can respond to different scenarios of usage. In C#, you'll learn how to use `if..else` statements, loops, and methods to control the behavior of the software.

This chapter will cover the following topics:

- Introduction to flow control
- Introduction to `if` statements
- Introduction to loops
- Introduction to methods
- Solving the Fizz Buzz problem

By the end of this chapter, you'll have enough knowledge about C# and flow control to try the popular programming problem called "Fizz Buzz."

Technical requirements

To complete the exercises in this chapter, you'll need a computer, such as a laptop or a desktop computer, that has Visual Studio Code and .NET installed. Refer to *Chapter 5, Writing Your First C# Program*, for information on how to install them.

You can find the code files for this chapter on GitHub at `https://github.com/PacktPublishing/Fundamentals-for-Self-Taught-Programmers/tree/main/Chapter7`.

Introduction to flow control

Most programming languages run linearly, where code runs from top to bottom, line by line. The following example shows the console application built in the previous chapter, which follows this order:

```
decimal balance = 75.45M;
string balanceMessage = "The current balance is: $";
Console.WriteLine(balanceMessage + balance);
balance -= 40;
Console.WriteLine(balanceMessage + balance);
balance -= 5;
Console.WriteLine(balanceMessage + balance);

decimal bookPrice = 25;
bool canAffordBook = balance > bookPrice;
```

If you have ever kept a personal budget, you're likely aware that expenses can be unpredictable at times. Regarding this problem with managing the ending balance, the cost of the groceries can vary, where it may be higher or lower than 40. This example currently has the price of the groceries hardcoded as 40 and the cost of tea as 5. Let's change it so that these values are stored in variables of the decimal data type:

```
decimal balance = 75.45M;
decimal groceries = 40.00M;
decimal tea = 5.00M;
string balanceMessage = "The current balance is: $";
Console.WriteLine(balanceMessage + balance);
balance -= groceries;
Console.WriteLine(balanceMessage + balance);
balance -= tea;
Console.WriteLine(balanceMessage + balance);
```

If you run the code, including the lines containing the book price, you'll see that the code runs the same and has the same behavior. Now, we have more control over handling the uncertainty of the prices by storing them in variables. Next, let's focus on the Boolean value in the program – that is, the line that checks whether you have enough for the book you want to buy:

```
bool canAffordBook = balance > bookPrice;yes
```

This comparison reads as *"balance is greater than the book price."* Based on the current costs, the program calculates a Boolean value of true. What else can we do with this value other than printing it to the console? As we learned in the previous chapter, Boolean values can either be true or false. This data type, which can only have two possible values, is what allows a program to have various behaviors based on its conditions. Boolean values are used in flow control because of their ability to evaluate particular conditions of a program and have it branch off into different parts of the program. In other words, Booleans are what programmers write to deal with uncertainty and different scenarios that may arise under certain conditions. However, Booleans are most powerful when combined with other methods of flow control. The majority of this chapter will use Booleans in combination with other statements to break away from the linear progression of the code, starting with the common `if..else` statement.

Introduction to if statements

Software engineers write conditions based on certain criteria to alter the flow of code. They do this by writing code that performs different tasks based on whether that condition evaluates to true or false. One of the most common ways to create these options, or branches of code, is with the `if` statement with the following syntax:

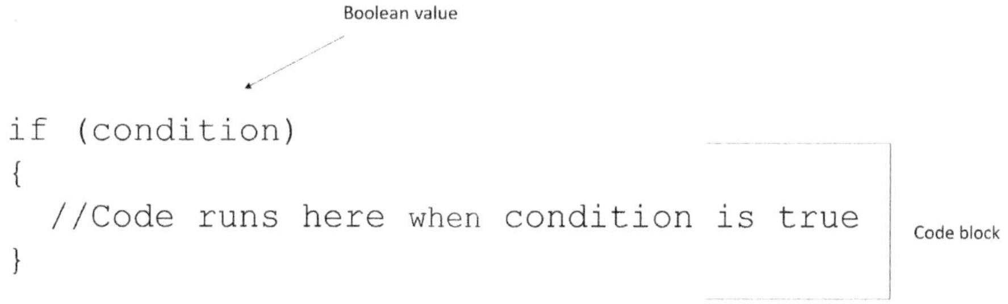

Boolean value

```
if (condition)
{
    //Code runs here when condition is true
}
```

Code block

Figure 7.1 – Identifying parts of an if statement

The code between the curly braces of an `if` statement will only run if the condition is true. If it's false, then the code will be ignored. Let's apply this `if` statement to the end of the `MyBudget` application, where we evaluate if we have enough for the book in the `canAffordBook` Boolean value. If we do, we'll subtract the price of the book from the balance:

```
decimal bookPrice = 25;
bool canAffordBook = balance > bookPrice;

if (canAffordBook)
{
    Console.WriteLine("You can afford to buy the book!");
    balance -= bookPrice;
}
Console.WriteLine(balanceMessage + balance);
```

With the current values in the program, we know that `canAffordBook` is true. Setting it as the `if` statement's condition means the message will print to the console. The updated application now informs you when you have enough for the book and will, but what if you also want to be informed when you don't have enough? We can add more to the `if` statement to perform tasks when the condition is false.

Using if..else statements

The `if` statement can be used to handle scenarios when the condition is true, but sometimes, code needs to be written for scenarios where the condition happens to be false. You can add an `else` statement immediately after the `if` statement to add code that will only run when the condition is false. An example of an entire `if..else` statement is shown here:

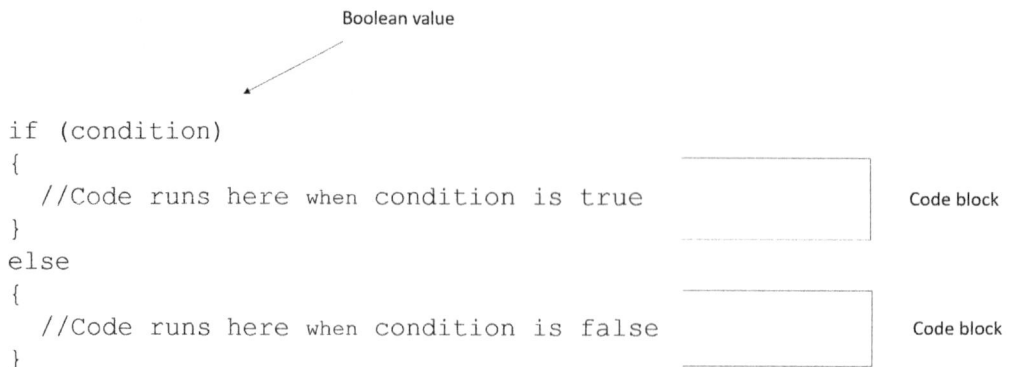

Boolean value

```
if (condition)
{
  //Code runs here when condition is true        Code block
}
else
{
  //Code runs here when condition is false        Code block
}
```

Figure 7.2 – Identifying parts of an if..else statement

In an `if..else` statement, two different lines of code will run based on either outcome of the condition. Keep in mind that while `if` statements can be used without `else`, `else` statements can't exist without `if` statements, so you can't apply `else` alone. Now, let's apply the `else` statement to MyBudget:

```
if (canAffordBook)
{
    Console.WriteLine("You can afford to buy the book!");
    balance -= bookPrice;
}
else
{
    Console.WriteLine("You can't afford the book!");
}
Console.WriteLine(balanceMessage + balance);
```

Now, the program alerts you about either condition, but will also subtract the price from the book if you have enough for it. Try to experiment with the program by changing the values and discovering what happens when the condition is false.

`if..else` statements can be categorized as a type of flow control called branching, where not all the code that exists will run because of the conditions that are put in place. Branching statements allow the program to make decisions, enabling software engineers to build different outcomes that can handle uncertainty, where they don't have control over the values in the program. Now, we'll keep MyBudget aside for a while and move on to another type of condition-based flow control that allows you to execute lines of code repetitively.

Introduction to loops

One common problem software engineers face when building software is repetition. Sometimes, they need to build code that needs to do repetitive tasks, such as reading from a database or analyzing blocks of text. This type of flow control is called iteration. Loops are blocks of code that run repeatedly until a condition, such as a Boolean value, is met. The loop continually runs when the condition is true and stops when it becomes false. C# has a few different types of loops, also called iterators, but this section will focus on the `for` and `while` loops. You can read more about the other loops by looking at the links provided in the *Further reading* section.

Using a for loop

The syntax of a `for` loop includes three parts, as shown here:

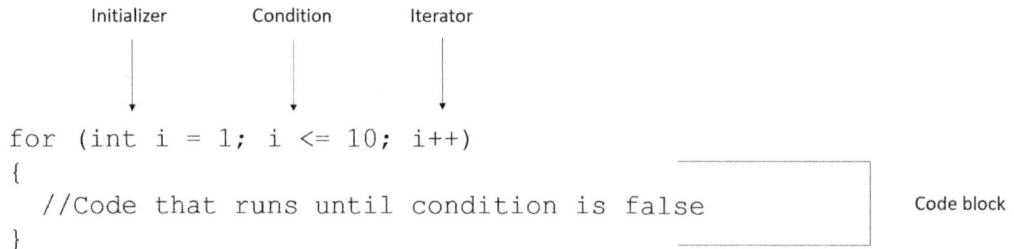

```
       Initializer          Condition          Iterator


for  (int  i  =  1;  i  <=  10;  i++)
{
    //Code that runs until condition is false                    Code block
}
```

Figure 7.3 – Identifying the different parts of a for loop

The initializer creates and sets the initial starting value of a variable that can be used within the code block of the `for` loop, within the curly braces. Next, the condition controls whether the loop continues to run by evaluating to true or false, where it will continue until false. Finally, the iterator is used to define behavior at the end of the loop's iteration, when all the code in the block has finished running. There are many use cases for the `for` loop, where it's often used with numbers and arrays. Let's look at a small example of a `for` loop that prints the numbers 1-10. You can copy this code and try it in a new console application:

```
for (int i = 1; i <= 10; i++) {
    Console.WriteLine(i);
}
```

Here, the initializer is an integer called i that has been set to 1, and the condition keeps the loop running so long as i is less than or equal to 10, and then increases i by 1 with the increment operator at the end of the loop after the current value of i is printed to the console. Imagine that this loop is at the end of its 10th iteration, where i is equal to 10 and has been printed to the console. At this point, the iterator increases i by 1, and its new value is 11. The i <= 10 condition is tested to verify whether the comparison is true. However, 11 is not less than or equal to 10 and equates to false, ending the loop.

Now that you understand how to use loops, we can apply this knowledge to the concept of arrays and iterate over them too.

Using a for loop with arrays

`for` loops can contain numerical initializers, and arrays contain numerical index values, where the initializer value can be set as the index of the array. You can also loop through the entire array by setting a condition that checks if the iterator is less than the length of the array. The length of an array refers to how many items are in the array and can be found with the `arrayName.Length` statement, where `arrayName` is the declared name of the array. Knowing the length of an array is key information to traverse or visit all the items of an array in a `for` loop.

Here's a small example of an array from *Chapter 6, Data Types in C#*, which is followed by a line returning and printing its length:

```
string[] primaryColors = {"red", "yellow", "blue"};
Console.WriteLine(primaryColors.Length);
```

The number 3 would print to the console because there are three strings in the array. Now, let's continue by using the same array in a `for` loop:

```
for (int i = 0; i < primaryColors.Length; i++)
{
    Console.WriteLine(primaryColors[i]);
}
```

The `primaryColors` array has three items in it, but the index of the last item, blue, is 2. So, the loop ends when i reaches 2 after it prints the value at the index, the iterator increases i by 1, updating the value to 3 and compares the condition where 3 is not less than or equal to 3, equating to false, and ends the loop. `for` loops can be used with arrays, but `foreach` is another loop that works for data types such as arrays. Refer to the *Further reading* section to learn more about the `foreach` loop.

Using a while loop

A `while` loop differs from a `for` loop as it only requires a condition, where the programmer must manage how the condition in the loop will evaluate to false and end. A while loop is shown in the following figure:

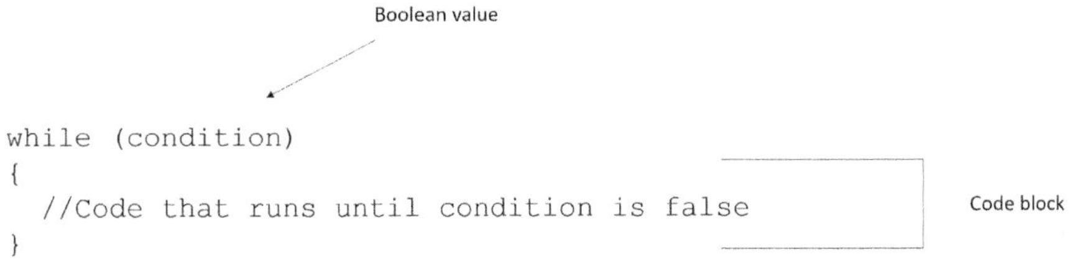

```
                                Boolean value


while (condition)
{
    //Code that runs until condition is false         Code block
}
```

Figure 7.4 – Identifying the different parts of a while loop

Notice that there are no initializer or iterator values. Let's use the same example of counting from 1-10 but with a `while` loop:

```
int j = 1;
while (j <= 10)
{
    Console.WriteLine(j);
    j++;
}
```

This example starts by creating a variable called `j` to manage the condition in the `while` loop. Inside this loop, `j` is increased by one at the end. Because there are no initializer or iterator values, you'll have to create them yourself.

Loops allow you to do repetitive tasks based on a Boolean condition, where `for` loops provide a way to track the condition with initializer and iterators, and `while` loops provide more flexibility in defining how the condition is met. Many different types of C# loops were not covered here, but you can learn more about them by looking at the resources in the *Further reading* section. In the next section, we'll explore another form of flow control: methods.

Introduction to methods

Methods are blocks of code that are built to execute specific tasks by the programmer. Methods can be categorized as a form of flow control because they typically do not have to be in a program's linear order to be executed. There may be cases when the code within a method doesn't execute at all. One of the benefits of using methods is reuse, where the same lines of code can be executed again by referencing the method, also known as calling the method. This saves time by reducing the time programmers spend writing repetitive lines of code to do the same task by running linear lines of code without it. It also helps reduce the risk of error by having less repetitive code. As we learned in the software engineering process, more code means that there is the possibility for more errors. Unlike loops, where the lines of code run repetitively until the condition is false, the lines of code in a method only run when they are called in the program, so they may only run once, or not at all depending on certain conditions.

While there are special types of methods that will require unique placement and syntax rules in C#, this section covers the basics of a common method. In addition to this, while you learn more about C# and other languages, you may come across the terms *function* and *method* used interchangeably. You can learn more about the difference between the two terms by looking at the resources provided in the *Further reading* section at the end of this chapter, but the concept is nearly the same across all popular programming languages. Now, let's return to `MyBudget` and continue building on the application by adding some methods to it.

How to create a method

Creating a basic method requires the method's definition, whose syntax starts with the data type and the method name. For now, we will use void, which is a method without a data type:

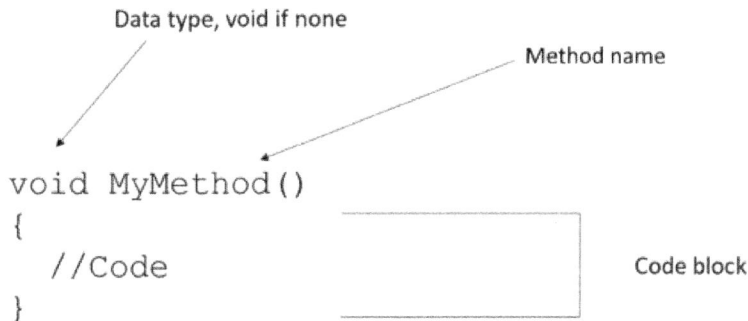

Figure 7.5 – Identifying the different parts of a method without a data type

In the preceding figure, the blocks of code between the curly braces will execute when the function is called.

Let's edit the MyBudget app so that it uses a method to replace some of the repetitive code. The following line, which prints the balance, shows up four times in MyBudget:

```
Console.WriteLine(balanceMessage + balance);
```

This line seems like a great candidate for a method. Here's a method that executes this line that can be added to the bottom of the MyBudget application:

```
void PrintBalance()
{
    Console.WriteLine(balanceMessage + balance);
}
```

Now that the application has one method called PrintBalance that can replace the four lines of code, it's time to use it by calling it in the application.

How to call a method

Calling a basic method requires using its name, followed by parentheses. Here's an example of calling the method you just created:

```
PrintBalance();
```

With this line of code, all the code inside of the `PrintBalance` method will run until it reaches the end of the method; then, the program will continue to the next line of code after where the method was called. Let's apply these method calls to `MyBudget` by replacing the repetitive lines:

```csharp
decimal balance = 75.45M;
decimal groceries = 40.00M;
decimal tea = 5.00M;
string balanceMessage = "The current balance is: $";

PrintBalance();
balance -= groceries;
PrintBalance();
balance -= tea;
PrintBalance();

if (canAffordBook)
{
    Console.WriteLine("You can afford to buy the book!");
    balance -= bookPrice;
}
else
{
    Console.WriteLine("You can't afford the book!");
}

PrintBalance();

void PrintBalance(){
    Console.WriteLine(balanceMessage + balance);
}
```

We have replaced the repetitive `Console.WriteLine` messages with a simple method call. Now, if you want to change the entire string inside the `WriteLine` message, it only needs to be changed in one line of code.

Notice that the location of PrintBalance does not matter in this example, just that the method needs to be defined in the application. You can experiment with the application by moving the method definition of PrintBalance around the application, where the behavior of the application will stay the same. Now that you have a basic understanding of methods, you'll build on your knowledge of parameters and return values.

Using method parameters and arguments

Sometimes, when performing tasks within methods, you may need to rely on extra information from values. These values are called parameters, which are optional values that are used within a method that includes a data type, and are referenced in the function definition. Let's look at an example by creating another method with parameters in MyBudget:

```
void CalculateNewBalance(decimal expense){
    balance -= expense;
}
```

This new method, CalculateNewBalance, takes a parameter called expense to calculate the cost of the new balance. Now, when we call the CalculateNewBalance method, we need to include a parameter that is of a decimal data type. The MyBudget app contains three lines of code that calculate the new balance, but the values that are calculated are different, which makes a method with a parameter a great replacement for these lines. First, let's replace the first line, which contains the function call.

Take a look at the following line:

```
balance -= groceries;
```

It now looks like this:

```
CalculateNewBalance(groceries);
```

The value of groceries replaces the expense parameter, which is now called the argument, or the value that takes the place of the parameter. Now, the value of groceries is defined as an expense in the method, but the value stays the same. Let's apply this method to the rest of the lines:

```
decimal balance = 75.45M;
decimal groceries = 40.00M;
decimal tea = 5.00M;
string balanceMessage = "The current balance is: $";
```

With all the variable values created in the first four lines, we can use them as arguments in the CalculateNewBalance method. Notice that groceries and tea have been used as arguments:

```
PrintBalance();
CalculateNewBalance(groceries);
PrintBalance();
CalculateNewBalance(tea);
PrintBalance();


decimal bookPrice = 25;
bool canAffordBook = balance > bookPrice;
```

The bookPrice variable can also be used as an argument for CalculateNewBalance when the balance is enough to buy the book, as shown in the following if..else statement:

```
if (canAffordBook)
{
    Console.WriteLine("You can afford to buy the book!");
    CalculateNewBalance(bookPrice);
}
else
{
    Console.WriteLine("You can't afford the book!");
}


PrintBalance();
```

Finally, all of the methods that were used in this example have been defined at the end of the program:

```
void PrintBalance(){
    Console.WriteLine(balanceMessage + balance);
}


void CalculateNewBalance(decimal expense){
    balance -= expense;
}
```

The lines that calculate the balance with the expense of the tea and book have been replaced with the method, and the values have been set as the argument. If you run the application again, you'll notice that it still runs the same way.

How to return a value from a method

There are times when the value that's calculated within a method needs to be used outside the method itself. These values can be returned from a method by defining a method with a data type. Let's write a small example in MyBudget that checks if the cost of an item is less than the balance:

```
bool VerifyAffordable(decimal cost)
{
    bool canAfford = balance > cost;

    return canAfford;
}
```

Note that the methods you have been writing up until now start with void, but because this one returns a Boolean value, it begins with the bool data type. This defines the data type of the value that the method will return, as seen in the code within the method, which ends with the return statement, followed by the return value. Now that the method returns a value, you can use the value outside the method by saving it to a variable, for example. Let's apply this to the MyBudget application:

```
bool canAffordBook = VerifyAffordable(bookPrice);
```

If you replace the existing line with the previous line and run the code, you'll notice that the code behaves the same. You now have a method that can calculate whether you can afford to buy anything else based on your current balance, including the book.

Methods are powerful tools for reuse in a software application; they help manage the flow of control in an application by keeping repetitive and/or specific tasks in one place. With parameters and return statements, functions can be reused with multiple values or used to create new ones.

That concludes this introduction to different methods for flow control. Now, we will apply what we have learned in this chapter to a common programming problem as an exercise in flow control.

Solving the Fizz Buzz problem

Fizz Buzz is a common programming problem that is a great way to challenge yourself at flow control. Before you begin, there are two C# concepts you should know about that will help you solve the problem. The first is else..if, which is another addition to the if..else statement, while the second is the remainder operator. Let's briefly return to the if..else statement in MyBudget, where we have added a Boolean called bookOnSale.

Using else..if

else..if statements allow for more branching, where you can add conditions that can be tested if the condition in the if statement is false. In the following example, the if..else statement in MyBudget has been modified to include an else..if statement:

```
decimal bookPrice = 25;
bool bookOnSale = true;

bool canAffordBook = VerifyAffordable(bookPrice);


if (canAffordBook)
{
    Console.WriteLine("You can afford to buy the book!");
    CalculateNewBalance(bookPrice);
}
else if(bookOnSale)
{
        Console.WriteLine("You can't afford to buy the book,
        but it's on sale!");
}
else
{
    Console.WriteLine("You can't afford the book!");
}
```

In this example, when canAffordBook is false, the bookOnSale condition is tested, and the code will execute because the statement is true. However, if bookOnSale happened to be false, then the code in the else statement would execute. You can add multiple else..if statements to an if..else statement.

Using the remainder operator

The remainder operator allows you to collect the remainder of two numbers when they are divided. In the following example, two numbers that divide evenly will result in 0:

```
int noRemainder = 10 % 5;
Console.WriteLine(noRemainder);
```

10 divided by 5 is 2, which leaves no remainder behind. This will print the number 0 to the console. Let's try another example with a remainder:

```
int remainder = 10 % 7;
Console.WriteLine(remainder);
```

10 divided by 7 does not divide evenly, leaving a remainder of 3 behind; it will print the number 3. It can be assumed that when a calculation with the remainder operator results in a remainder of 0, the number on the left of the operator can be divided by the number on the right evenly.

Now that you have these helpful additions to your programming skills, let's look at the problem. Try to solve it yourself before walking through the solution.

Write a console application that prints the numbers 1 to 10. For multiples of 3, print the word Fizz instead of the number, and for multiples of 5, print the word Buzz instead of the number.

Fizz Buzz solution

Here's the solution for the given problem:

```
for (int i = 1; i <= 10; i++) {

    if (i % 3 == 0) {
        Console.WriteLine("Fizz");
    }
    else if(i % 5 == 0){
        Console.WriteLine("Buzz");
    }
    else
    {
        Console.WriteLine(i);
    }
}
```

This solution first prints the numbers 1 to 10 in a for loop. Then, inside the loop, it checks if the initializer is divisible by 3, and checks if it's divisible by 5 if the first condition was false. If both conditions are false, then it prints the number.

The output should be as follows:

```
1
2
Fizz
4
Buzz
Fizz
7
8
Fizz
Buzz
```

How did you do? If you were not able to solve it this time, give it another try after a day or two. If you figure it out, you can search the internet for the full version of the challenge, which prints a longer range of numbers and the word `Fizz Buzz` when a number is a multiple of 3 and 5. You'll need to read up on logical operators for those versions.

With that, we have come to the end of this chapter. Let's summarize what we have achieved so far.

Summary

In this chapter, you learned the many ways you can control the flow of a program in C#. The benefit of learning flow control is that it's a common concept across a variety of languages and learning them now will help you learn to use them in different languages and platforms as well. We started by learning that conditions play an important role in flow control regarding Boolean data types. Next, we applied the `if..else` statement to branch out to different lines of code based on a condition. Then, we learned how to iterate and repeat executing lines of code with `for` and `while` loops, and compared and contrasted the two.

Later, you learned about how methods achieve flow control by organizing multiple lines of code that focus on a particular goal or task with the added benefit of reusing code, including being able to use multiple values with parameters and their matching arguments and extracting values with the return statement. Finally, you put your flow control skills to the test with a small Fizz Buzz exercise.

With that, you have learned enough C# to be able to use it to solve problems, as you have already been doing by tracking your expenses with `MyBudget`. In the next chapter, we will focus more on problem-solving with some common algorithms.

Questions

1. What data type is commonly used for flow control?

2. An `if` statement always needs to have a matching `else` statement. True or false?

3. What makes a loop stop?

4. What is the difference between a method parameter and a method argument?

5. Why would you create a method that begins with `void` instead of a data type?

Further reading

- Learn more about `if` statements: `https://learn.microsoft.com/en-us/dotnet/csharp/language-reference/statements/selection-statements#the-if-statement`

- Try out `if` statements and loops in this interactive tutorial: `https://learn.microsoft.com/en-us/dotnet/csharp/tour-of-csharp/tutorials/branches-and-loops`

- Learn more about C# methods: `https://learn.microsoft.com/en-us/dotnet/csharp/methods`

- Refer to this popular Stack Overflow question about the difference between a function and a method: `https://stackoverflow.com/questions/155609/whats-the-difference-between-a-method-and-a-function`

- Learn more about C# loops: `https://learn.microsoft.com/en-us/dotnet/csharp/language-reference/statements/iteration-statements`

- Learn more about the remainder operator: `https://learn.microsoft.com/en-us/dotnet/csharp/language-reference/operators/arithmetic-operators#remainder-operator-`

8
Introduction to Data Structures, Algorithms, and Pseudocode

When it comes to software engineering, there are many ways to solve one problem. Teams get together to break down complex problems into multiple subtasks, and some of these subtasks are things that software engineers do quite often. In *Chapter 3, Roles in Software Engineering*, we covered that software engineers often write code that will create, read, update, and delete data in their software programs. What happens when it's a large set of data that a user needs to filter, sort, or search through for something? When we look at a large amount of data on a web page or any other software, we often don't think about how much resource it takes to complete these types of tasks. As an example, let's consider a software program that retrieves a list of first and last names. A software engineer will write code that reads these names from a database and then loads them onto the screen in a readable format. If the list is quite long, the software engineer may need to handle how many names you see per page or view, also called paging, where you may see a list of numbers at the bottom of a list to see where you are in the list. They may also consider infinite scrolling, which you see on social media apps, where new text and content are often displayed as the user scrolls through an app or web page. As the list gets larger, you'll need to search for any specific names you're looking for, and you may want to have the ability to reorganize the list or search the list. Again, this is a common problem that software engineers face, and have different options on how to approach. A software engineer will most likely pick the most efficient solution, which is the one that allows you to quickly search through and sort the names.

Each of these options a software engineer has is called an algorithm, a set of tasks that solves a particular problem. However, many problems often have details and caveats that may make the problem complex. In other words, the problem is solvable based on a certain set of conditions, which is why a software engineer picks the best one for the problem that they are trying to solve. Data structures refer to the specific way that data is organized, which allows the data to be easily accessed and searchable. In general, a computer program is made up of algorithms and data structures. Topics relating to algorithms and data structures are quite vast, so much so that there are entire courses and textbooks dedicated to the subject. While this may sound overwhelming, just remember that any code you write can be considered an algorithm. Furthermore, it's impossible to remember every popular algorithm and data structure out there and software engineers will often refer to the internet or a textbook to refresh their memory. If you tried out the exercise in the previous chapter, you have successfully written an algorithm.

This chapter will walk through popular algorithms and data structures and show you how to conceptualize algorithms with pseudocode, which enables you to write algorithms in English or whichever written language you're comfortable with before you write it in code. Next, you'll dive deeper into popular data structures and algorithms, starting with learning about the array data structure and then exploring various sorting and searching algorithms.

This chapter will cover the following topics:

- Planning with pseudocode

- The importance of data structures and algorithms

- Introduction to the array data structure

- Introduction to the selection sort algorithm

- Introduction to the linear search algorithm

- Introduction to the binary search algorithm

By the end of this chapter, you will be able to write pseudocode and write algorithms with it.

Technical requirements

There are no technical requirements for this chapter.

Planning with pseudocode

Have you ever tried to plan out your day before starting to do the things you plan to do? Think about whether you have ever done this for a large trip or whether you do so every day when you start work at your job. Planning helps you prepare for what's to come and, in many cases, can make things such as your trip or workday successful. Programmers sometimes need to do this for complex problems they're trying to solve. Pseudocode enables you to plan out the task you're attempting to accomplish by writing out the computational steps in English, or any other preferred language. With no programming language, you can freely plan and document how you plan for your program to run, step by step. Unlike programming syntax, there is no "right" way to write pseudocode, and there are many guides on how to write it well, but a general rule of thumb is to not to introduce actual code into your pseudocode; save it for the actual program you're trying to write. You can write pseudocode with a pen and paper, in a document, on your phone, or even in the comments of the program you're creating.

Pseudocode can be broken down into two concepts: tasks and constructs. Tasks are the things that you'd like your program to do, such as increasing the numerical value of a variable or retrieving information from a database. On the other hand, constructs are representations of common programming operations, such as `if else` or loops. The combination of the two generates a sequence of progression of your tasks and constructs that describe the logic of the program you'd like to create.

Because pseudocode doesn't require syntax as a programming language does, we can dive right into writing it. Let's try it out in an exercise with the FizzBuzz problem from the previous chapter.

Exercise – FizzBuzz in pseudocode

One of the key things in pseudocode is to understand the problem you're trying to solve, so let's first revisit the prompt in FizzBuzz from the previous chapter.

Write a console application that prints the numbers 1 to 10. For multiples of 3, print the word `Fizz` instead of the number, and for multiples of 5, print the word `Buzz` instead of the number.

In the first sentence, we can ignore the console application part, as it doesn't apply to pseudocode, but here is where our first task is introduced – printing. In this program, we'll be printing numbers 1 through 10, which you have learned in the previous chapter that you can do with a loop, a construct. The next sentence contains another construct, where the number will be checked for multiples of 3 or 5, which means that the program will need to evaluate a condition, where an `if..else` statement would be a reasonable fit and counts as a construct. Now that we've identified the tasks and constructs in this problem, we're ready to write it out in the following example:

1. Set the counting number to 1.

2. Keep increasing the counting number until the counting number is 10.

3. When the counting number is a multiple of 3, print Fizz.

4. When the counting number is a multiple of 5, print Buzz.

5. When the counting number is neither a multiple of 3 nor 5, print the number.

6. Increment the counting number by 1.

7. End the program after the counting number prints 10.

While this is an acceptable example, we can improve on this by introducing common constructs as keywords in the pseudocode, where these keywords resemble the syntax you would write in the actual program. Combining keywords with formatting such as indentation, spacing, and cases will closely resemble the syntax of a programming language without writing code. The following example introduces keywords and formatting:

1. Set the counting number to 1.

2. WHILE the counting number is 10 or less.

3. IF the counting number is a multiple of 3.

    A. Print Fizz.

4. IF the counting number is a multiple of 5.

    A. Print Buzz.

5. ELSE, print the number.

6. Increment the counting number by 1.

7. End the program after the counting number prints 10.

Notice that the `while` and `if..else` keywords have been added and capitalized to stand out. Also, the steps under `while` have been indented to notate that these tasks should be repeated until the loop is complete. Either version of this pseudocode can be considered complete, but keywords and formatting enhance it with more structure without introducing programming syntax.

Recall earlier in the chapter that writing a program such as FizzBuzz is considered an algorithm, so writing pseudocode allows you to plan out your algorithm before you start writing it and can be a helpful tool to break down complex problems you may face when creating software. The following sections will focus on data structures and algorithms, why they are important, and some popular ones out of the many that exist.

The importance of data structures and algorithms

You'll find that an important part of programming is practice and experience, where you continually improve your skills, try new things, and apply what you have learned from past mistakes and wins. As an example, in *Chapter 5, Writing Your First C# Program*, you have probably learned that you need to add a semicolon at the end of every C# statement; otherwise, your code won't run. As you practice, you may find that you discover new ways to do something, a new solution to an old problem. When it comes to solving problems with software, algorithms create solutions.

Algorithms solve problems, where problems can vary in complexity from adding two numbers to finding text in a picture. You have probably used software that has solved these problems and you may not have noticed how fast it was and how accurate it was in doing so. These are things that software engineers face daily, and not only is it important to find a solution but it's also important to do so efficiently so that it takes up the least amount of resources: time and space. The thing about tasks on computers is that any operation will cost resources, whether it be time and/or space in computer memory, and software engineers will use algorithms to find the best balance.

Fortunately, many software engineers have faced similar problems and have built algorithms that others may use to quickly solve and move on to the next problem. The same goes for data structures, where efficiency means using the least number of resources to do something with data, whether that be reading, searching for, or inserting data. Algorithms save time for the programmer and computer alike so that they don't need to worry about how long it takes for autocomplete to appear in a search engine such as Google when the user starts typing, for example.

The rest of the chapter will focus on data structures and algorithms. There are many different ones that have been discovered and used in software that you probably use today. The following sections will focus on some popular ones, starting with a data structure you learned how to implement in C# in *Chapter 6, Data Types in C#*, the array.

Introduction to the array data structure

Arrays are a popular data structure represented in various software languages, including machine code. You learned how to write them in C# in the previous chapter. Arrays are a set of spaces in computer memory that have been saved for data, where each space has a fixed size for the data. When you create an array in a computer program, the computer saves or allocates space for the data, a collection of spaces that live next to each other and can be found in a single location in computer memory, and gives each space a memory address, which is a unique location in computer memory, similar to a typical address. So, when you create an array with five items in it, the computer allocates five spaces for your data and gives each of them a memory address and index. This defines an array as a contiguous data structure, where the data is in one location and each item is in subsequent order. The opposite of this is a linked data structure, where there may be space allocated for data in different locations, where these locations are identified in pointers. As you learned in the previous chapter, data that takes up space inside of an array is labeled and can be identified by its index, starting with the number 0. The following is a visual representation of an array, where the data will be pictures stored in computer memory:

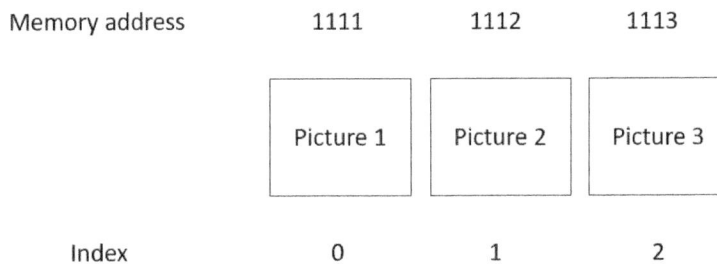

Memory address	1111	1112	1113
	Picture 1	Picture 2	Picture 3
Index	0	1	2

Figure 8.1 – Example of an array

There are some advantages of arrays that provide programmers with an easy way to store and find data. As you learned earlier in this chapter, space is a valuable resource in computation. A computer program must not waste space, which can affect any other operations happening on the computer and may slow it down and affect user productivity. Arrays are of a fixed size that is allocated for the data, so no space is wasted. When it comes to time, arrays provide a way to directly access data when the index is known, so there's no need to spend time searching through the entire array to find something if you already know where it is. One disadvantage is that arrays cannot be modified while a program is running, so you can't add additional data to the array while you're looping through it, although there is a type of an array called a dynamic array that does allow these types of operations.

You can read, search for, insert, and delete data within an array. Let's walk through some examples of what this looks like, starting with an example of the read operation. Here is an example of a picture in the array being read:

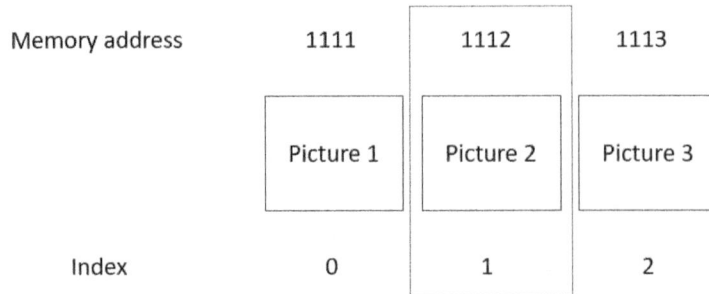

Memory address	1111	1112	1113
	Picture 1	Picture 2	Picture 3
Index	0	1	2

Figure 8.2 – Reading an item in an array

Computers can easily read data in an array thanks to the index, where the computer can increase an index by 1 to find the next item. When you want to find a specific item in the array by index, the computer has already made note of the memory address of the first item, where the index is 0. So if you wanted to retrieve data where the index is 2, the computer can easily jump to the item by adding 2 to the memory address, returning **Picture 3**. In other words, it takes the computer one step to find a value by its index. Steps refer to the work the computer has to do to carry out a particular task, which will most likely be instructions from a block of code. More steps mean more time to complete a task, where time is a resource that we try to preserve when possible. Now, let's try the opposite of reading, which is searching an array.

The difference between searching for data in an array and reading the data in it is that reading uses the index to find the value, while searching uses the value to find the location or index. To find a value, the computer will need to search through the array to find the value there. As mentioned before, the computer stores the memory address and index of the first item, so it knows where the value is but not what it is, so it must go through the array to find the value. To find the location of **Picture 3**, the computer will visit each item in the array until it's found, starting with index **0** in the following example:

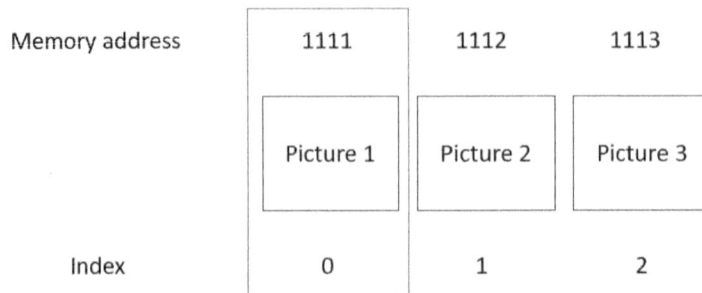

Memory address	1111	1112	1113
	Picture 1	Picture 2	Picture 3
Index	0	1	2

Figure 8.3 – Searching for a value by visiting the first item of an array

The computer does not find **Picture 3** at the location visited, so it moves on to the adjacent location, as seen in the following example:

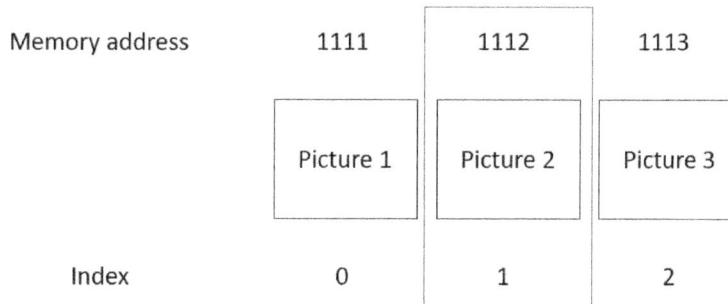

Figure 8.4 – Searching for a value by visiting the second item of an array

Again, **Picture 3** does not exist at this location, so the computer moves on to the next one:

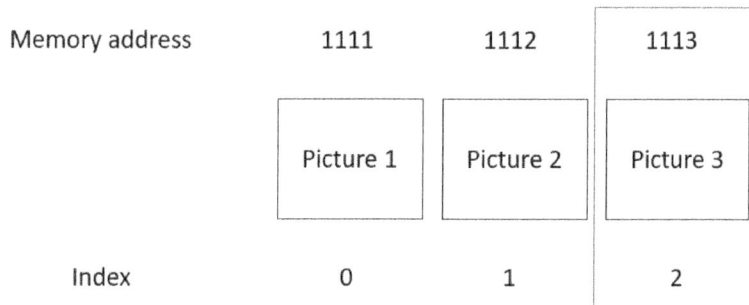

Figure 8.5 – Finding a value by searching in an array

Finally, **Picture 3** is located at index **2**. The computer took two steps to find it, but it would take much less if we were searching for **Picture 1**. This means that depending on where the value is, it may take less or more time to retrieve the value. Let's move on to how insertion works in an array by looking at the following example:

Memory address	1111	1112	1113	1114
	Picture 1	Picture 2	Picture 3	
Index	0	1	2	3

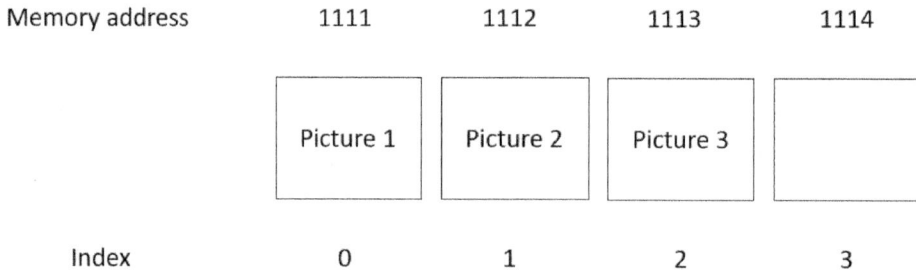

Figure 8.6 – Allocating new space in an array

Because arrays are of a fixed length, insertion operations require the computer to allocate additional space for a new value. A space is added at the end of the array, then the value is inserted into the array. The value can be inserted into any part of the array, but to do so, the existing items may need to shift to a different space or index. The previous example showed how to allocate space for a new value to be inserted. Let's explore scenarios for inserting a new value.

When new space is allocated, a new memory address and index are added to the end of the array, where a new value could be inserted. Here's an example of adding a value to the end of the array:

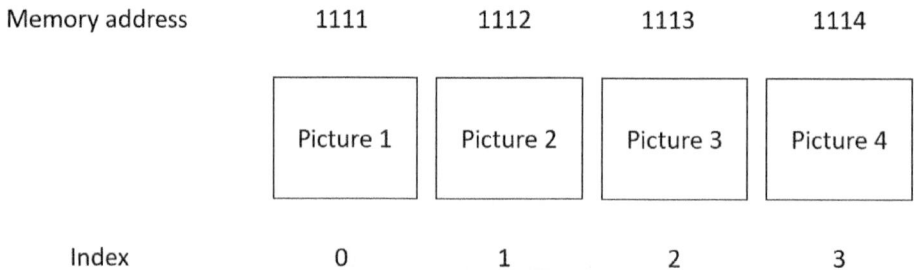

Memory address	1111	1112	1113	1114
	Picture 1	Picture 2	Picture 3	Picture 4
Index	0	1	2	3

Figure 8.7 – Inserting a new value into an array

What if we wanted to insert **Picture 4** into another part of the array, such as into index **1**? To do this, we must first return to the first example with the empty allocated space and shift the existing values to the right to make space for it. Here's the first step of moving the last item, **Picture 3**, to the right:

Memory address   1111   1112   1113   1114

Picture 1	Picture 2		Picture 3

Index   0   1   2   3

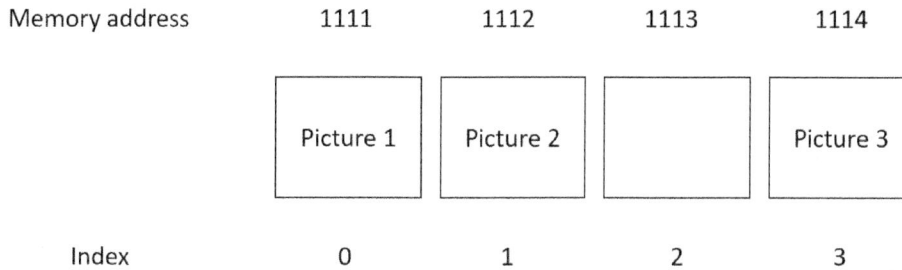

Figure 8.8 – Shifting the Picture 3 value to the right in an array

There's now an empty space, but that's not the index where we'd like to insert the new value, so let's move the item on the left to the right in the following example:

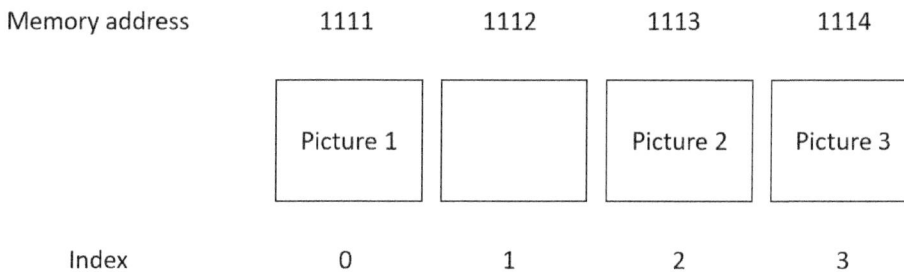

Memory address   1111   1112   1113   1114

Picture 1		Picture 2	Picture 3

Index   0   1   2   3

Figure 8.9 – Shifting the Picture 2 value to the right in an array

The empty space is now at index **1**, and we can insert the new value there. Here's an example of the completed insertion:

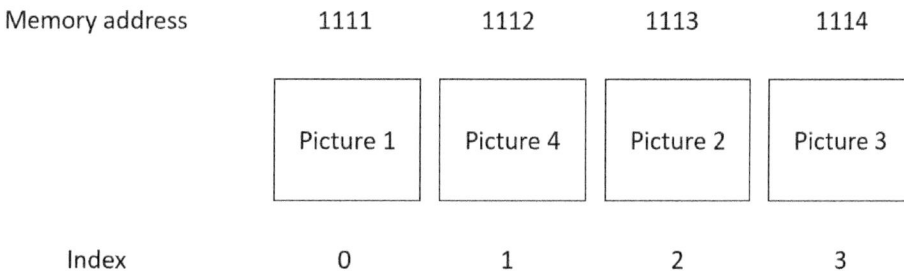

Memory address   1111   1112   1113   1114

Picture 1	Picture 4	Picture 2	Picture 3

Index   0   1   2   3

Figure 8.10 – Inserting a new value into index 1 of an array

This took four steps to complete: new space was allocated for the value, then **Picture 3** and then **Picture 2** were shifted to the right, and, finally, **Picture 4** was inserted into the empty space. In the insertion scenario, the smallest number of steps in this operation would have been two if we had inserted **Picture 4** into the last space. Let's move on to the final operation, deletion. In the following example, **Picture 2** has been deleted from the array:

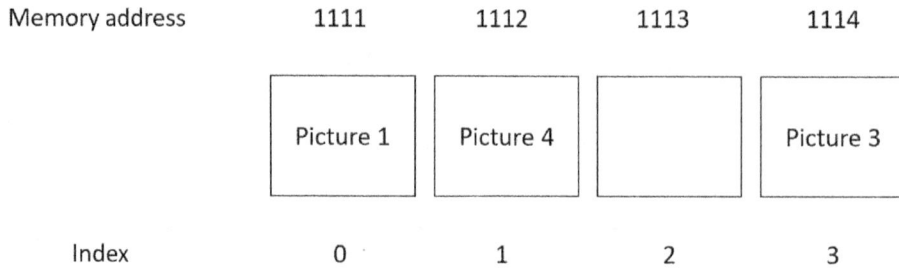

Memory address	1111	1112	1113	1114
	Picture 1	Picture 4		Picture 3
Index	0	1	2	3

Figure 8.11 – Deleting an existing value from an array

There's now an empty space in the array, which will make search operations less efficient because visiting each item will reveal an empty value. We can make any search operation a little faster by filling it in with the neighboring values by shifting everything to the left, as in the following example:

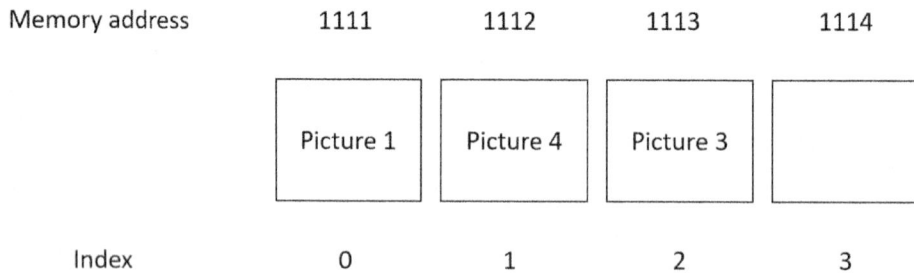

Memory address	1111	1112	1113	1114
	Picture 1	Picture 4	Picture 3	
Index	0	1	2	3

Figure 8.12 – Shifting the Picture 3 value to the left in an array

This operation took two steps, deleting **Picture 2** and shifting **Picture 3** to the left. Now, searching through the array will take less time, because the empty space is at the end, and if the value we are looking for exists in the array, we'll find the intended value before the computer visits the empty space.

Now that you have learned about the array data structure, we'll explore algorithms for organizing and searching data, starting with the selection sort algorithm.

Introduction to the selection sort algorithm

In the previous section, we saw that the steps to complete array operations can vary based on the position of the data. We sometimes arrange and organize data in such a way that it is more readable and faster to find what we're looking for, and computers can benefit from this too. A data structure that contains sorted data, such as a numerical sequence stored in an array, takes fewer steps to complete an operation such as reading or insertion. Sorting algorithms also take several steps to complete the sorting process. We will explore the selection sort algorithm, which is a common sorting algorithm that finds the smallest element in a data structure and moves it to the front. Let's dive in by exploring an example of an array that contains four integers:

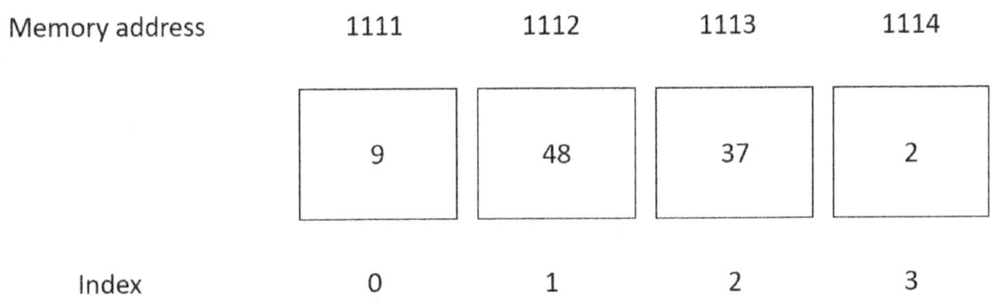

Memory address	1111	1112	1113	1114
	9	48	37	2
Index	0	1	2	3

Figure 8.13 – An unsorted array of integers

We can easily organize this sequence in our heads, but writing an algorithm to do this will involve writing code that takes a few steps, which we can write in pseudocode:

1. Store the value as the "smallest."
2. Compare the value to the other items in the array by visiting each one.
3. Find the smallest of the values.
4. IF the smallest value is found, swap the location of the smallest value with the first item.
5. Store the new value as the smallest one.
6. Visit the next value at index **2**.
7. Repeat *steps 2-6* until all values in the array have been visited and compared.

In this example, the value at index **0** is **9** and will be compared against the other values, where **2** will be the smallest. The positions of **2** and **9** will be swapped, placing **2** at the beginning of the array at index **0**, and **9** at index **3**:

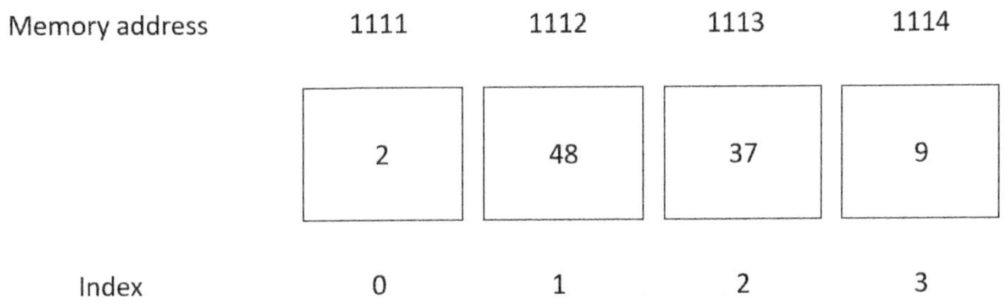

Memory address	1111	1112	1113	1114
	2	48	37	9
Index	0	1	2	3

Figure 8.14 – Swapping integers in an array with selection sort

The algorithm will now move on to index **1**, where the value is **48**. It is compared against the remaining values, where **9** is the smallest and swaps positions so that **9** moves to index **1** and **48** moves to index **3**.

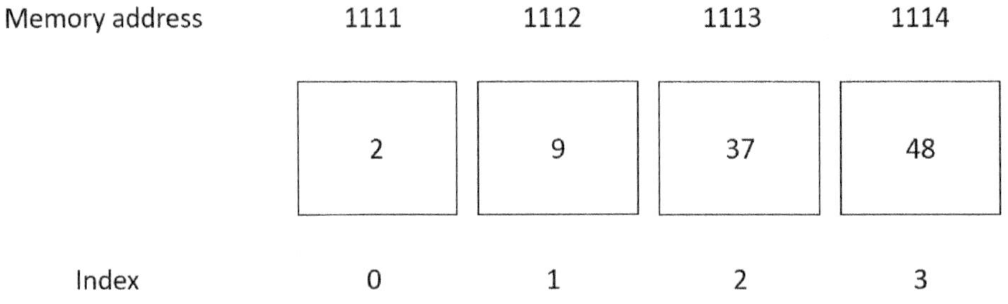

Memory address	1111	1112	1113	1114
	2	9	37	48
Index	0	1	2	3

Figure 8.15 – An array that has been sorted with selection sort

While we can see that the array is now obviously sorted, the algorithm is not aware that the sorting is completed and visits index **2** and value **37**, and compares it to the remaining value, **48**. At this point, the algorithm ends because the algorithm has reached the last item in the array and has no more comparisons to make.

The selection sort algorithm is a common way to sort values. There are various other sorting algorithms, such as bubble sort and quick sort, with various levels of complexity and efficiency.

Having learned the importance of organizing data, we'll move on to searching algorithms, starting with linear search.

Introduction to the linear search algorithm

The linear search algorithm is a basic search within a data structure that begins by visiting the data at the beginning and visits each value until it's found or reaches the end of the array, where the value does not exist. In the *Introduction to the array data structure* section, we did a linear search to find a picture in the example array. We'll experiment with it more by using the same array of integers used in the selection sort algorithm. First, let's write the algorithm in pseudocode:

1. Store the value being searched for.

2. Start at index 0.

3. WHILE the value is not found and is not at end of the array.

    A. IF the value is equal to the value being searched for.

        i.   Return the index

    B. ELSE

    i.   Increase the index by 1 and move on to the next value.

  C.   IF at end of the array.

    i.   Print value not found.

In the following example, we will be searching for the integer **48**, so the algorithm will visit the value at index **0**:

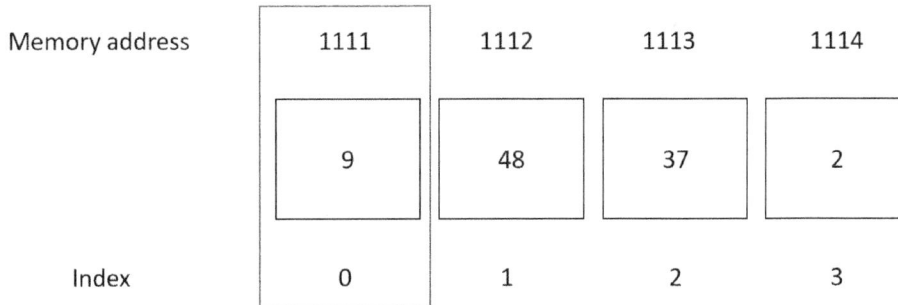

Figure 8.16 – An array being searched with linear search

The value at index **0** is **9** and is not the required value, so the algorithm increases the index by 1 and visits the next value.

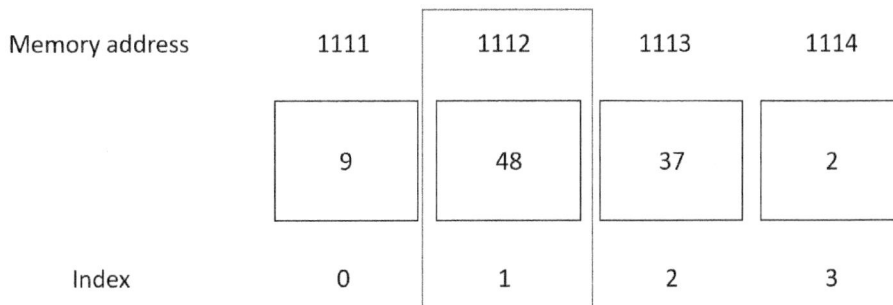

Figure 8.17 – The linear search algorithm finding a value in an array

48 is at index **1**, so the algorithm ends the search. While this is a straightforward algorithm, it can get quite lengthy depending on how the items are organized. Let's try this algorithm again with the sorted version of the array and search for **48**. We'll fast forward to the final step in this example, where **48** is found:

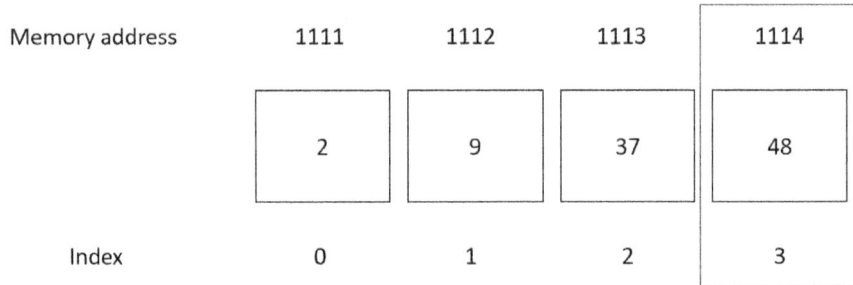

Figure 8.18 – The linear search algorithm finding a value in a sorted array

To get to the value being searched for, the algorithm needed to visit all the other values to find it, taking more steps. This could be costly in time and resources, so depending on the situation, a software engineer may pick this search algorithm or another to reduce the steps and time. The next section explores another search algorithm, binary search.

Introduction to the binary search algorithm

The binary search algorithm differs from the linear search algorithm in that the data structure, like an array, needs to be sorted to apply the algorithm. Binary search works by finding the middle value of the array and comparing it to the value that is being searched for. This narrows down the list of values so that every item in the array won't need to be visited because they are higher or lower than the middle value. First, let's set up the algorithm in pseudocode:

1. Store the value being searched for.
2. WHILE the value is not found.

   A. Take the array length and divide it by 2.
   B. Set the value as the midpoint index.
   C. IF the index value is less than the search value.

      i. Stop visiting values that are less than the midpoint index.

   D. IF the index value is higher than the search value.

      i. Stop visiting values that are larger than the midpoint index.

   E. IF the index value is equal to the search value.

      i. The value has been found, return the index.

   F. IF no more indexes to visit exist.

      i. Print value not found.

Now, we will revisit a previous example of the sorted array in *Figure 8.18* and add an additional number so that it has an even number of elements. The following example searches for **9** and highlights the middle index and value of the array, but because **9** is less than **37**, we can ignore the values to the right, including the one at the middle index.

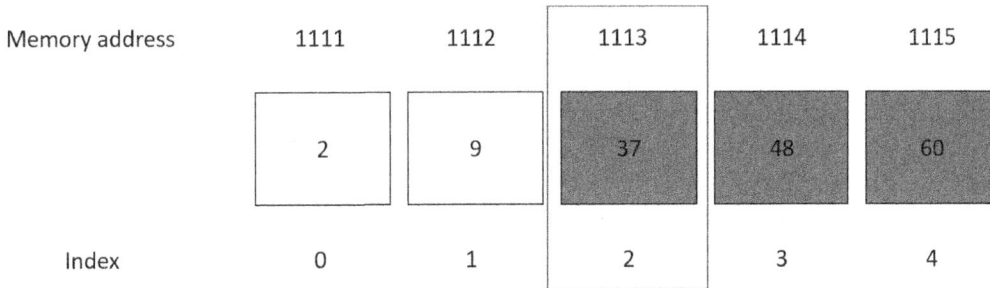

Figure 8.19 – The binary search algorithm finding the middle index

The algorithm has now narrowed down the possible location of the value. Next, the algorithm selects the next median value, which would be **1**, and finds that the value at the index is the one that the algorithm is looking for:

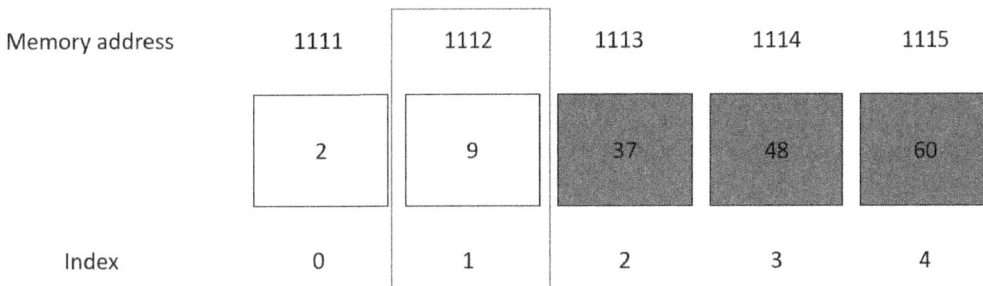

Figure 8.20 – The binary search algorithm finding the search value

Like the other algorithms, the amount of data and the value being searched can change how long or how many steps it takes to find a value in a binary search. This concludes our exploration into data structures and algorithms.

Summary

Data structures and algorithms save software engineers' time with efficient ways to complete tasks and solve problems. You can get started with writing algorithms in plain English with pseudocode, where you can write what you'd like your program to do as tasks and incorporate them into common programming tasks as constructs. You have already learned about the array data structure and how to write it in C#, and in this chapter, you learned more about it as a data structure and about using read, search, insert, and delete operations on them. Finally, you learned about some popular sorting and searching algorithms, where binary search required an array that had already been sorted.

Software engineers rely on and will select different algorithms and data structure operations based on the problem they're trying to solve and how efficiently they use computer resources. In the next chapter, we'll return to programming in C# to create these algorithms.

Questions

1. What is the difference between tasks and constructs in pseudocode?
2. Why would software engineers seek to reduce the number of steps it takes to perform an operation on an array data structure?
3. In an array, what is the location of the first value where the selection sort algorithm begins?
4. What are the two outcomes of using the linear search algorithm?
5. What are some differences between binary search and linear search?

Further reading

- *The Algorithm Design Manual* (2nd edition, 2010) by S. S. Skiena, Springer
- *A Common-Sense Guide to Data Structures and Algorithms, Second Edition: Level Up Your Core Programming Skills* (2017) by J. Wengrow, Pragmatic Bookshelf
- *Pseudocode Standard.* (n.d.): http://users.csc.calpoly.edu/%7Ejdalbey/SWE/pdl_std.html

9

Applying Algorithms in C#

In the previous chapter, you learned about a few algorithms, and also how to use pseudocode to get a high-level view of how each algorithm is applied. Software engineers may use this method to understand how an algorithm works, or as practice for a technical interview for a role they may be pursuing. Whatever the case may be, the next step after working with pseudocode is to implement the algorithm in a programming language. After an algorithm is built, software engineers can make the choice to improve it. They can take another look at the code they wrote and decide which parts need improvements to make the algorithm more efficient or its code more readable. In a team setting, this is usually done through a code review, where another software engineer who wasn't the original author of the code will look over it and make the recommended performance and readability changes. The process of applying changes to code such as an algorithm is called refactoring. In this chapter, you'll build the algorithms you learned about in the previous chapter and learn ways to make them better in terms of readability and performance with refactoring.

This chapter covers the following topics:

- Writing a selection sort algorithm in C#
- Writing a linear search algorithm in C#
- Writing a binary search algorithm in C#
- Building your own algorithms
- Improving algorithms with refactoring

By the end of this chapter, you will know how to write the algorithms from the previous chapter in C#. You will also have learned how to build your own algorithm and make it better with refactoring. As a reminder, there are many ways to solve a problem when it comes to programming. With that said, the examples in this chapter won't utilize all the possible features built in the C# language, and you may discover new ways to write the solutions here. These solutions can be revised with much fewer lines of code, and some of these algorithms can be done in one line. It's highly encouraged to take these examples and try and learn new ways to make the code more efficient in terms of readability and performance. Refer to the *Further reading* section to learn about techniques for doing this.

Technical requirements

To complete the exercises in this chapter, you'll need a computer, such as a laptop or a desktop computer, that has Visual Studio Code and .NET installed. Refer to *Chapter 5, Writing Your First C# Program,* for information on how to install them.

You can find the code files for this chapter on GitHub at https://github.com/PacktPublishing/ Fundamentals-for-Self-Taught-Programmers/tree/main/Chapter9.

Writing a selection sort algorithm in C#

To recap what you learned in the previous chapter, the selection sort algorithm searches for the smallest value within the array and then moves the smallest value to the front of the array so that the array will be sorted in ascending order. Let's identify a few things about this algorithm that will help us build it in C#. First, we'll need to search the entire array until the smallest value is found, so we'll need some iteration, such as a `for` loop, to visit every item in the array.

> **Tip**
> It's important to note here that algorithms are meant to be abstract, meaning that this algorithm will be able to work with any numerical array. The array in the example is a test array to make sure we're on the right track.

Let's begin by creating a small array and a loop to do this:

```
int[] testArray = {13, 55, 0, -4, 80, 7, 20};
for (int index = 0; index < testArray.Length; index++)
{
    Console.WriteLine(testArray[index]);
}
```

Next, notice that when the smallest number is located and moved, the array is now split into sections, where the front of the array is sorted and the other end remains unsorted until the algorithm is complete. With this knowledge, we know that once the first item is found and moved, the value at index 0 is sorted and the algorithm doesn't need to visit the value stored at that index anymore. This will be the case for each subsequent sorted item. How can we search through the unsorted part of the array exclusively so that we don't waste resources visiting sorted items? We can use a technique called nesting to do this, where we can insert an additional `for` loop within the first `for` loop and search through the unsorted section. Nesting can be a useful tool in building algorithms and can be used with other statements, such as `if..else`. Let's use nesting here by adding another `for` loop:

```
int[] testArray = {13, 55, 0, -4, 80, 7, 20};
```

```
for (int index = 0; index < testArray.Length; index++)
{
    Console.WriteLine(testArray[index]);

    for (int unsortedIndex = index + 1;
        unsortedIndex < testArray.Length; unsortedIndex++)
    {
        Console.WriteLine("Unsorted value:" +
            testArray[unsortedIndex]);

    }
}
```

This inner loop is visiting the unsorted parts of the array by increasing the current index by 1. The loop starts by visiting index 0, then visiting all the items at index 1 to the end. The algorithm is incomplete as is, but the goal is that when the smallest item is placed at index 0, the inner loop will visit all items starting at index 1, finding and placing the smallest item at index 1, and moving on to the next items until it reaches the end.

At this point, it sounds like the algorithm will need to make some comparisons within the array to find the smallest value and the index of where it's stored, which can be captured in a variable. From what we learned about arrays in *Chapter 7, Flow Control in C#*, we can use the index variable to keep track of the index and use it to find the value stored there. Here's a snippet of the outer loop and the values to keep track of:

```
for (int index = 0; index < testArray.Length; index++)
{
int minIndex = index;
int minValue = testArray[index];
```

Now that we are storing the key values we need to keep track of, let's compare the value to the rest of the unsorted array with an if statement. This should happen within the inner loop, as it's visiting the unsorted values within the array. Here's a snippet of the inner loop and the comparison:

```
for (int unsortedIndex = index + 1; unsortedIndex < testArray.
Length; unsortedIndex++)
{
    if (testArray[unsortedIndex] < minValue)
    {
```

```
        minIndex = unsortedIndex;
        minValue = testArray[unsortedIndex];
    }
}
```

When a smaller value is found, it will replace the currently stored index and value and keep going until the smallest value is found within the unsorted part of the array. At this point, it's now time to swap the smallest value with the value of the index stored in the index variable, if it exists:

```
int tempValue = testArray[index];
testArray[index] = testArray[minIndex];
testArray[minIndex] = tempValue;
```

The index variable is the location of the value that needs to be swapped with the smaller variable. However, we need an extra variable to store the old value at the initial location in a temporary variable, which is the variable called tempValue, so that the next line can swap the two values by replacing the current value at the current index with the newly discovered minimal value at minIndex. Finally, we use the tempValue variable to store the previous value in the index variable and set it to the old location of the minimal value. With that, the algorithm is completed and will sort any array that is used. The algorithm can be tested by printing the entire array. The following line is a quick way to print the contents of the array and can be added to the end of the algorithm, outside of both loops:

```
Array.ForEach(testArray, Console.WriteLine);
```

The output will return the following:

```
-4
0
7
13
20
55
80
```

You can test this out in a new C# console app and experiment with different values. This solution only works with numbers, but you can edit the data type to try it with decimal values.

Writing a linear search algorithm in C#

The linear search algorithm is a basic search algorithm that starts from the beginning of an array and visits each value until it matches the value that's being searched. In the previous algorithm, selection sort, a linear search already takes place where values are compared with the less than (<) comparison operator to find the lowest value. The basic version of linear search only needs one loop and will use the equality operator (==) to find the value. If the loop reaches the end of the array, then the value does not exist within the array. Let's build a short example of linear search within an array:

```
int[] testArray = {13, 55, 0, -4, 80, 7, 20};
int searchValue = 0;

for (int index = 0; index < testArray.Length; index++)
{
    if(searchValue == testArray[index])
    {
        Console.WriteLine("Value found!");
        break;
    }
}
```

This algorithm will need a loop to visit each item in the array so that the value being searched for, named searchValue in this example, is compared for equality in an if statement. When a value is found, the search is over, and the loop should end. Loops can be interrupted and exited with a break statement inside the code block. If you run this example as is, the output to the console will show the following message:

```
Value found!
```

This message prints because the value of searchValue is 0, which exists in testArray. Now, let's move on to the binary search algorithm, which is a bit more complicated but can be faster than a linear search.

Writing a binary search algorithm in C#

Binary search requires that an array be sorted first before searching for the value. The reasoning behind this is that binary search doesn't visit all the values within the array, but instead will find the midpoint value, sectioning the array into values to the left or right of the midpoint, continually splitting the array in half to narrow down the search. If the value is higher than the midpoint, the algorithm narrows the search to values to the right of the midpoint, known as the upper half, and to the left if it's lower, known as the lower half. There is also the possibility that the value could be the midpoint. To calculate the midpoint, we'll need the beginning index and the last index of the area being searched within the array, which will be the whole array at first. The following example shows this calculation:

```
int[] testArray = {-4, 0, 7, 13, 20, 55, 80};
int lowerHalfIndex = 0;
int upperHalfIndex = testArray.Length - 1;
int midpointIndex = lowerHalfIndex + (upperHalfIndex -
lowerHalfIndex)/2;
```

In the midpoint calculation, dividing the difference between the lower- and upper-half indexes will first be evaluated before adding the lower-half index. The lower half is then added to skip over any values that have been already visited. Try calculating it yourself, ignoring any decimal places and not rounding up. This calculation will return index 3 and the value 13.

The value at the midpoint index can now be compared against the search value, so let's add more to this calculation by creating a search value and comparing it against the midpoint value in the next example:

```
int[] testArray = {-4, 0, 7, 13, 20, 55, 80};
int lowerHalfIndex = 0;
int upperHalfIndex = testArray.Length - 1;
int midpointIndex = lowerHalfIndex + (upperHalfIndex -
lowerHalfIndex)/2;
int searchValue = 55;

if (testArray[midpointIndex] > searchValue )
{
    upperHalfIndex = midpointIndex - 1;
}

else if(testArray[midpointIndex] < searchValue)
{
    lowerHalfIndex = midpointIndex + 1;
}

else
{
    Console.WriteLine("Your value was found!");
}
```

When the midpoint is larger than the search value, the search can be narrowed down to the left of the midpoint, or the lower half of the array. The highest point will then need to be adjusted to only values to the left of the midpoint, by subtracting the midpoint index by 1 and keeping the lower-half index the same, shortening the search range. If the value is larger and the values can be narrowed down to the right, or upper half, the lower-half index needs to be adjusted to an index range that is higher than the midpoint, by adding 1 to the midpoint and setting it as the lower-half index. In either case, we can ignore the midpoint because it is not equal to the search value. If the midpoint is neither higher nor lower than the search value, then the only possibility is that the midpoint is the search value and the value has been found.

With a search value of 55, the new search range is now a lower index of 4 and a value of 20, and the upper index remains at 6. It's now time to find the midpoint of this range with the same calculation we used earlier, but instead of rewriting it, we can put this in a loop, as seen in this next example:

```
while(lowerHalfIndex <= upperHalfIndex)
{
    int midpointIndex = lowerHalfIndex + (upperHalfIndex -
      lowerHalfIndex)/2;
    int searchValue = 55;

    if (testArray[midpointIndex] > searchValue )
    {
        upperHalfIndex = midpointIndex - 1;
    }

    else if(testArray[midpointIndex] < searchValue)
    {
        lowerHalfIndex = midpointIndex + 1;
    }

    else
    {
        Console.WriteLine("Your value was found!");
        break;
    }
}

if (lowerHalfIndex > upperHalfIndex)
{
```

```
        Console.WriteLine("Your value was not found!");
}
```

The upper and lower halves are adjusted in each iteration, and when the lower half ends up being larger than the upper half, the algorithm has run out of spaces to search, and the value has not been found. The test array does contain the search value of 55 and will print that the value was found, but you can experiment with other numbers and add more numbers to the array to see different outputs. Just remember that the array must stay in sorted order. You can also measure performance by counting the iterations with a counter variable: the lower the iterations, the faster it is, but this primarily depends on the value that is being searched. Now that you have learned how to build a few popular algorithms in C#, you'll learn tips on how to create your own algorithms and improve them with refactoring.

Building your own algorithms

As you learned in *Chapter 8*, *Introduction to Data Structures, Algorithms, and Pseudocode*, algorithms are computer programs that solve problems. From this, we can conclude that programmers who build computer programs (including you if you have tried any of this chapter's exercises and previous chapters on C#) can build an algorithm. Algorithms won't always be the common sorting and searching problems that were built in this chapter or ones you may discover in other algorithm books but can be customized to solve unique problems that a programmer may face. Algorithms not only solve problems but also need to solve the right problem within a reasonably estimated time frame. When you're building algorithms, you'll want to take this into consideration, in addition to reviewing it to make sure that any input and data that it works with will produce the same result, and whether it's an efficient way to solve the problem. To help understand how to build a good algorithm, let's focus on the topics of correctness and performance from the earlier quote.

When algorithms solve a problem, they must be able to produce the same output with any input they take. As an example, all the algorithm exercises from earlier chapters used smaller arrays as sample input but would also work with arrays that are much larger. However, there are cases where algorithms will only be correct with specific input, which you may have noticed in the binary search algorithm, which requires a sorted array. Correctness doesn't always mean that an algorithm should be correct for all input, but that input can come in different forms and some algorithms will solve specific problems relative to the input. With that said, you will discover that some algorithms will be a better fit, and you may find that you compare the pros and cons of each when making a decision on which one to choose. You'll also find that one of the biggest factors in making this choice is the input you're working with.

When it comes to performance, algorithm efficiency primarily relates to how long it takes for an algorithm to run and the resources it uses. Have you ever tried using a slow app, or maybe a computer program that froze your machine while it completed a task? It was probably pretty frustrating! Algorithms that take too long and use too many computer resources can create a negative experience for the user. While a fast computer may make an algorithm run faster, an algorithm that runs efficiently will often be a sufficient way to handle performance. The larger the input used in the algorithm, the longer it will take to complete, and input size is usually out of the software engineer's control. Algorithm performance can be measured and analyzed with big O notation, a mathematical representation of the complexity of an algorithm. Big O takes into account time and space complexity, measuring how long the algorithm takes and how much memory the algorithm needs to run. This calculation is dependent on a few factors, such as input size and how the input is organized. For example, an array that is already sorted and is used with the selection sort algorithm would not see an improvement in performance because each value would still be compared. However, the insertion sort algorithm, which was not covered in this chapter, would benefit from a sorted array because it takes a different approach by comparing adjacent values and swapping them into ascending order. These two algorithms would have different calculations of big O complexity despite using the same input. Complexity can usually be categorized into three types, described by using the linear search algorithm as an example:

- Best case, where the algorithm runs the fastest or uses the least resources. If the value being searched for is the first value in the array, the algorithm will end and take less time to run.

- Average case, where the algorithm runs in the expected amount of time and uses the expected number of resources. If the value happens to be in the middle of the array, this could be categorized as an average case because there's a higher probability that the value is in between the first and last values in the array. Average case scenarios for algorithms are based on complex calculations of probability.

- Worst case, where the algorithm runs the slowest and uses the most resources. If the value being searched for is at the very end of the array or doesn't exist, the algorithm would spend time visiting every value in the array until it reaches the end.

Big O is a very extensive topic, and entire books have been written about the details of how to deeply evaluate any algorithm. While this is useful information that will help you in the long run, it's not expected from you to be an expert at it to be a great software engineer, and as you improve your skills and knowledge in algorithms, you will become more familiar and comfortable with it. If you're curious about big O notation, visit the resources in *Further reading*.

Here are some questions a software engineer may ask themself when building their own algorithm:

- Do I have all the information I need to build a solution?

- What is the problem I am actually trying to solve?

- What could go wrong?

- Are there any restrictions on the inputs this algorithm can take?

- Have I considered all types of input that the algorithm will use?

- How can I test the algorithm with a large variety of inputs?

- Is it possible to make this run faster?

- Is there anything I can do to reduce the chances of a worst-case scenario?

- Am I using computer resources wisely?

- Am I leveraging the full capabilities of the programming language I am writing with to make my algorithm efficient?

As stated earlier in this section, while there are many tried and tested algorithms, any computer program can be an algorithm. When building an algorithm, there are many options that a software engineer may consider to improve its correctness and performance. The final section is focused on improving an algorithm with a technique called **refactoring**.

Improving algorithms with refactoring

Chapter 2, The Software Engineering Life Cycle, covered the maintenance phase of the software engineering life cycle, where improvements in the code are made. During this phase, a software team may revisit code that could use some performance improvements or have better maintainability. This technique, known as refactoring, involves changes made to the code in a software program that don't change its behavior. The maintenance phase of the software engineering life cycle includes fixing bugs that arise in the code, which is not the same as refactoring. Both techniques require code changes, but bugs are unexpected behavior in code that needs to be fixed, while refactoring changes the structure of the code. The code may work and look different after a refactor but will behave the same way.

Refactoring is a common practice in a software team, and there are various reasons for doing a refactor. As you have learned in this chapter, there are many ways to build one thing and it's common for teams to set standards on how things should be built to maintain consistency and readability. Sometimes, these standards may slip, especially when working to a demanding deadline, which makes the code less maintainable because the code is harder to understand. This can be a problem if a team is trying to add new features to the software because it will now take more time to understand it and build on top of what exists. In addition to these standards, software projects may change hands often, including changing software engineer leads, who make big decisions about the code and may have differing opinions about how code should be built from previous leaders.

Despite the reasoning for needing to do a refactor, it can produce benefits in the following ways:

- Making the code more readable so that any software engineer can easily understand it and apply new changes or fix a bug
- Discovering new bugs before they cause severe issues
- Discovering more effective and efficient ways to do something, thus saving time and increasing performance
- Allowing teams to adopt new software libraries or newer versions of the programming language to improve the code to modern standards or improve performance

There are many approaches to refactoring, including choosing the appropriate time to do it or where to start first. This will vary between teams, but some common times when a team might discover parts of code that could use some refactoring is when they're adding a new feature or fixing a bug.

Now that you have an idea of what refactoring is, we'll walk through two exercises based on some examples you've seen. First, we'll revisit the example of the MyBudget app from *Chapter 7, Flow Control in C#*. The program was a small budget management app for calculating the remaining balance after buying a few items. It also had a method called VerifyAffordable for checking whether the remaining balance was enough to buy a book. The following example includes some of the solution from the chapter:

```
decimal balance = 75.45M;
decimal groceries = 40.00M;
decimal tea = 5.00M;
string balanceMessage = "The current balance is: $";

PrintBalance();
CalculateNewBalance(groceries);
PrintBalance();
CalculateNewBalance(tea);
PrintBalance();

void PrintBalance()
{
    Console.WriteLine(balanceMessage + balance);
}

void CalculateNewBalance(decimal expense)
{
    balance -= expense;
}
```

> **Note**
>
> To view the complete example, visit the GitHub repo at https://github.com/ PacktPublishing/Fundamentals-for-Self-Taught-Programmers/tree/ main/Chapter7.

One common approach to refactoring is following the **don't repeat yourself** (**DRY**) principle, where code that will be repeated throughout a program should only be written once. A great approach to resolving this is using methods to reuse blocks of code. Methods have been used in this example, but notice we have a bit more repetition in the following blocks of code. Is it possible to reduce the repetition?

```
PrintBalance();
CalculateNewBalance(groceries);
PrintBalance();
CalculateNewBalance(tea);
PrintBalance();
```

The `PrintBalance` method is called immediately after each `CalculateNewBalance` method so that the balance prints the new calculation. We can reduce the repetition here by calling `PrintBalance` within `CalculateNewBalance`, which is done in the following example:

```
void CalculateNewBalance(decimal expense)
{
    balance -= expense;
    PrintBalance();
}
```

This updated method eliminates the need for calling `PrintBalance` and the updated code now has fewer lines of code, as shown in the following example:

```
PrintBalance();
CalculateNewBalance(groceries);
CalculateNewBalance(tea);
```

Now, let's try refactoring the selection sort algorithm, where a sorted array is split into halves and one half is eliminated to narrow the search of the value:

```
int[] testArray = {-4, 0, 7, 13, 20, 55, 80};
int lowerHalfIndex = 0;
int upperHalfIndex = testArray.Length - 1;
while(lowerHalfIndex <= upperHalfIndex)
{

    int midpointIndex = lowerHalfIndex +
        (upperHalfIndex - lowerHalfIndex)/2;
    int searchValue = 55;
```

```
    if (testArray[midpointIndex] > searchValue )
    {
        upperHalfIndex = midpointIndex - 1;
    }

    else if(testArray[midpointIndex] < searchValue)
    {
        lowerHalfIndex = midpointIndex + 1;
    }
    else
    {
        Console.WriteLine("Your value was found!");
    }
}
if (lowerHalfIndex > upperHalfIndex)
{
    Console.WriteLine("Your value was not found!");
}
```

Notice that the example already has a search value and array assigned. This is called hardcoding, which is inserting values directly into the code, which prevents it from being reusable for other values. This algorithm is not reusable as is because it only works for a specific array that is searching for a specific value. How can we make this more reusable?

Another practice in refactoring is the extract method technique, which takes large blocks of reusable code and turns them into methods. This entire algorithm could be turned into a method, which is done in the following example, showing the parts of the code that would be affected by the change:

```
void SelectionSort(int[] inputArray, int searchValue,
                   int lowerHalfIndex = 0){
int upperHalfIndex = inputArray.Length - 1;

while(lowerHalfIndex <= upperHalfIndex)
{
    int midpointIndex = lowerHalfIndex +
        (upperHalfIndex - lowerHalfIndex)/2;

    if (testArray[midpointIndex] > searchValue )
```

```
    {
        upperHalfIndex = midpointIndex - 1;
    }
    else if(testArray[midpointIndex] > searchValue)
    {
        lowerHalfIndex = midpointIndex + 1;
    }

//Rest of the code here ...
}
```

The method can now use any array of integers and search for any integer value with the inputArray and searchValue parameters. The final parameter is called an optional parameter, a feature that can be used in C#. This allows you to set a default value for a parameter and skip it as an argument. This type of parameter was used because the starting index of the lower half of the array is usually the beginning of the array, at index 0. However, there may be cases where this differs. The following example shows how the method could be called with the test values we used in the initial example:

```
int[] testArray = {-4, 0, 7, 13, 20, 55, 80};
int searchValue = 55;
SelectionSort(testArray,searchValue)
```

Notice that the third parameter was not used because of the choice to have the lower-half index begin at 0. To use a different value for this parameter, a third parameter could be added to change the default value of 0. Refactoring is a practice that takes reviewing code that's been written and asking the question, "How can I make this better?" where better means more efficient and easier to read. Discovering places to refactor code takes practice, and there are even tools that analyze code to find these places for you. There are many ways to approach refactoring; you could even do more to these examples to make them even more reusable and readable. If you have code you have written or have tried any of these exercises, try to apply some refactoring to it with what you have learned here or with the resources under *Further reading*. This is the end of the basics of applying and building algorithms and using refactoring to improve them, but there is much more to learn about this topic, some of which will become clearer as you continue to practice writing code and making programs that become more complex over time.

Summary

In this chapter, we applied C# to selection sort, linear search, and binary search algorithms, but these are only some of many solutions and can be rewritten to be even better. Selection sort relies on visiting every value to compare them against each other and swap them to organize an array in ascending order. Linear search also requires visiting every value in an array until the value being searched for is found. These two algorithms use loops to iterate through arrays to find and compare values. The binary search algorithm does not need to visit every value within an array when it's sorted and can narrow down the values with calculations and some iterations. While these algorithms are quite popular, there are many built-in features and methods within C# for searching for and sorting values rather quickly and with less code. There are also even more sorting and searching algorithms to explore.

Computer programs are algorithms that solve specific problems based on the input and create the same expected output in an expected amount of time. You can create your own algorithms and evaluate what it takes to make your algorithm correct and have the best performance. You can improve your algorithms by refactoring and rewriting the code to improve their readability, reusability, and performance. A great way to explore any algorithm is to test it out and experiment and think about what changes you can make to make it more efficient and readable.

Congratulations, you have gotten through one of the more complex chapters of this book! Don't feel discouraged if it felt overwhelming: algorithms are a very extensive topic and have a lot of research behind them. Some of the popular algorithms out there are already integrated into programming languages. For example, you can write the line `arrayName.Sort()` in C# and it will apply the heap sort, insertion sort, or quick sort algorithm depending on its size. However, it's helpful to understand how these common algorithms work as it will help you get better at problem-solving with code. If you felt a little lost, it's encouraged to give the examples another try by going back to *Chapter 8, Introduction to Data Structures, Algorithms, and Pseudocode*, and drawing out the examples in the figures or writing the pseudocode yourself.

You have learned how to write a few popular sorting and searching algorithms in C# with the knowledge you gained in *Chapters 5-8*, where you learned how to work with variables with different data types and apply flow control. You have also learned considerations for making your own algorithms and how to use refactoring to make them even better. The next chapter will return to learning more about the C# language to leverage its full potential through object-oriented programming.

Questions

1. Why is a loop needed for a selection sort?
2. What is nesting?
3. In the linear search algorithm, what assumption can be made if a loop reaches the end of the array and ends?
4. What statement can you write to interrupt and end a loop early?

5. True or false: The binary search algorithm visits every value in an array.

6. What happens to the time it takes for an algorithm to run when the size of the input increases?

7. What's the most important benefit of refactoring?

Further reading

- *C# Data Structures and Algorithms* by Marcin Jamro, Packt Publishing

- *Algorithms, 4th Edition* by Robert Sedgewick and Kevin Wayne, Addison-Wesley Professional

- *Five Lines of Code* by Christian Clausen, Manning Publications

- *What is Big O Notation Explained: Space and Time Complexity*, Shen Huang, Free Code Camp, `https://www.freecodecamp.org/news/big-o-notation-why-it-matters-and-why-it-doesnt-1674cfa8a23c/`

10
Object-Oriented Programming

Software can help its users be productive. This is achieved by building solutions that reflect users' expectations, such as being able to sort a list of names, where software engineers will apply algorithms to build systems that enable users to make the most of the software. However, algorithms alone cannot help users be productive, especially when it comes to users accessing several types of data. Something such as a list of names usually comes with a particular context, such as a list of patient names that needs to be secure to ensure patient confidentiality or a list of the names of students in a class that needs to be filtered by students who are at risk of failing the class. Users need their software to meet their expectations, including how it will help them be productive in their everyday tasks. How are software engineers able to reflect these expectations in code? There are various techniques within **object-oriented programming** (**OOP**) that enable software engineers to develop solutions by creating an abstract view of the real world so that a list of names, whether it be for a doctor's office, classroom, or something else, can be easily represented in code.

So far, you have learned the building blocks of programming in C# and how algorithms solve computational problems such as sorting and searching. In this chapter, we'll explore how OOP allows software engineers to create an abstract view of the real world. You will use special techniques, keywords, and syntax built into the C# language to apply OOP concepts.

This chapter covers the following topics:

- Introduction to object-oriented programming
- Understanding objects
- Introduction to inheritance
- Introduction to encapsulation
- Introduction to polymorphism
- Introduction to abstraction

By the end of this chapter, you will know about the pillars of OOP and be able to write C# using object-oriented concepts to add a level of abstraction to your code.

Technical requirements

To complete the exercises in this chapter, you'll need a computer, such as a laptop or a desktop computer, that has Visual Studio Code and .NET installed. Refer to *Chapter 5, Writing Your First C# Program*, for information on how to install them.

You can find the code files for this chapter on GitHub at `https://github.com/PacktPublishing/Fundamentals-for-Self-Taught-Programmers/tree/main/Chapter10`.

Introduction to object-oriented programming

OOP enables programmers to build software systems that reflect the world we live in. Objects are central to OOP because they're how we represent these real-life entities in code. To summarize what OOP does, it allows us to build an abstract model of the people, places, and things that the software user interacts with every day. This allows software developers to build applications that are tailored to solve specific problems and keep any data or information associated with it relevant and secure.

C# is an OOP language, and there are many other OOP languages out there, such as Java, C++, and Python. OOP is only one type of programming. Other popular types are logical, imperative, and functional, which all have a long list of languages that fit under these categories. The difference between each type is the difference in approaches to how a language approaches and organizes a problem in code. As you learned in *Chapter 3, Roles in Software Engineering*, programmers evaluate and use the best language for the job based on various criteria and no language or language type is better than the other; it's just a way to approach a problem.

OOP can be categorized into four pillars:

- Inheritance
- Encapsulation
- Polymorphism
- Abstraction

The rest of this chapter will be dedicated to introducing and demonstrating how these pillars work within the C# language.

Understanding objects

As you learned in the previous section, OOP is centered around the concept of **objects**, which are abstract representations of things in the real world. Anything that can be considered a noun, such as patients, landmarks, or an address, can be represented as objects in code.

In the C# language and most OOP languages, the process of creating any object begins with a class, which is a code block containing values and methods that are used to describe what an object is and what it does. Consider the C# variable in the following example:

```
string animal = "Cat";
```

A cat is an animal, but it would be helpful to have more information about it. How old is it? Where's its natural habitat? How can it be described? A variable in this state can't really provide many details about it. What if we converted the variable into an array like in the following example?

```
string animal[] = {"Cat", "White", 2};
```

With an array like this, a little more detail can be stored about the animal, but this is not a sustainable way to store information about a lion. Imagine a programmer creating software for an animal hospital. They would have to keep track of which value within the array index describes a unique part of the animal in the array. In other words, you can't label indexes as type, color, and age in an array. How can we accurately describe what type of animal this is, and any other identifiable features in a convenient way where this information is easy to access and clearly identifiable? This is a perfect fit for class, which is a code template used to describe a specific object. You'll now learn more about how to create classes and objects.

Working with objects, classes, and types in C#

Creating an object in C# begins with creating a class. Classes are also defined as types, because classes create an object of a certain type. The following figure describes how to define a class, using the same animal example that has now been converted into a class:

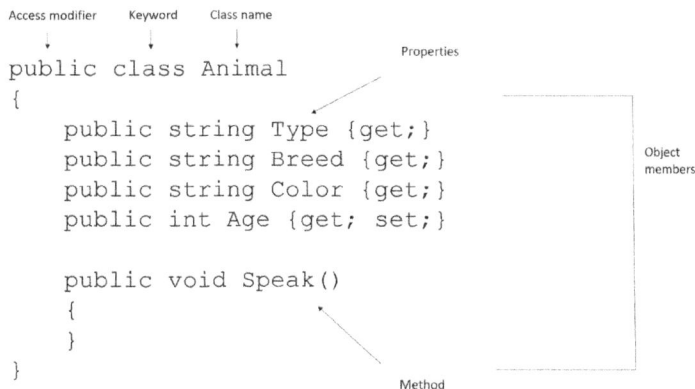

Figure 10.1 – A class named Animal with properties and one method

A basic class is defined with the following:

- An access modifier, which defines which parts of an object are available to be used by other objects and classes.

- The class keyword, which is a reserved word that informs the C# compiler that the upcoming lines of code are for creating a class.

- The class name, which is a unique identifier that is up to the programmer to define. Class names represent the object type that will be generated. In other words, objects that are created by the Animal class will be of the Animal type. You'll notice that once an object is created, it will normally be referred to by its type.

- Properties, which define the type, describing what it is. Properties can be defined as built-in data types, such as a string or even another customized object type. Properties may seem like they store data, but they simply provide access to data. C# creates a special variable to store the value of the property. You'll learn later how to create your own variables to control the values that properties use.

- Accessors, the get and set keywords, which enable the property to be read or assigned a new value. These are also known as getters and setters. Properties that only have a get accessor can only be read and their values cannot change after the object is created, while ones with both get and set can be read and updated.

- Methods, which operate the same way that methods in the previous few chapters did, as reusable blocks of code that can take parameters and return values. However, in most cases, you can only use them with the objects they belong to. There is an exception to this rule with a different type of class called static classes. You can read more about them from the resources listed in the *Further reading* section of this chapter.

- Members, which are all properties, methods, and any other declarations within the class, basically anything that has a name that you must define. To learn more about additional members found within a class, refer to the resources listed in the *Further reading* section of this chapter.

Before this class can be used, we'll need to provide a way for this class to set the values of the properties. Remember that once the object is created, you can change any read-only properties. We can set these values when the object is created with a **constructor**, which is a special method within the class that is executed when the object is created. A constructor will always have the same name as the class, including the same casing. The constructor is often used to set the properties of an object. Here's the complete example of the Animal object, including the constructor that is setting the property values:

```
public class Animal
{
    public string Type {get;}
    public string Color {get;}
```

```
    public int Age {get; set;}

    public void Speak()
    {
    }


    public Animal(string animalType,
                  string animalColor,
                  int animalAge)
    {
        Type = animalType;
        Color = animalColor;
        Age = animalAge;
    }
}
```

This completed code can now create an object. Note that the `Speak` method is still empty but can still be called despite it having no functionality at the moment. The following example shows how to create an animal object:

```
Animal cat = new Animal("Cat", "White", 2);
```

Creating a new object starts with defining the object type with a name on the left of the equal symbol, then using the new keyword on the right, followed by the type, and then setting the properties in the order that they appear in the constructor argument, like calling a method. The following example shows how to access the object to read properties that only have getters and update properties that have setters and execute methods in the class:

```
Console.Write(cat.Age);
cat.Age = 3;
cat.Speak();
```

Creating a new object, also known as creating an instance of a class, or **instantiation** of an object, involves using the class as a template for creating an object and executing the code within its constructor inside it. You can create as many objects as you'd like. Try this experiment: make a few objects and try to store them in an array.

Does any of this seem familiar? Believe it or not, you've already used objects before this chapter! Recall arrays, where you could write `arrayName.Length` to find out how many items were in the array. When you create an array, you're creating or instantiating an array object. There are many built-in objects in C# and you can use all the members it contains to your advantage when working with them.

Now that you have learned the basics of classes, objects, and types, you can dive deeper into OOP, starting with learning how to extend the capabilities of classes with inheritance.

Introduction to inheritance

So far, the `Animal` class does a fine job of providing a way to differentiate between different types of animals. However, not all animals will have the same characteristics. A cat will not have gills, so having an `Animal` class have a property named `NumberOfGills` would be a waste of space for any animal that is not a reptile or sea creature. However, we know that all the animals will have an age, color, and type. Can we make a new animal with unique properties? Could we do it without having to recreate the `Animal` class again, which already contains members that could be used?

Inheritance enables the reuse of classes to create new classes that generate objects with modified members. Classes that inherit properties and methods from another class are called derived, or child, classes, while the original class is called a base or parent class. The following figure shows how to implement inheritance in C# with a base and derived class:

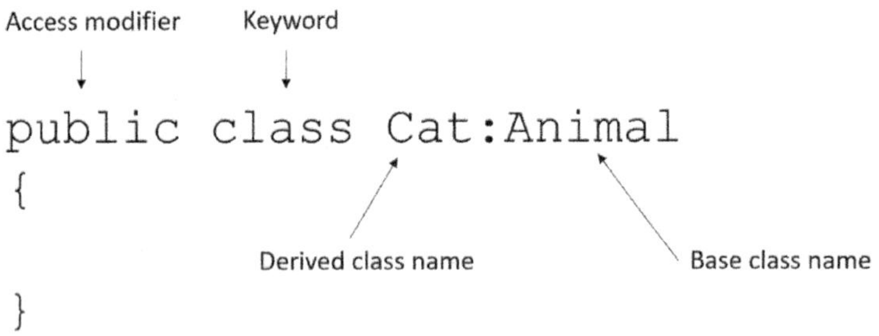

Figure 10.2 – A class that has been derived from the Animal class

Let's create a new `Cat` class that is derived from `Animal`. The following example has additional members that describe cats that have five or more toes on each paw and their breed:

```
public class Cat : Animal
{
    public bool Polydactyl {get;}
    public string Breed {get;}
    public Cat(string animalType,
            string animalColor,
            int animalAge,
            bool polydactyl,
            string breed) : base(
```

```
        animalType,
        animalColor,
        animalAge)
    {

        Polydactyl = polydactyl;
        Breed = breed;

    }

}
```

The derived Cat class inherits the constructor from the base Animal class with the base keyword so that when the Cat class is instantiated, it also sets the base members located in the Animal class as well. The following example shows how the Cat class is instantiated:

```
Cat milo = new Cat("Cat", "White", 3, true, "Shorthair");
Console.Write(milo.Age);
Console.Write(milo.Breed);
```

Through inheritance, the base Animal object was able to be reused to create a specific type of Animal object. You can derive as many classes as you'd like from the base class. With this knowledge, you can give yourself a challenge and try to make a derived class for another animal type, or you can make an entirely new custom base class with a derived class.

You can prevent classes from being base classes by using the sealed keyword, as seen in the following example:

```
public sealed class Animal
```

Inheritance can be a powerful concept in the C# language to encourage code reuse and extend the capabilities of your objects. Next, we will look at another powerful OOP pillar, called encapsulation.

Introduction to encapsulation

When working with objects, there is a lot of focus on how information is expressed and described in code. Sometimes, the information, or members within a class, needs to be controlled so that it's protected from causing issues when the object is instantiated and shares its information across complex programs. This form of protection is called encapsulation, where not all members within a class are accessible to other parts of the code, particularly to other classes. Encapsulation prevents issues such as data loss, security breaches, and bugs in your code. Encapsulation can be applied to any members within a class. In C#, encapsulation is done with **access modifiers**, all of which have their own levels of protection, as well as fields, which are variables that exist and are only accessed within a class.

Working with access modifiers in C#

The access modifiers available in C# are the following:

- `public`
- `private`
- `protected`
- `internal`
- `protected internal`
- `private protected`
- `sealed`

You have already used the `public` access modifiers, but they may not be the best option for the problem at hand. Here's a table that details what can be accessed within a class based on its modifiers:

> **Note**
>
> This table only refers to classes that are in the same assembly. Refer to *Further reading* for a complete list that includes member access outside of assemblies, including definitions and resources on assemblies in .NET.

	Inside class	Derived class	Non-derived class
`public`	Yes	Yes	Yes
`private`	Yes	No	No
`protected`	Yes	Yes	No
`internal`	Yes	Yes	Yes
`protected internal`	Yes	Yes	Yes
`private protected`	Yes	Yes	No

Table 10.1 – List of access modifiers for members and where they can be accessed

Let's revisit the idea of software engineers creating software for an animal hospital, where it would generate an invoice for the care the pets receive to be delivered to the owners. At first glance, these invoices will most likely need to be associated with an animal in the hospital, where an `Invoice` object would need to be associated with `Animal` but also includes personal information such as names and payment methods. The following example is an `Invoice` class that includes members describing this object:

```
public class Invoice
{
    private int _invoiceId;
    public Animal Pet {get;}
    public string OwnerName {get;}
    public double Balance {get; private set;}
    private string DefaultPaymentMethod {get;}

    public int InvoiceId {
        get { return _invoiceId; }
    }

    public Invoice(Animal pet, int invoiceID){
        //Private code that validates invoice ID
        //If invoice exists in database...
        //it sets each property.
        _invoiceId = invoiceID;
    }

    public void MakePayment(double paymentAmount)
    {
        bool transactionSuccessful =
                Calculate(paymentAmount);
        if(transactionSuccessful)
        {
            UpdateBalance(paymentAmount);
        }
    }

    private bool Calculate(double amount)
    {
        //Code that makes some calculations
        //Code sets success variable to true or false
        bool success = true;
```

```
        return success;
    }



    private void UpdateBalance(double amount)
    {
        Balance = Balance + amount;
    }
}
```

The `Invoice` class sets members that have private information with the private access modifier. First is the `_invoiceID` field, which is private and only to be used within the method. The previous example assumes that the invoice data comes from a database, though this logic is not included in the code. The `Invoice` constructor grabs this information by first validating `invoiceId`, which was passed into it, and then sets the other properties with data from the database. Fields are typically used to encapsulate information from other classes by making it only accessible through a property. As mentioned before, properties allow you to access values but don't store them. Fields give you more control over how those values are stored or accessed. Fields can have public access modifiers, but this is generally discouraged. The `InvoiceId` property may need to be accessed outside of the class, so the property is public and its matching `_invoiceId` field is used to access the value, but these invoice IDs will not change, so the `set` accessor has been omitted from the property.

With private members, other classes won't be able to access everything within the class, so if a software engineer were to try the following example, they would get an error:

```
Cat milo = new Cat("Cat", "White", 3, true, "Shorthair");
Invoice invoice = new Invoice(milo, 123 );
invoice.DefaultPaymentMethod;
```

Before we move on to what's happening here, notice that the example is using inheritance again to create the `Invoice` object. The `milo Cat` object is a type of animal, and therefore can be used to instantiate `Invoice`. The third line of code in this example would have a syntax error since `DefaultPaymentMethod` is a private member. However, the class definition allows an external part of the application to use the public `MakePayment` method to update the owner's balance with the `Balance` property, which is public, but whose `get` accessor is private so it cannot be set by an external class. The `get` and `set` accessors are like special methods for properties to retrieve and update values. So, if someone wanted to implement code to update a balance, they'd need to pass in the amount to `MakePayment` so that `Calculate` can calculate their remaining balance and update it if the transaction is successful. Otherwise, they can only view the balance.

Encapsulation gives software engineers control over what can happen to any data that is represented in an object. You will now move on to the next pillar of OOP, which is polymorphism.

Introduction to polymorphism

The term polymorphism applies to many scientific and mathematical concepts, but the meaning is generally the same across all definitions. It refers to the ability to change into many different forms, and when it comes to OOP, it refers to changes that are made to classes and members that transform into something different that may deviate from their original form. This can be a powerful tool to encourage code reuse and create many types of objects that come from the same base class. Polymorphism can be grouped into two forms: static and dynamic.

Static polymorphism

Static polymorphism refers to methods that are determined at runtime, or code that is compiled before the program begins execution. One example of static polymorphism is method overloading, where two methods with the same name are created but have different parameters. The following example shows an example of overloading, where a decision has been made to round all future payments up to a whole number, but it must also handle older balances that accepted change for the time being. The software engineers at the animal hospital decide to overload the `Calculate` method in the `Invoice` class, as seen in the following example:

```
public class Invoice
{
    //Code...
    private bool Calculate(double amount)
    {
        //Code that makes some calculations
        //Code sets success variable to true or false
        bool success = true;
        return success;
    }

    private bool Calculate(int amount)
    {
        //Code that makes some calculations
        //Code sets success variable to true or false
        bool success = true;
        return success;
    }

}
```

Notice that the difference between the two methods here is the data type. This class can now calculate the different types of balances that may come in.

Dynamic polymorphism

Dynamic polymorphism happens at runtime, where the method of a base class may take a different form in a derived class. Dynamic polymorphism can be applied to methods with the `virtual` keyword in C#. With this information, we can revisit the empty `Speak` method from earlier:

```
public virtual void Speak()
{
}
```

Without the `virtual` keyword, this method would have had the same behavior when the `Animal` class was instantiated or derived. We know that animals make different sounds, but now the method can be reused to display different behavior that will differ among each derived class. Here are two different examples with two derived classes using the `Speak` method:

```
public class Cat
{
    //Code...
    public override void Speak()
    {
        Console.Write("Meow");
    }
}
```

The previous example uses the `override` keyword to create a new custom `Speak` method. Here's the other example:

```
public class Dog
{
    public bool Agitated {get;}

    //Code...
    public override void Speak()
    {
        if (Agitated)
        {
            Console.Write("Growl");
```

```
        }
        else
        {
            Console.Write("Woof!");
        }
    }
}
```

This example has a bit more added to it with some logic, but again will need the override keyword to use the Speak method.

Polymorphism allows you to keep your objects consistent but apply details to them that allow you to create accurate abstractions of how they should behave. You will now move on to the final pillar of OOP, which is abstraction.

Introduction to abstraction

You have learned in this chapter that OOP creates an abstract view of the things that we interact with so that we can use them in code. However, you can apply an additional level of abstraction to your classes in C# with abstract classes.

Let's use our existing animal example to explain the concept. We now know that the Animal class doesn't have enough members to describe all animals, but we also know that some members from derived classes of animals will not make sense in other derived classes. For example, a Cat or Dog class shouldn't need a property for gills, like a Lizard class would, but all three animal types will have an age. It seems that the Animal class won't ever be used by itself, only as a base class. It can be inverted into an abstract class so that the following apply:

- The class will never be instantiated, since we know it's best used as a base class and should only be used for that purpose

- The base class has members that can be applied to all classes derived from it

To create an abstract class, the abstract keyword is added to the class definition, as in the following example of the Animal class:

```
public abstract class Animal
{
    //Rest of code here...
    public abstract void Speak();
}
```

Derived classes can continue to inherit members from the base class and add new members, but the only difference here is the following:

- The abstract class cannot be instantiated, so `Animal pet = new Animal();` will produce a syntax error

- Any abstract methods within the abstract base class must be implemented in the derived class

- Abstract methods don't have a body

Implementing methods in derived classes is not a new concept, as we saw in the *Introduction to inheritance* and *Introduction to polymorphism* sections of this chapter, where the `Speak` method was inherited and rewritten using dynamic polymorphism with the `virtual` and `override` keywords. The original `Speak` method had a body without any code in it, so it didn't do anything, and any derived classes would have the same behavior. Then, it was made virtual and was overridden in derived classes to add some implementation. With an abstract class, abstract methods can be added to make sure that all derived classes implement the expected behavior based on their type. These methods will also use the `override` keyword in each derived class, as seen in dynamic polymorphism. The following example makes another derived class from this new abstract class:

```
public class Spider:Animal
{
    //Code...
    public override void Speak()
    {
    }
}
```

Although spiders generally don't make noise, the class must be implemented, so the body stays empty to indicate that this animal type doesn't make any sounds. The `Animal` class could be refactored so that `Speak` is virtual, as you can have a mix of virtual, abstract, and normal methods in an abstract class. There is a special modifier called `sealed` for protecting overridden methods in derived classes from being used in any classes that may use the derived class, which can be used as in the previous example:

```
public class Spider:Animal
{
    //Code...
    public sealed override void Speak()
    {
    }
}
```

Now, if a class, such as `Tarantula`, were derived from the `Spider` class, the `Speak` method would not be available for inheritance or to be overridden. This will cause a syntax error. Because some tarantulas hiss, there is a way to implement the method with the new keyword, as seen in the following example:

```
public class Tarantula:Spider
{
    //Code...
    public new void Speak()
    {
    }
}
```

If the `Tarantula` class needs to implement `Speak`, it will need to use the new keyword to do so to differentiate it from the base class where this method is sealed.

Here's a table of the method types that you can use in OOP:

Method keyword	Usage
virtual	Allow the method to be reimplemented in derived classes
abstract	Enforce a method that must be implemented in every derived class
override	Use to implement methods that have the abstract or virtual keyword in the base class
sealed	Prevent any methods that have the override keyword from being inherited in any classes that are derived from that class

Table 10.2 – List of method keywords and how they are accessed in other classes

This is the final pillar of OOP covered in this chapter.

Summary

OOP enables software engineers to apply what they know about the language and use it to represent the real world through the pillars of abstraction, inheritance, encapsulation, and polymorphism. It all begins with the object, which can be created with classes, where objects represent something that software users need to interact with in their daily lives. Inheritance allows objects to be reused and have different characteristics and behaviors. Encapsulating these things gives software engineers control over how it's used and shared. Polymorphism, on the other hand, allows software engineers to add more details to these behaviors and characteristics so that they can be the same object with distinct parts.

Because C# is an OOP language, applying OOP to your projects enables you to look at the full capabilities of the language. With everything that you know about programming and C# up to this point, you have enough knowledge to improve the examples in this book and learn more about programming, as well as do some self-guided learning and build some projects.

The next chapter will focus on careers in tech, starting by learning about how software engineers work from software engineers with various levels of experience and backgrounds, including their typical workday and how they got into programming.

Questions

1.   What can be considered an object?

2.   From where are objects created in C#?

3.   A base class can inherit members of a derived class. True or false?

4.   What access modifier will keep member access within the class?

5.   What is the difference between static polymorphism and dynamic polymorphism?

6.   What is the difference between virtual and abstract methods?

Further reading

- *Object-Oriented programming (C#)*: https://learn.microsoft.com/en-us/dotnet/csharp/fundamentals/tutorials/oop

- *Members (C# Programming Guide)*: https://learn.microsoft.com/en-us/dotnet/csharp/programming-guide/classes-and-structs/members

- *Access Modifiers (C# Programming Guide)*: https://learn.microsoft.com/en-us/dotnet/csharp/programming-guide/classes-and-structs/access-modifiers

- *Hands-On Object-Oriented Programming with C#* by Raihan Taher, Packt Publishing

Part 3: Software Engineering – the Profession

This part connects you to the software engineering profession with a range of information. It starts with software engineers sharing how they work, then covers the benefits of best practices in coding by adopting widely accepted conventions and styling with the C# language, and finally, ends with tips and tricks for breaking into the industry.

This section has the following chapters:

11
Stories from Prominent Job Roles in Software Development

So far, you have learned about the software engineering profession, including the types of roles it comprises, but have not learned about the progression into these roles or what they entail. The path to a career in software engineering is not linear; there are many stories from engineers who did not even see it as a potential career, while others knew it was something they wanted to do from the beginning. The best way to learn about these paths is from people who have been there.

So, in this chapter, some of these experts share their experiences in the industry. These are real software engineers (names with an asterisk have been anonymized) who have been interviewed about their careers spanning different specialties and backgrounds. They describe their job and what they do and share some advice with you about programming. You'll find that each of these stories is unique and that the path to software engineering is a unique mix of various opportunities, people, and challenges that you may face along the way. This chapter is intended to inspire you to think about ways to pave your own path.

This chapter covers the real stories of the following software engineering roles:

- Android software engineer
- iOS software engineer
- Generalist software engineer
- C# software engineer
- Frontend web developer
- Data engineer
- Salesforce software engineer

By the end of this chapter, you'll have learned about what challenges real engineers face in the industry and received advice on how to progress in your career.

Technical requirements

There are no technical requirements for this chapter.

Android software engineer

Brianna Smith* is an Android engineer with over 10 years of professional experience. She works at a company in the retail industry that has over 10,000 employees worldwide. Brianna is on the mobile team of six engineers with a mix of Android and iOS developers.

Brianna discovered that she wanted to be a software engineer back in high school, when she was a junior and heard her calculus teacher say something funny. *"My teacher said, 'A girl in computer science can write her own ticket.' I was 16 at the time and didn't know what that meant, but it sounded good."* At that time, she was already spending a lot of time on the computer and phone and became more interested in the computer science field. She quips, *"Someone will pay me to do things that I love? Sounds like a great deal!"* She decided to take some computer science classes offered at her high school and went on to major in computer science in college. Her college offered a few specializations, but none of them were interesting to her. *"I went to a college that was attached to a hospital, so there was a big pipeline to get into software for medicine, but none of that interested me. So when I found out there were other aspects of computer science, I was excited."* Brianna enjoyed mobile apps and was curious about how they were made and so decided to pursue a career in mobile development.

In *Chapter 4, Programming Languages and Introduction to C#*, you learned that some software developers end up choosing a language or technology due to their current circumstances. This was the case for Brianna, who decided to pursue Android development because she already had some of the things she needed to get started: a PC and skills in Java. *"I was a student at the time, and Apple products were expensive for me. You needed a MacBook to develop iOS apps."*

She began her professional career during her junior year of college, where she began a part-time internship at a small consultancy and then worked full-time after graduation. She spent her time working on various projects. Brianna has been deeply focused on her specialization her entire career, working exclusively on Android applications. She built Android apps before Android Studio was available, when the only development environment was in the IntelliJ IDEA IDE. It became so large that the functionality needed to be moved to its own standalone development environment, which is now Android Studio.

Today, Brianna is a staff Android engineer, working on features and the infrastructure of Android applications. The typical professional progression of a software engineer will start from junior or entry-level to mid-level, senior, and staff, a title that may differ between companies. Brianna shares her experience with these titles, *"When I was a junior, I spent 100% of my time doing coding and completing tickets. Mid-level is when you start getting brought into stakeholder meetings because you have a better understanding of the code and how long things take. Senior is when you can take a task and fill in the gaps yourself, where you make decisions and feel confident about them. Staff takes a holistic view, so when you add a feature, you're thinking 'Am I adding this feature in a sustainable way? Did I build this in a way that is extensible, or do I just need to get it out the door?".*

As a staff engineer, Brianna talks about her current responsibilities, which are meeting with managers and product managers to determine timelines and feasibility for features as well as making a quality assurance plan to make sure all requirements are met. She says she spends about 20% of her time coding, which is when she's building the underlying foundational parts of a new feature that other engineers will build on, which is non-user-facing code. She prefers working in the backend, *"I like the less user-facing parts because I find it more complex and richer."* She mentions it took about 6 months for her to feel comfortable with the large code bases that are common to work with in her job. She also spends about 40% of her time pair programming with other engineers and doing code reviews. Pair programming is a practice where two software engineers work together to write some code, which can be fixing a bug or building a feature. Usually, one person, known as the driver, writes the code, while the other person, known as the observer or navigator, observes and catches any pitfalls or problems that the driver may be facing. They may swap these roles during their pairing session. Pair programming is a great way for teams to work through complex problems and allow members to learn more from each other and share knowledge. For code reviews, Brianna is tasked with looking at her team members' code to check for correctness and proper coding standards. Code reviews are a common practice in a software engineering team, where if there are changes that need to be made, the author will apply them until their code is approved for merging, which is a process in source control for adding code to the code base.

40% of Brianna's time is spent in meetings, where she works through things such as engineering plans, where large tasks are broken down and distributed to the team. She describes engineering plans as details on what the feature is and what needs to be done, and creates a high-level design of tasks in the UI, implementation, and backend, and breaks them down into tickets, which are then assigned to team members. These features come from a roadmap that product managers and leaders of the team will plan out and make decisions on what to build next.

Despite being responsible for tasks that don't require as much coding, she enjoys the implementation part of the software engineering process the most. She beams when talking about the things she enjoys as a programmer, *"I love coding. It's a creative outlet for me. It's an art."* She spends time outside of work building personal projects, as she finds she learns best that way.

In her experience so far, 15 versions of the Android operating system have been released. She's faced many challenging problems, from being on a team of one and handling multiple parts of the development process to keeping UI styling cohesive when an app goes through rebranding. Brianna's expertise in mobile development extends into her everyday life. During our meeting over video, my phone's speaker starts to crackle. She asks, *"Is your phone overheating?"*

She talks about her professional experience and the unnecessary stress that technical interviews put on potential employees. She reluctantly talks about her experiences going through the technical interview process before graduating college. She remembers the stress of being asked complex questions that have nothing to do with the role she was applying for and having to solve them in an open-concept office, writing them out on clear glass windows, where interviewers and everyone in the office could see. *"I have never used linear algebra on the job. I think the interview process is so negative."* She decided to stop interviewing and take a full-time role in the same company that hired her as an intern. She still avoids technical interviews and has been able to skip them because she has a strong technical portfolio and experience. *"I never really apply at places; they seek me out. I purposely avoid the terrible interview process I have come to know about."* If she were to search for a job today, she would get up to date on the latest Android technologies and then build a sample with it. Though she's not looking, she enjoys building personal projects and will take the time to stay up to date by using the latest tools. She's built projects such as a flashcard app and an app for her sister's business to help her manage her store's inventory.

Brianna thinks a common misconception about programming is that it's a lot of math, *"Engineering is so big; even just for Android, if you just work on the UI and don't do any animations, you're not doing any math. Animations use calculus, but it's as much math as you want, honestly. I could get away with not doing any math."* She also talks about the misconception that programmers only spend their time coding. *"Communication skills are actually way more important than engineering skills."*

Brianna's advice to someone who is learning to program is to make sure you are learning it because you enjoy the act of programming. *"Or else you're going to feel unfulfilled. You can make money, but I think what I do is so fun that I do it when I don't get paid."* She also shares, *"There's nothing wrong with being a generalist. It depends on where the company is and how you want to apply your skills. You can be extremely successful having a surface-level knowledge of multiple technologies, or some like to focus on one specific thing. It's up to you; there are options for all."*

iOS software engineer

Alex Margate* is a senior iOS software engineer with over 7 years of experience. She works at a technology company that has over 100,000 employees. She's on a sub-team of 3 software engineers, within a larger team of 50 engineers.

She grew up working with computers, during a time when you could easily customize your personal websites and social pages. In college, she was deciding between psychology and computer science, *"I ended up going into psychology because I really enjoy psychology and still study it today but thought the math in computer science wouldn't be something I would be interested in."* After a while, she decided that she needed to make a change and switched her major to computer science. *"For me, money meant safety, and I knew that this career path would provide me stability. And I enjoyed being on computers, so why not get paid to do it?"* During that time, she started getting involved in the start-up world, when a lot of popular companies today were just getting started. *"I was a young person who got swept up in that and it seemed like a space for me to do well."*

Alex started taking part in entrepreneurship competitions. *"This was back in the day when everyone had an app idea."* She started to teach herself how to make apps by taking a course online for iOS development. *"I kind of just stumbled into it. I felt like Apple stuff was expensive and fancy. I didn't have access to that growing up. I had to buy a Mac, which was the first one I bought. I just kind of fell into it because in the United States, the customers that businesses typically wanted to go after were Apple customers."* She took this course as she was working on her computer science degree and dedicated her time to improving her craft. *"At that time, I was very ambitious. I had a chip on my shoulder and really wanted to prove myself and I wanted to be where the best worked. I had a job offer in my home state, but I had worked so hard and was so ambitious that I felt like I needed to go to Silicon Valley. I went there but I didn't have many connections."*

She stayed with a family friend while she went for interviews. *"I tried to line them all up in a 1- or 2-week period, then I would take the train up to San Francisco and interview at companies. When I wasn't interviewing, I would go to tech events and meetups, networking and being aggressive, and I eventually got a job at a start-up."*

On the topic of networking, Alex thinks it's very important. *"Networking is huge. For example, I went to this meetup for iOS engineers, and I bumped into this person who was trying to start his own start-up and was looking for iOS engineers. I didn't have enough experience, but we exchanged numbers. And then, when I was at my first job, I was laid off. It was a really scary and traumatizing experience. I reached out to that person I met; he was working at another company at the time. And that's how I got my next job, through his referral."* She was able to do the same thing for her current job; she reached out to some contacts on Twitter, got into a conversation with an iOS developer she admired, and managed to get a referral. *"I think referrals are probably the number one way to get noticed at a company; otherwise, it's very competitive because the more popular the company, the more applicants are coming in, so knowing someone through networking is huge."*

The interview process for her current role was through technical phone screening, then she went through six rounds of interviews that took all day, some of which were technical. The technical interview was project-based, where she built an app from scratch throughout the day.

Today, she works on services for a mobile application, mainly on the backend. *"There's a bit of frontend and backend, like the web, where there are two kinds of mobile engineers. There are infrastructure or platform engineers, and then there are feature or frontend engineers, but there isn't a clean split between the two; it's more of a pattern. I've been more interested in platforms or infrastructure, where I'm creating things that feature engineers consume to create those features."*

She's been in her current role for a few months and is still learning about the code base, so she spends most of her time coding and reading documentation. *"I read books, I watch tutorials on things I'm trying to achieve, and I use Stack Overflow."* She says she spends about 80% of her time coding and the remaining 20% in meetings and sending and responding to emails. In her previous senior role, she spent more time in meetings, so she thinks that split will shift in the coming months as she gets more acquainted with the code base.

She thinks programming can be challenging. *"It can really make you doubt yourself and think you're not smart enough, or just not enough basically. There can also be this toxic culture around how smart you are or how better you are than others, and you may work with people who are like that if you're unlucky enough. Combine this with the fact that technology is ever-evolving, but it is something you have to stay on top of, so there's this constant grind of continually learning."*

She thinks aspiring programmers should set realistic goals and not overwhelm themselves. *"It's a marathon, not a sprint."*

Generalist software engineer

The next two engineers are people who have worked with multiple programming languages throughout their careers, making them generalists. Today, both engineers work on backend development, which involves writing code that other parts of the code base and software will use to carry out tasks such as displaying data to users and keeping software services running.

Engineer #1

Greg Thompson Jr. is a software engineer with 10 years of experience, who has worked in many technical specialties, considering himself a generalist. Currently, he works at an IT company focused on web networking that has over 2,000 employees. Greg is on a team of eight engineers who work on a part of the code base that manages the security of information being exchanged between servers. This team is a mix of frontend and backend engineers, as well as a project manager.

Greg's first programming language was the mIRC scripting language, also known as mSL, where the language was interpreted by an **internet relay chat** (**IRC**) client, also called mIRC on Windows 98. He started using the language in middle school, when he was seeking translations for a trading card game that was originally in Japanese. From there, he found a community of other players in mIRC and noticed that some users' messages would stand out with different styling, *"They would type 'LOL' on the screen, but instead of it showing up as text, it would be ASCII art across the screen. I thought that was cool."* These users had the word "scripted" added to their usernames, and he started reaching out to them to learn how they were doing it. After getting access to the mIRC user manuals, he started building his own things, and within a few months, he had built his own text-based games.

He started to build scripts for other games he would play, and eventually moved on to websites, when forums and personal website platforms started to become popular. He picked up HTML and JavaScript to customize his personal social pages, which led him to learn more about web security, where he picked up more languages such as C and Perl. By the time he started college, he already had programming experience from writing code in his spare time, so he decided to pursue a position without a degree. He decided to put together his professional portfolio and started applying for jobs until he landed his first role and started his professional career.

He bounced around to other technical roles and specialties until he found his comfort zone, which primarily focuses on backend development. *"It just seemed to be the area I was most familiar with, so it was a lot easier to be productive. I remember going into interviews saying, 'I'm full stack but lean toward backend.' I've been saying that my whole career, but I'm a generalist. I can learn the language I need and solve the problem; that's the attitude I've always had."* But when he started talking to recruiters, he learned he had to align with a particular tech stack to move ahead in interviews. If he had to define what he focuses on, he would say it's distributed systems, where he builds software that is scalable, which enables a high volume of usage at any given time, preventing it from having errors or being inaccessible due to too many users. *"I like it because it's a broad term."* He currently writes in Rust and Python and works with a lot of other technologies and tools, such as PostgreSQL, Docker, and **Amazon Web Services (AWS)**.

Today, Greg is a senior software engineer who builds and maintains security services. He's currently working on fixing a lot of bugs and carefully integrating a new code base into his company's and making it as smooth as possible without any issues. It takes a lot of configuration when he integrates code that has older versions of the language and needs to be modernized. *"It's complicated because it's a monolithic code base. If you make a change in one place, it can affect another part of the code that has nothing to do with that change. We don't have enough test coverage, and it's very delicate."* He has to plan how to manage these issues while building new features. He starts and ends his day by checking what backend services failed and have errors. He'll receive any errors via chat messages. Greg has faced this challenge many times before, working through older code bases, each of which comes with its own set of issues. He usually spends 80% of his time writing code. Some of his coding time is spent researching, where he's trying to figure out the source of errors, including who to contact about the code base when something goes wrong. The other 20% of the time is spent meeting with other engineers to discuss things such as planning and regular syncs. He's also currently onboarding a new team member and meeting with them regularly to get them comfortable with the code base.

Greg is passionate about design, finding patterns, coming up with conventions, and figuring out how best to build a software system. *"Those are always fun problems to me. How can I build this right the first time?"* He finds coding creative, especially when he's building something new. *"I didn't see it as a technical endeavor until my first year as a professional software engineer. Before that, it was more about the craft. I see programming as painting, where you're coming up with these systems to solve a problem; you're painting a picture and different areas of the picture require different paints and brushes. I take a lot of pride in that; it's fun. It's more free form when you're able to look at everything with a blank slate and solve the problem."*

To this point, he thinks that software engineers are pigeonholed into assuming they have a more rigid mode of thinking, but *"the best programmers I've known are not as rigid as you would expect them to be. They are very curious and open to gray areas. In fact, they live in them and try to pull rigidity from the boundaries of those gray areas so that they can make more sense of the world. I think more people should think of programmers as creative because most of the time, you don't have a straightforward problem to solve; you have to come up with all the in-betweens that require you to think outside of the box."*

Greg's interview for his current role started off with an interview screening asking a variety of questions, where an emphasis was placed on what projects he had done. He applied through a job platform, where a recruiter reached out to him. He had a few rounds of interviews, which were a mix of algorithms and database questions. He remembers one of his first interviews, which was an intimidating experience. *"I walked in, and he asked me a number of trivia questions about computer science. At some point, we go to the whiteboard and I'm thinking I'm about to get a programming problem, but the first thing he asks me is to graph x squared. I will never forget it because I was so nervous. I graphed it, but that was the tone of the rest of the interview."*

He didn't get the job, but he shares that you don't need to be considered a genius to be a programmer, but: *"You need to be pedantic about what you're doing and the problem that you're solving. It's something that people normally overlook; you need to be someone who can at least orient themselves around whatever effort and curiosity are required to figure out these problems. Genius is not required; I think that's a common misconception."*

If Greg were looking for a job today, he says it would be important to *"have something to show for what you say you can do. Have two or three projects, even if they're not complete or well written to the best of your abilities and well documented."* Greg took these steps when he was applying for roles but also talked about blogging: *"I blogged my different areas of learning and my various thoughts. It doesn't take much to write 200 words about some new concept that you've learned. I think there's a lot of value in showing that you can articulate very technical thoughts so that they're understandable for various crowds. I think the engineer of yesteryear that can be fully technical is gone. Right now, I think what we'll evolve into is the communicating engineer. You can no longer go in the back and build something technical."* He says that it helped him in his career, especially as he applied for roles without a degree. He also says that networking is important, *"People talk. I think a lot of people don't want to acknowledge it but it's a very small world. If you're that person that people think of as a technical person who can solve a problem, that's a good thing."*

Greg thinks the hardest thing about programming is finding out what projects to build on your own that you can learn from. *"You want to come up with something creative that's not too easy but not too tough that you can't make progress."* He continues by explaining what it means to "know" a language. *"I think people conflate syntax with learning the programming language. It's like learning the general structure of a natural language. When you learn a language, you're trying to learn how to construct gracefully written paragraphs and essays. You're trying to construct complete expressions of thought. You can learn all the syntax you want, but you're not really learning the language until you can write a full-fledged program from start to finish and you can do it in such a way that the code is maintainable, something that you can generally change and distribute if you wanted to. I strongly believe that."*

If Greg could give advice to someone today who is new to programming, it would be, *"Coding is the last part; first, draw out and clarify the problem. Figure out what you're trying to solve and write out a solution in plain natural language before you try to code. Often, folks jump right into the code, but forget all that for a sec and think about the general algorithm, write some pseudocode, and connect the dots. Think of the code as the last 10% of the project you're engaging in. If you write that code the wrong way, you'll end up with bigger problems than you started with."*

Engineer #2

Patrick Oduro is a senior software engineer at a financial technology, also known as FinTech, company and is based in western Africa. He has over 7 years of experience and is a self-guided developer who has worked across many technical stacks and has managed and led teams.

Patrick studied industrial chemistry at university but had a couple of friends who were into software engineering, graphic design, and web design. *"They were doing very well but I wasn't sure if I was going to take that path."* However, he struggled to find a job after graduating. *"Where I'm from, you need to know someone, who knows someone, who knows someone to connect you to the industry. I tried everything that I could, but it wasn't working."* However, he had a laptop that his father gifted him in his third year of college. *"So I said to myself, 'I'm kind of wasting time going about looking for a job. I should try to build a kind of skill so I can make myself employable.'"*

Patrick started by learning PHP. *"It was a bit difficult then because at that time, there wasn't much knowledge, books, or information about PHP out there. I could only rely on a friend who had experience using that language, but he was also busy."* Patrick is used to solving problems on his own, *"It's good when you are learning on your own, but sometimes you just need to call on the person you think can help so that you can move fast."* He relied on YouTube for learning; he says he watched and downloaded about 200 videos. *"At that time, we didn't have the internet as it is now. I had to go to an internet café and then download the videos."*

In the meantime, he earned income by helping mothers in a humanitarian village by running errands. He'd spend his income at the café. *"I did this for about a year. And then I developed my first personal website."* About a few months later, he got a call from a company for an interview and got the job. *"I was employed as a database developer, where I managed their database."* During this time, he also learned Java. *"I had a friend around who was very helpful and very experienced with Java."* He ended up using Java at his company and developed a desktop application. He decided to move on after a year and a half. He felt like the company didn't value software development as they should and he wanted the opportunity to grow. *"They were a networking company. When I'm working in a company, I would rather be an asset, not a liability. I realized that I was considered a liability in that role. They can get rid of you at any time and I saw I was not much of a priority. I observed this as I realized that they were employing very good network engineers and prioritized them. So I moved on to another company."*

He moved on to a software engineering firm that had affiliations with most of the banks in the area, as well as IBM. *"That created a great platform for me to actually learn, improve, and also expand and explore. I think that this company really nurtured me into understanding object-oriented programming because we used mostly .NET and a bit of PHP, so I got the opportunity to learn C# there and use the .NET Framework."* He would spend his days at work learning and exploring, sometimes leaving the office at 12:00 A.M. and then coming back in the morning to work. He moved around a few more times before he landed a role that led to a leadership position.

Patrick became the lead of the technical department for a large telecommunications company. *"What they offered me was quite huge. For the first time, I was in a company that provided all the tools that I needed. They provided me with the best laptops, phones, and allowances that I needed, which created a very good environment for me. Their philosophy was 'whatever tool that you need, you will be provided with so that you can be effective.' So it was a bit more comfortable. And after every year, you were given a bonus depending on your performance. It was good. It was exciting."* However, he fell on difficult times as his direct reports and colleagues began to leave the company. *"One day, one of our products was hacked. I was left to handle it alone. I needed to handle about four servers and three applications. I needed to fix all the bugs that were causing hackers to have access to our server."* Another time, a server went down before a product launch, right at the end of the working day. Patrick let his colleagues and reports go home and stayed behind. It took six hours to get it running again and he had to sleep at the office. *"I wore a lot of hats, doing a lot of things. Whatever problem was thrown at me, I wanted to take it on even if I had no experience with it."* Patrick used it as an opportunity to learn more. *"That helped me because I ended up understanding how telecommunication services worked."*

Patrick learned about server administration and networking, load balancing, and containerization with Docker. He also learned how to use **virtual private networks** (**VPNs**) and was able to use cloud platforms such as AWS to set up VPN connections. *"It was exciting but a lot was demanded of me."* In addition to his technical responsibilities, he would train new engineers. In the next few years, he would continue learning new technologies that spanned many technical stacks and problems, from backend web development to migrating applications to new technologies.

Today, Patrick is a senior software engineer at a Web3 company that uses blockchain technology to send and receive money without the need for an internet connection. *"What I do is just manage the backend. We have a couple of APIs that are used by our partners to distribute currency and crypto."* Now, he's only focused on one part of the system. *"The programming aspect always takes priority. I don't know much about planning, but I'm getting to a point where I can't run away from planning – yes, because I realize that it's helpful. It gives you a better picture of what you are going to do and you are able to evaluate the risk factors and the tools you will need to use. I would always prefer programming first and then planning, but now I need to gradually learn to plan first before programming."* Patrick talks about how **test-driven development** (**TDD**) helps him be more planful. TDD is a type of software development where you write code that tests the features that you will build so that each part of the code has test cases and test coverage.

Patrick has experienced a lot in his 7 years working in the industry and shares what he's learned so far with new developers. *"Make sure that you understand the basics; don't just learn it, work with it. Develop a project with it. You need to work with what you have learned because that is the only way you will be able to register some of these skills to your memory. Having these skills at your fingertips will help you be able to effectively work with them."*

C# software engineer

Ernesto Ortiz is a software developer with 2 years of professional experience as a software engineer consultant. He's currently in between roles as he waits for a new project. He works on various projects as a full stack web developer using C#, which is the ASP.NET framework.

Ernesto went to college for software engineering. He wanted to be a programmer since secondary school, mainly because his dad was a systems engineer, who worked on hardware support but did a little programming as well. He's getting ready to graduate soon with a bachelor's degree. When he was in high school, he believed college was the only way to get a good job. *"I think now, with more experience and a little more perspective into the industry, it's not necessary to go to college; you can totally be a self-taught programmer and still be able to make very good projects."* He recalls his experience in university that helped him come to this realization, *"When I was in university, I didn't have good teachers but I still wanted to learn. I started learning by myself and discovered that I could have done this since secondary school. I could have been a self-taught programmer years ago and it's something that I kind of regret, though I can't change the past. There are kids that are coding at the age of 10. I would have liked to be that kid. I didn't know. I didn't have the information; I didn't have a mentor to guide me."* He mentions that though taking the self-guided route takes longer, *"It's worth it."* Despite his regret, he's glad he got his degree because he mentions that a degree is usually a requirement for getting a job out of the country, which he would like to do.

Today, in his current role, he's realized that although he's still quite flexible in his career at the moment, he's drawn to backend web development. *"I agree that the UX/UI is very important when you're working on a project when you have end users, but personally, I don't like developing that side of a project. I like the abstract side of the backend and working with data and databases and all of the necessary background services for the frontend. In my experience with full stack projects, I focus on the backend, but I participate in frontend projects where I work on the logic, which I enjoy more than the styling."* He is also interested in data engineering and data science and worked on a thesis that involved numerical analysis that required some coding. But he recognizes that he doesn't have professional experience and hasn't had the opportunity to apply for these roles. He's currently postponing pursuing this because he will most likely have to start at a lower level than his current position, which will mean earning less money, so he's decided to stay focused on his current experience and skills. In terms of experience, he thinks that while internships can define your career path, *"I would say that it's not your destiny but it will say a lot about what you focus on."*

Ernesto explains how consultancy works. *"You have a lot of projects to work on. Sometimes you choose them, sometimes you don't. When you are hired as a software engineer in a consulting company, you get interviewed by clients that hire development teams through the consultancy."* The person who interviews you will typically be an engineer from the client that is hiring. He hasn't had an interview that has asked him about algorithms and data structures. *"It's not very common. It's more about technical knowledge. They usually ask you, 'What's C#? What's a class?'"* He says joining a team is like any other software project, *"There's a development team, a project team, and a security team that will give you the necessary credentials for a project. The process of getting into the project is the difference. If the project ends or you want to switch projects, which you can do if you don't like the project, you have to be interviewed again."*

He describes how, when he moved between different projects, he noticed that teams solve each problem differently. *"You can get a project without standards, a project with very strict standards, a project with legacy versions that need to be maintained, or a project with the most recent technology."* He spends most of his time coding and doing code reviews, which he notes will sometimes take time. He has to carefully look through the code because he did not write it, which takes time and focus.

He enjoys planning and designing, though he used to enjoy programming the most. As he's gained more experience, he has started to encounter "boilerplate" situations where there is reusable code or templates to solve a problem. He says this follows the Pareto principle, where *"you're going to see 80% of the most important code 20% of the time. But with planning and designing, you have more creativity because it depends on the problem you're trying to solve. I haven't led any planning or designing but I have enjoyed participating."* He doesn't enjoy maintenance as much: *"It's not that fun. It feels like holding up a building so that it doesn't fall apart."* He recalls a few times when he had to make a tough decision on getting a completed project out of the door or spending more time to make the code more readable, but had to meet the deadline in the end. He says unreadable code presents the biggest challenges.

Ernesto recalls his first job as a software engineer, where he started as an intern at a very small start-up that didn't have an IT team. He felt really proud of the experience because he was the only software engineer. He wanted to show what software would do for the company by building a mobile app and automating manual processes within the company, showing how applying technology is more reliable.

Ernesto's experience in learning coding has given him a lot of insight to share with self-guided learners. *"Don't limit yourself with learning; you can learn anything. Thankfully, the resources are infinite thanks to the internet, but our time is not. Take advantage of that fact. Don't wait. Even when it comes to a job, you don't need a job to solve problems. You will fail. You will get bugs, but keep going."*

Frontend web developer

Kandance Ferguson is a software engineer at a very small start-up, on a team of two, including herself. This is her first software engineer role and she started a little over 6 months ago. Kandance is also a part-time programming instructor. She's consistently crossed paths with programming in her 15-year professional career across various roles.

Although her father was an engineer and a math teacher, Kandance wanted to be a nurse. After facing extreme discrimination in her nursing degree program, she decided to try something different and change majors, *"but never considered computer science. I had a few friends in that department but never really saw myself in it."* She completed a bachelor's degree in psychology. She went to graduate school for information systems management and had to learn Python to get into the program: *"I applied as I was learning Python and spent nights in my dorm room learning it after studying for my classes."* She learned more Python as well as how to use databases in her degree program. She went on to work in the healthcare systems field after graduating. She started working with hospitals to help launch their internal healthcare software, but eventually left the field. She decided to return to school after that to pursue being a doctor, but she already had two children, and the demands of med school put stress on her family, so she decided to stop. *"Maybe for later in life, who knows?"*

She picked coding back up again, planning to return to the healthcare systems field. It was at this point that she discovered a women-focused programming community and found and applied for a position as a computer science teacher on a job board at the same time as applying for a programmer position at an oil company. Both jobs extended an offer to her and she found herself at a crossroads, *"Honestly, the programmer job would have been better for my life and the lifestyle I wanted in my head at the time, but when I went to my final interview again and looked around, I knew I didn't fit in that room."*

She decided to decline the offer and became a computer science teacher. She taught various topics, such as web development and how to build a computer. *"I had students put together computers and donate them to schools that needed them."* The principals at the school picked up on how her class was excelling and how great of a teacher she was, as students received consistently good grades. She was asked to sit in on the math classes and eventually was transferred to teaching math. *"My students did really well. In the 2 years that I had them, they increased their test scores from 30% passing to 90% passing. So, I was asked to lead the math department."*

She moved on to become the STEM chair at a high school and taught Python. *"But it was a tough year for students, coming back from the pandemic."* During her time there, she ended up joining a bootcamp and taking classes, splitting her time between being online for her classes, monitoring the hallways, and interacting with students. Her principal was initially supportive, but one morning, Kandance received a negative text message from her principal about her priorities and decided to quit on the spot. *"I was like alright, today's my last day! That was it. I went to work and packed up my stuff."* She thought about holding out until the upcoming holiday weekend to receive holiday pay but decided it wasn't worth it. *"No. I wasn't going to sacrifice my mental state anymore for this when I knew something bigger and better was out there for me and I could go into something that I'd been doing for all these years."* She decided to take the time to recover from the physical and mental stress of her last position, then dedicate her time to finishing her bootcamp. About 5 weeks before the bootcamp ended, she was offered a position as a software engineer.

She mentions that support from her mentor, an instructor at the bootcamp, helped her find the courage to dedicate her time to pursuing a career in software engineering. *"I called him and said, 'I can't do this anymore.' And he said, 'You need to just do the program now.'"* She applied the same day and was offered a seat in the next cohort. She had to take a programming assessment to be accepted, though she hadn't written code in a while. *"It felt refreshing."*

Today, in her current role, she and her manager are the only two software engineers. She focuses on frontend development, but she's been taking the time to learn the entire development stack since the team is so small. In her bootcamp, she learned the popular frontend framework called React, but the current project uses another, called Angular. The two take very different approaches to frontend development. *"I've been spending a lot of time learning the stack. It's taken me a while to learn how to do things in Angular versus React. It is a long road getting from zero to now."* She spends most of her time programming: *"I'm either working on something and pushing code or trying something and breaking stuff to see what happens in our code base."*

Her experience in healthcare systems followed her software engineering role, and she worked the tasks centered around maintenance and quality assurance. *"We had to do a lot of quality analysis to see where issues were, and also detect fraud."* She also had to work on design and remembers a time when she had to work out ways to have multiple healthcare systems communicate with each other. She didn't find it very interesting because it took a lot of time and meetings with no significant progress.

Kandance talks about how networking helped her land her first job. *"As someone who has been in and out of tech and didn't take the traditional route to a particular position, networking worked really well for me and my personality. On paper, I may miss what I'm trying to convey to somebody about my experience and my passion for software engineering and tech, but once you meet me, you'll understand and probably develop a greater appreciation for what I bring to the table. I really don't care what someone says. 'No.' It was no in the beginning before I even asked. I will ask for whatever I want. It's been something that's worked for me over the years, being vulnerable enough to ask, and demand in some cases, 'Why?' I can see why some may be uncomfortable with it."*

"My interview processes were really unique. I was shamelessly reaching out to people on LinkedIn. I made it a point to send a certain number of messages per day. I sent one to someone I went to high school with and he responded to my message." They continued the conversation over the phone and learned that his business partner was looking for an engineer. He referred her to the current manager for an interview. *"We talked about tech, we talked about what I knew, and I had already sent him some of my projects."* She ended up doing a small project for the next phase of the interview. After that, she had another interview and was offered a position. *"I wasn't sure if I was going to take it because I was well paid as a teacher, and because this was a start-up, you're typically paid less, but they made it work."* She decided to keep applying anyway because she wanted to practice interviewing and finding a second source of income as she had recently had a big move with her family. She remembers one interview where she had made it to the second-to-last interview round and was given an hour to complete a coding assessment with a small project. However, she couldn't finish it in time and didn't get the role. *"That would have been a cool position but I'm happy with where I am now because another company wouldn't have given me the time and space to learn this much."*

The hardest part of learning programming for Kandance is being comfortable with failing. *"You have to understand this is how you learn more."* She also shares that programmers don't sit in front of a computer all day. *"Do you know how hard I'm thinking? Do you know how many times my IDE tells me I'm doing something wrong, I have 23 errors, my server isn't running right, and my code doesn't compile? Then, you find out you had a random comma somewhere because you accidentally added one in your code when you were trying to lock your computer screen, or your cat walked across the keyboard."* For advice, she shares one of her favorite phrases: *"ABC – always be coding. Do it all the time! Keep doing tutorials and do them again because you might notice something different the next time. Also make sure you're doing it for the right reasons because if you really don't enjoy it, you will struggle."*

Data engineer

Max Blum is a data engineer working in a team of 8 for a financial company with over 400 employees and has a year and a half of experience. He's currently working and finishing his master's degree in information systems.

Max went to college and started his bachelor's in business administration, but then he took a course in C++ and moved on to business intelligence. He discovered that he enjoyed it and began working in the field. While he enjoyed building reports, he also enjoyed the process of preparing data to build reports. During his master's, he joined a data science bootcamp and learned Python, and then went to an AI bootcamp while completing his master's. He was given the opportunity to switch from business intelligence to data engineering at his current company. *"Most of the things that I learn in university now are computer science topics."* He's currently applying his skills to his thesis, where he's tracking the sustainability of goods with data. He thinks what pulled him into the direction of coding as a profession was that he was already working on side projects but then discovered that he enjoyed working with real-time data. *"Because the data you get from the real world is all mixed up and uncleaned. Cleaning the data and the automation or orchestration of data pipelines is what drew me most to data engineering."*

In his current role, *"I take data from different sources needed for a report, load it into a data lake, then transform the data so that it fits right, which is most of the work to get the data in clean shape, and then I build reports. Most of the time, they are not as complex as a data scientist would create, but just a basic report to visualize the data."* More of his time is typically spent planning than coding: *"I think it's most important to first plan what steps you want to carry out. The programming is the fun part, but the planning is the important part."* The first step is always data governance, which is a set of processes and tools that make sure that the data is being handled securely and within regulations. Max's company has documentation on standard procedures. If there isn't documentation, then the planning process takes a little longer because a standard procedure needs to be created, as well as deciding whether it's something that will be used in the future. Once governance is in place, then the planning process continues with deciding how to load and transform the data. He typically does transformations with Python. While he enjoys programming and thinks it's like solving puzzles, he also enjoys the design parts. *"The programming still excites me the most because you can really get into your zone. On the other hand, in the design part, you really need to do a lot of thinking. 'How can this work now? How can this work in the future?"*

During the interview, Max didn't have any coding questions. He's based in central Europe and says it's uncommon there. *"It depends on the company, but for me, it was an application with your CV, including your grades, because I started as a student, and then there's an assessment center to test your verbal and cognitive abilities. It's like pattern matching and small word problems, not really coding-related tests. After the tests, if you do well, then you get invited to an interview with the team and HR where they ask about your experience."*

Max explains how a bug works in data engineering, where it's usually a problem in a data pipeline. He explains one particular case that he spent a lot of time trying to fix. *"It worked when I created it but didn't work the next day, though nothing had changed in comparison to yesterday. I tried to ask the senior engineers for help but they all said they didn't know, so it was a lot of searching for the problem. Then finally, a senior data engineer discovered that a setting needed to be turned off. The fix was minor but finding the error and correcting the error was the hard part."*

The most challenging part of programming for Max is object-oriented programming. *"In most cases, Python works without object-oriented programming. Especially in data engineering, you can just write scripts without it, so you don't really need it."* He thinks that a common misconception about data engineering is that many think it's data science. *"There is a difference between the two. Data scientists would do more with machine learning models while data engineers work with models sometimes, but not often. The biggest difference between the two is in machine learning."*

As for advice, Max thinks that you shouldn't let your fear block you from getting started with programming. *"There was this big block that made me think that coding was only for very intelligent people. Which is wrong. So just start."* He also shares that you should start a project with a mentor. *"It's like working with a senior engineer because it's someone you can ask for help or who can point you in the right direction. My mentor helped me get better at searching for the answers I needed."*

Salesforce software engineer

Nayonna Purnell is a Salesforce engineer at a consulting company with over 10,000 employees. She's a career switcher who started in the education field. She's been a software engineer for 2 years.

Nayonna had her first experience with code in her undergraduate degree, where her first career of choice was to become a lawyer. *"I remember, in my undergraduate experience, they gave us the opportunity to work on a program, where we made a Dreamweaver website for a science course. I loved it; I believed I was a developer."* After graduating, Nayonna went on to become a teacher. She recalls the second encounter she had with coding. *"I became involved with a women's group that was looking to advertise a conference and they asked, 'Does anyone know web design?' So I raised my hand because in my mind, if I could build it in Dreamweaver, I could learn it there."* She learned about opportunities in tech while at an alumni brunch at her alma mater, where she discovered an organization for women who are software developers or aspiring to be one. The person responsible for starting a chapter in her city was an alumna of the university as well and spoke about her experience. *"She was sharing how her life had changed. I was at a crossroads in my life, where I was ready to leave teaching, and I saw it as an out. She told us how she found this group, learned how to code, created a company, and was thriving, and I thought, 'Why can't I have that?' So I did some research. Although I have two master's degrees, I did more research to become a developer than I did with my master's program."*

Her real start in software development was through the organization's workshop classes. *"I became inspired. I found a start-up and knocked on their door thinking, 'The research says you can become a developer in 3 months,' and I believed it. The start-up gave me a chance as an intern, so I thought I could take the 3 months during my summer break off, and then quit my job."* She spent 3 months coding and learning. It didn't turn out the way she had planned, except for the fact that she did end up resigning from her post as a teacher. *"Trying to adapt to a three-month coding program with the belief that I would get a job right away was unrealistic. I think the 3-month plan might have really worked for some people. My kids are programming now and that 3 months might be their story, but it wasn't mine because I wasn't introduced to coding until later in life."* When asked about her experience at the internship, she says she learned how to work in a technical group but felt that she needed to find the right learning environment to thrive. *"I couldn't connect with them because I also had a family. I have a husband and children. They didn't come into the office until 10 A.M. to start the workday and they didn't leave until 7 P.M. or later. I arrived at the office every day at 8 A.M. The times that they were leaving the office, I was already having dinner with my family."*

Nayonna went on to take a 2-year software engineering program at a community college. *"But it was virtual, which was a mistake because I knew that in-person was better for me, but I was desperate. Desperation is hard when you're surviving."* She talks about the isolation she felt during the program. *"I didn't take to the virtual route because with no prior background, who are you bouncing your ideas off of? Who are you speaking to? Who is giving you advice? So you know what ended up happening? Most of my time, I went to see the tutor in person, taking my kids with me. What was the point of me doing a virtual program if I was still going into the building? I learned more from the tutor than I did from the teacher!"* Nayonna is critical of this outcome because of her background as an educator. She recalls the teacher not giving her a lot of direction. *"They'll give you the book and say, 'Just do it.' How am I supposed to know what I'm doing? I don't know what I'm doing. I didn't know what I didn't know and I didn't know what I knew. With no prior knowledge of coding, the self-taught route can be difficult because you have to sift through information."*

Through that program, she joined a job board and got a technical consultant role while doing the program. *"All this time of me thinking 'I'm a developer,' but meanwhile I'm a developer in training at school and a technical consultant doing software development and other things centered around technical work."* This gave her a technical edge but she also saw some gaps in the learning content and thought it was inconsistent with what she was learning in the industry. *"So now I'm arguing with the professor – the book is saying one thing but the industry is doing something different. It was outdated and it wasn't making me competitive."*

Nayonna moved on to a bootcamp and is graduating in a few months. She reflects on this time that intersected with her discovery of a community of people like her learning how to code. *"You need community because it can be lonely. It can be discouraging, especially if you're self-guided. With the bootcamp, I'm able to raise my hand and speak because I've already been exposed to these topics, I already understand things, and although it's virtual, it's not hard for me now. All of the fear is gone. I'm not lost and I'm not scared. I think fear is an issue with being a developer. You have the fear of not knowing, fear of not understanding, fear of what people will think of you, and fear of not getting a job. It's all centered around acceptance and that's what makes it difficult. When you remove the fear and say, 'I don't know but I'm going to ask questions and figure it out,' I think that's where the strength lies, but it takes time to get to that point."*

Nayonna goes into more detail about networking and what it's done for her. *"When I first started learning how to network, it was because I wanted a job, and in the tech industry, they tell you to network."* She describes networking at tech conferences: *"I did not have the money to pay for attendance for conferences, so I volunteered and got to go to the conferences for free."* These opportunities led her to mentors and interviews. She recalls one mentor that helped her navigate her new career. *"Every Saturday morning, we would connect. We weren't doing programming tutoring. I needed the soft skills. He taught me how to negotiate my salary. I think that networking means going to those conferences. You need to go to those workshops that are of interest to you and that are available to you. Go to the meetups that are in your local area now. There are lots of virtual meetups, so you could even do that. Have conversations, even if you don't know what to talk about. Pay attention to what other people are talking about. Watch videos on YouTube if you can on how to network and get yourself a LinkedIn account. I don't think that's a should but a must. Your LinkedIn is your business card. My LinkedIn has been my power move."* It's true – Nayonna points out that we had a conversation over a year ago via LinkedIn.

Nayonna is currently a Salesforce engineer consultant. She learned about Salesforce through the women's coding community she found through the alumni brunch. *"When I was doing those workshops, Salesforce wanted to give a demo on how to be a Salesforce developer, so they had someone come in to do so. And I couldn't attend."* She researched and found the person who gave the demo that day. *"Eventually, she connected with me and gave me a bunch of resources. But at the time, I was deep into the software engineering program and felt like I was struggling with that. So how am I going to struggle in a program that I'm paying for and try to learn Salesforce?"* Nayonna decided to come back to learning more about Salesforce later. However, she discovered that the company she was working for had a Salesforce department and decided to pivot into that role. *"They didn't have me developing at first. I was doing testing and I hated it. Then, in the second project, I was doing configuration, which had development aspects."*

Nayonna describes coding with Salesforce technologies, where the Apex coding language is written on top of Java. She learned Java in the software engineering program. *"It was easier for me to understand the Java concepts because I didn't understand it then and now I get it because now it's hands-on."* Apex is at the backend of a Salesforce application, while Salesforce Lightning is at the frontend. *"They call it the Lightning Web Component, which is written on top of JavaScript. You can integrate frontend frameworks such as Angular and React and not use Salesforce components. You could still use other code and make a regular website over the top of Salesforce."*

Nayonna's bootcamp focuses on full stack development, although she's a Salesforce developer. She describes why she went down that route. *"You want to be in spaces that are highly needed because strategically, to me, if it's a high-need area, it's less likely that you will lose your job, or you can pivot. If you're a full stack developer and you understand the frontend or the backend, you can pivot. Also, I love to help, which means that if I understand both angles, I know how to speak the language of frontend and backend and I know how to help."* Nayonna is focusing on finishing her bootcamp and not really thinking about specializations. *"I hadn't thought about it until you brought it up because this has not been an easy journey for me."* While she feels more experienced, she also feels like she's got a long way to go. *"It's been 2 years of me being on the job, and even with those 2 years, it doesn't feel consistent. This is the first time that I've been able to connect with architects and other senior engineers. And now, because I'm in the bootcamp, I'm able to piece together what the true experience is supposed to be. I think I was so focused on the code because I wanted to be secure and confident."*

She talks about the interview process, which didn't require a technical interview. With it being her first developer role, she had some difficulties ramping up and goes on to describe how she overcame her challenges. *"I was able to stay afloat because I'm used to surviving, and appear like I'm thriving when I'm surviving. I worked hard to understand how to do it because I felt like I had seen the most amount of money I had ever seen in my career and I'm finally getting what I've been working for years to get into. I didn't want it taken away from me, so I was scared to speak up."* She talks about making it through that difficult time in her career by looking back at where she's come from. *"When you start really looking at your successes, it can help you change your mindset. I have 2 master's degrees and I've taught over 400 students at once, so if I can do that, I can do this. When you can pull the power from your experience and put it in that perspective, it changes your mindset. You have to change your mindset. I realized how much value I bring; I'm more than just a developer. So, because of that, it was easier for me to rise to the challenge and speak up."*

This mindset helped Nayonna through her toughest bug where she was tasked with an integration. *"There are algorithms that prevent duplicate insertion and I was still in the process of learning algorithms, so they had me do a lazy loading algorithm, but I didn't know what I was doing. Algorithms are important. I struggled because I didn't understand."* On top of that, the code was not written in a way that was easy to understand. *"I feel like when you write your code, you need to make sure that it's easy for the person after you to go in and build on it. I worked with a more senior developer who was struggling to understand it too. I was going line by line and pulling both of my architects in to help me."* Eventually, she was able to solve the problem. She says it was because she asked for help from multiple colleagues. *"I feel like another thing I had to learn is you need to seek out more than one guide in the workplace. Because sometimes just because a person has a specific title, doesn't mean they will know everything."*

She ends with some words of encouragement for new developers, especially ones with families. *"I'm not just a career changer. I'm a mom and a wife. I've built a family; I've built a team. It's more than just software development. Just remember it's not a competition and your job doesn't define you. Don't miss out on life because that's all you're doing."*

Summary

In this chapter, you learned a lot about software engineering from professionals who are currently tackling problems with code. As you can see, there are many paths to software engineering, even if you're well established in another profession. It can even help boost your skills to have that background. Despite the unique stories, experience, and technical expertise of each software engineer, there are some main points to draw from each story:

- You do not need a degree to become a software engineer

- Coding can be creative

- Math is not required for a software role

- You can generalize your specialization, but you may need to highlight certain skills for a particular role
- You should have some projects to show future employers
- Networking can be an important part of moving forward in your career

These stories can help you navigate your career and carve your own path in the industry. By reading this book, you're already creating your own path and story. In the next chapter, you'll learn about best coding practices with C#.

Further reading

- The Dev.to community's beginners tag contains many resources and stories of beginners in software engineering: `https://dev.to/t/beginners`
- Hear stories from developers of all backgrounds on the CodeNewbie podcast: `https://www.codenewbie.org/`

12
Coding Best Practices

Software engineers who enter the workforce and work on building complex software applications with a team are constantly learning. As they progress in their careers, they pick up new ways to write code and habits and preferences along the way, and sometimes these habits are hard to let go of. Part of joining a new team is adapting to the team's procedures and adapting your coding style to stay consistent with the project they're focused on. A common joke among programmers across all years of experience is returning to code they wrote a few months ago and having no recollection of what or why they did it. So, it's important to make code as clearly written and documented as possible to make it easier to return to, especially if there's a critical bug that needs to be fixed immediately. As you learned in *Chapter 9, Applying Algorithms in C#,* and *Chapter 10, Object-Oriented Programming,* consistency in code makes it more readable so it's easier to follow. This is why software teams will adapt to a coding style that they all must agree on so that each member knows what to expect. But where do these rules and standards come from?

Most programming language compilers ignore any unclear formatting because they're focused on whether the syntax is correct. However, you might have noticed that C# has special keywords, such as `if` and `private`, that can only be used in special circumstances. There are also many rules in the syntax, including rules for naming variables, classes, or anything else that might need an **identifier**, which is a name that you must define and assign to something. Despite all of the rules, there's still a lot of flexibility in how you can write code, as long as the syntax is valid. This is the case for many languages.

The C# language documentation gives guidance on ways to standardize code in an application, which many software engineers, including professional teams, will adopt. However, there are no hard rules on which to adopt, so many will pick and choose the ones that are the best fit for their code base. You'll learn that some of these choices stem from lead software engineers who brought the habits and style preferences they've learned to the team. A personal example is, when I used to use C# in a professional setting, I always instantiated objects like this example:

```
ClassName objectName = new ClassName();
```

However, I joined a team that standardized their code as done in the following example:

```
var objectName = new ClassName();
```

This line is the same as the earlier example, where the `var` keyword allows you to create implicitly typed values, which basically means the compiler will evaluate the right side to know what type of value the variable will store. You will also notice that some of the examples in this book deviate from the documentation standards, as they have been written based on my past professional experience.

First, let's define and differentiate the difference between style, standards, and rules, which may have different interpretations, depending on who you ask:

- **Style**: Refers to choices a programmer makes in how they write their code
- **Standards**: Refers to widely adopted choices that professional programmers make in writing their code
- **Rules**: Refers to implementation choices that will prevent compilation or stop code from executing, such as syntax

This chapter will focus on best practices from the C# language documentation, including how to name identifiers in your code and how to format it for readability. A lot of what will be covered in this chapter is common standards used by teams who are building with C#, and other OOP languages such as Java may have some similarities in standards.

This chapter will cover the following topics:

- Following naming guidelines
- Following syntax consistency guidelines
- Following reusability guidelines
- Following documentation guidelines

By the end of this chapter, you will know how to apply popular coding standards to your C# code.

Technical requirements

To complete the exercises in this chapter, you'll need a computer, such as a laptop or a desktop computer, that has Visual Studio Code and .NET installed. Refer to *Chapter 5, Writing Your First C# Program*, for information on how to install them.

You can find the code files for this chapter on GitHub at `https://github.com/PacktPublishing/Fundamentals-for-Self-Taught-Programmers/tree/main/Chapter12`.

Following naming guidelines

Identifiers are names that define things in code, such as a class or a variable. Identifiers are one of the main things that programmers have nearly complete control over in their code. When you're creating code that only you are building, you may have a clear idea of what each identifier is. But on a team, it may be hard for someone to decipher the meaning of it if there aren't guidelines on how to name things in a code base. This can cause multiple issues, including bugs and slower implementation times, as software engineers try to understand what other teammates have done, especially if the previous authors no longer work on the code base because they have left the team.

In C#, identifiers can be anything except duplicate names, where there may be exceptions, as is the case with overloaded methods, and they must start with a letter or an underscore. While this is the basic syntax rule for identifiers, let's explore some guidelines that some teams might follow in terms of naming conventions.

Naming identifiers

Naming identifiers should be clear in terms of what they are or what they do. As you already know, you must avoid using the keywords available in C#. You can't name a class `class` or an integer `int`. However, you can create a class called `Class` or an integer called `Int` and the compiler won't stop you. But is the meaning of each of these identifiers clear? What do they mean? Can someone who looks at what you wrote understand what you're trying to build?

When you're writing identifiers, you'll want to make sure they're readable and clear enough to understand, not only for yourself but also for others who are following along or enhancing the work. The C# language guidelines for identifiers take a similar stance, where it is suggested to avoid underscores, hyphens, and other symbols that can make them hard to read. It's also suggested to avoid abbreviations and acronyms if possible. Here's an example of two properties:

```
public double Lat {get;}
public double Lon {get;}
```

Does it make sense to you what they stand for? To the trained eye who may have used a map, it's clear that this is latitude and longitude. It's unsafe to assume that this would be the case for all programmers and that whoever is working with these properties will understand what they are by looking at the rest of the class. In this case, spelling out the entire words will add clarity to what they mean. Let's explore some conventions by identifier type.

Casing and capitalization

The C# language documentation suggests two main naming conventions when it comes to capitalization:

- **camelCase**, where the first character of the second word is capitalized in the identifier
- **PascalCase** where the first character in each word is capitalized

C# recommends that camelCase be used for all method parameters, and PascalCase used for any other identifiers.

Data should be nouns

Identifiers that contain or represent a value are some type of data, such as a variable, and a parameter or property should be given a name that describes what the data is. This will most likely be a noun or adjective. This guideline is a bit more detailed when it comes to Boolean values, which is a unique case as it should be named with an affirmative phrase, such as `IsApproved` instead of `NotApproved`.

A unique case for naming identifiers is fields, which you were introduced to in *Chapter 10, Object-Oriented Programming*. As mentioned earlier, identifier names should not have symbols in them and should also be nouns if they represent data. The C# guidelines recommend fields use nouns but also should use PascalCase only if they're using `static` public or protected fields. However, the documentation doesn't specify guidelines for fields that are internal or private, and many teams decide to prefix these with underscores and use camelCase, which is what the `private int _invoiceId;` field in *Chapter 10, Object-Oriented Programming*, did.

Methods should be verbs

Methods execute code, or in other words, take some sort of action. They should be nouns that describe this action.

Here's another example with three method names that all are meant to do the same thing:

```
public string Invoice()
```

This first method does not follow the noun guideline and it seems unclear that this is a method, as at first glance this could seem like a type or class. This next method attempts to make it a bit clearer:

```
public string GetInv()
```

This method starts with a verb, where it's clear that it's going to be retrieving something, but can we assume that it's an invoice that is being retrieved here? The next method makes the purpose of this method much clearer:

```
public string GetInvoice()
```

This method has an action and no abbreviations and therefore is a much better revision. Naming conventions help with expectations in identifiers and make it easier to understand what the identifiers mean. Now, we will explore more coding guidelines to keep code readability consistent.

Following syntax consistency guidelines

While syntax is something that we can't avoid in any language, there are options for organizing it so that it's much clearer to understand. As code bases get more complex and go through multiple changes, such as refactors or more features, understanding how they all work can get more complex. Just like naming, following a consistent layout for syntax can make complex code easier to read and maintain.

Organizing lines of code

You have most likely learned that every C# statement needs to end in a semicolon, or else it will not execute. However, did you know that you can have two statements on one line, like in the following example?

```
int myFirstNumber; int mySecondNumber;
```

This is valid syntax in C#, because the two statements are separated by a semicolon, but is it clear? Someone could certainly miss that there are two variables here. It's best to put all complete statements, which are lines that end with a semicolon, on their own separate line. The following example shows what this should look like:

```
int myFirstNumber;
int mySecondNumber;
```

It's much more obvious that these are two separate values now.

Did you also know that you can use `if..else` statements without braces and on one line? Here's an example of the variations of how `if..else` statements can be written:

```
if (myBool) Console.WriteLine; else Console.WriteLine;
```

This example has no braces, is all on one line, and is valid C# syntax. This is clear but might be confusing if the next line looks like the following example:

```
if (myBool) Console.WriteLine("True");
else Console.WriteLine("False");
```

Again, this is valid syntax but this only works for statements that only have one line of code, so how will another developer decide which is the correct way to write this statement? The C# guidelines don't give any guidance, so a team will need to decide on what they would prefer to keep their code consistent.

Although the official C# documentation doesn't give guidance on it, a popular layout for braces is to keep them on their own line, like in the following example:

```
if (myBool)
{
```

```
        Console.WriteLine("True");
    }
    else
    {
        Console.WriteLine("False");
    }
```

This applies to any code that needs braces, and you will see this applied often in C# documentation, except for properties that only have the { get; set; } accessors.

Indentation – tabs versus spaces, the historic debate

You'll notice in all code examples, there's an indentation in each block of code that lies between braces. If you've tried writing your own methods, classes, and control statements in Visual Studio Code, you probably noticed that they're automatically indented. This is because this is a default setting in the editor and is recommended in the language guidelines. However, there is a very long debate on how they should be applied, as some programmers and teams take a hard stance on this.

When it comes to differences between the two, spaces and tabs are displayed differently in a computer program, where it's represented as an actual character. Tabs can also be configured to variable lengths, where the default setting is four spaces, but different editors interpret them differently. This can become a bit of a cumbersome task to navigate when code has a mixture of both, which is why there's a strong reaction to how indentation should be applied, especially when it comes to languages that are dependent on indentation and will throw errors when it's incorrect. On teams where there are strict rules on spaces, this doesn't mean that you must manually make four spaces with the spacebar, only that you must be sure that your editor is configured to automatically make indentations that are equivalent to four spaces instead of a tab.

If you're new to programming, focus on just learning and eventually you'll decide what side of this debate you're on. In the end, it comes down to consistency and it doesn't matter much if you're writing code for your own personal projects.

Implicitly typed variables

You have worked with many types of variables up to this point and can tell the difference between a number and a string. You also know that the right side of the equal sign is the actual value of the identifier when assigning values. Let's look at some quick examples:

```
int index = 0;
Cat fluffy = new Cat();
string name = "Lisa";
```

You can clearly tell what value type the identifier holds. This is known as explicit typing, and the C# documentation recommends using the `var` keyword for instances where the type of value is obvious on the right side of the assignment operator (=). The next example shows these values with the `var` keyword instead:

```
var index = 0;
var fluffy = new Cat();
var name = "Lisa";
```

This is known as **implicit typing**, where the value can be implied based on what is written. This is a popular way to declare values since it can save some space and reduce the time it takes to declare values, though it may be less verbose. The best practice is for a team to decide how and when implicitly typed variables should be used and what should be done when the values on the right of the assignment operator are not obvious. Now, we will look at ways to make code more reusable.

Following reusability guidelines

As you have learned in this chapter, well-written code is easy to read and maintain, as well as bug free. Code like this should be reused when possible. This reduces development time and leaves less chance of introducing bugs in code. You learned in *Chapter 9, Applying Algorithms in C#*, about the **Don't Repeat Yourself** (**DRY**) principle, where solutions that have already been built shouldn't be repeated but reused instead. You'll find that although some parts of the code don't entirely solve all the problems, they are a great step in the right direction.

Method usage

Methods are a great way to practice reusability in a code base and practice DRY as it can be a path to a new solution. To recap from *Chapter 7, Flow Control in C#*, methods are blocks of code that are built to execute specific tasks by the programmer, where the benefits allow those blocks of code to be reusable. Sometimes there are parts of the code where it's not obvious that a method would be useful until the code base grows and you notice that there's a lot of duplication happening. Consider the following example of a calculator that does addition and subtraction:

```
int Add(int number1, int number2)
{
    if (number1 >= 0 && number2 >= 0 )
    {
        var sum = number1 + number2;
        Console.WriteLine(sum);
        return sum;
    }
```

```
    else
    {
        Console.WriteLine("Can't calculate negative
            numbers.");
        return -1;
    }
}
```

This Add method takes two integer parameters and calculates the sum. The following Subtract method takes similar parameters to calculate the difference:

```
int Subtract(int number1, int number2)
{
    if (number1 >= 0 && number2 >= 0 )
    {
        var sum = number1 - number2;
        Console.WriteLine(sum);
        return sum;
    }
    else
    {
        Console.WriteLine("Can't calculate negative
            numbers.");
        return -1;
    }
}
```

These two methods print the sum if both numbers are not negative (0 or higher). Imagine how this would grow if additional methods for multiplication and division were added. Seems that the code that checks whether the numbers are negative should be its own method. Here's an example that extracts the repetitive code and places it into a method:

```
bool CheckNegative (int number1, int number2)
{
    if (number1 >= 0 && number2 >= 0 )
    {
        return true;
    }
```

```
    else
    {
        Console.WriteLine("Can't calculate negative
          numbers.");
        return false;
    }
}
```

Now the repetitive code is in one place and can be reused by any method that needs to check for negative numbers.

Another benefit to using methods is to reduce complexity. Sometimes, large blocks of code can get very complex, and sometimes splitting them up into smaller parts makes them easier to manage. Consider the following example that calculates the volume of a cylinder:

```
double diameter;
double height;
var radius = diameter / 2;
var area = Math.PI * Math.Pow(radius, 2);
var volume = area * height;
```

Calculating a cylinder's volume requires the area of its base and the height. This block of code makes the calculation based on the given values of diameter and height. The radius and area calculations can also be used for a regular circle. Here's an example of what a refactor of this code could look like:

```
double GetCircleArea(double radius)
{
    return Math.PI * Math.Pow(radius, 2);
}

double GetCircleRadius(double diameter)
{
    return diameter / 2;
}

double CalculateCylinderVolume(double diameter, double height)
{
    var radius = GetCircleRadius(diameter);
    var area = GetCircleArea(radius);
```

```
    return area * height;
}
```

Now the complexity of calculating a cylinder has been split up into smaller methods that can be reused for calculating circles. Having learned about code reuse with methods, next we will focus on reusability through extensible classes.

Extensible classes

Code has the ability to be reusable in ways that make it more extensible, which is the case with classes. This is due to the ability of classes to have various levels of abstraction, as well as other pillars of OOP that make it more flexible for all types of objects. Extensibility refers to the ability to enhance parts of a code base without causing major issues in how it originally works. In other words, it's easy to add or remove code and features without introducing bugs. You have seen examples of this in *Chapter 10, Object-Oriented Programming*, through inheritance, where derived classes can inherit base class constructors, and polymorphism with `virtual` and `override` methods. Extensibility makes it possible to easily add or remove new features without disrupting any existing code that shouldn't be disturbed in the process.

Guidelines for extensibility apply to the topics covered in *Chapter 10, Object-Oriented Programming*, as follows:

- Base classes that should not be used as objects or should not be instantiated should be abstract classes to let others working on the code base know to avoid creating objects from it. Recall how in *Chapter 10, Object-Oriented Programming*, you learned that abstract classes cannot be instantiated and that any method signatures it contains that are marked as abstract must be implemented in the derived class.

- A type of abstraction not covered in this book is interfaces, which work similarly to abstract classes. The main difference between the two is that abstract classes may provide a default implementation in members that can be inherited through derived classes, whereas interfaces do not contain any implementation at all. The C# design guidelines mention carefully deciding between an interface and an abstract class.

- Methods in a class that use the `virtual` keyword should have the `protected` access modifier added to them to make sure that they're encapsulated from non-derived classes and have an additional level of security. The C# guidelines also suggest limiting the use of these types of members to only necessary use.

Software engineers usually use their best judgment to decide where to apply extensibility to classes and it sometimes depends on how much planning ahead is done. Sometimes, extensibility is applied after the code is implemented during a refactor to prepare it for future use and features. Next, we will look at the final guideline: documentation.

Following documentation guidelines

Documentation is an integral part of software development because it's how teams communicate with each other on how to work on a code base. It's also how users of the software learn how to be productive with it. Documentation should never be an overlooked practice within software development because the code cannot speak for itself. Documentation keeps the code maintainable and provides a manual of its usage.

One of the most common ways that developers create code documentation is through comments, where they can leave notes about the functionality in small lines. You have seen comments in many examples, where a comment starts with the // syntax, is only used to document the code, and is not executed in any way. The main guidelines are these:

- Comments should be on their own separate line and not at the end of any line of code

- Each comment should be a complete sentence, where it starts with an uppercase character and ends with a period

Creating documentation with comments in C#

You just learned that comments in C# are not executed in any way, but there is an exception to this rule where you can output the comments created to generate documentation about a code base. The way this works is through the C# compiler, which can identify the structure of your comments and code to build documentation based on what you wrote about the code. When you hover over the comment code that was described in the documents, the documentation appears over it. This generates an XML file, which can be used in other tools to read it and export it to other formats.

To being documenting your code, instead of using the typical // syntax for code, use three forward slashes, ///. Here's an example of the Animal class from *Chapter 10, Object-Oriented Programming*:

```
/// <summary>
/// This is a description of the animal class
/// </summary>
public class Animal
{
}
```

As seen in this example, the documentation must be placed above any code declarations you make. The <summary></summary> parts of this documentation are called tags, where the summary tag describes the class below. There are different types of tags that can be used to fully describe a class and its members. Refer to the full list in the *Further reading* documentation for the list of recommended tags. The following screenshot shows what hovering over the object will look like:

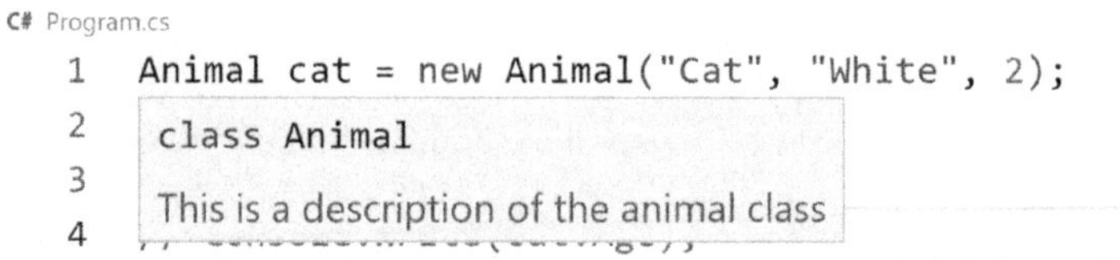

```
C# Program.cs
1    Animal cat = new Animal("Cat", "White", 2);
2    class Animal
3
     This is a description of the animal class
4
```

Figure 12.1 – Example of class documentation

Now, the Animal class is documented, and more details can be added to a class and its members to provide fully documented descriptions of its functionality. Let's explore a more complex example with an expanded Animal class:

```
/// <summary>
/// This is a description of the animal class
/// </summary>
public class Animal
{
    /// <value>
    /// Represents the animal type.
        /// <remarks>
        /// The <see cref="Type"/> is a <see
        /// langword="string"/>
        /// that you use to define any animal.
        /// <para>
        /// This property should not be used for
        /// a specific breed.
        /// </para>
        /// </remarks>
    /// </value>
    public string Type { get; }
    public string Color { get; }
    public int Age { get; set; }

    /// <summary>
    /// Mimics noises an animal makes.
    /// <remarks>
    /// Override this empty method.
    /// </remarks>
```

```
/// </summary>
public virtual void Speak()
{
}
```

Starting from the top, there is the `Type` property, which is documented with the `value` tag. Inside this tag are more details about how it should not be used to define a breed, but instead just define a generalized name of any animal, which is documented in the `remarks` and `para` tags, to separate the information. It also notes that the property currently has a value, by stating that it's not null. Note that you can use special tags such as the `see` tag to display more information about the property:

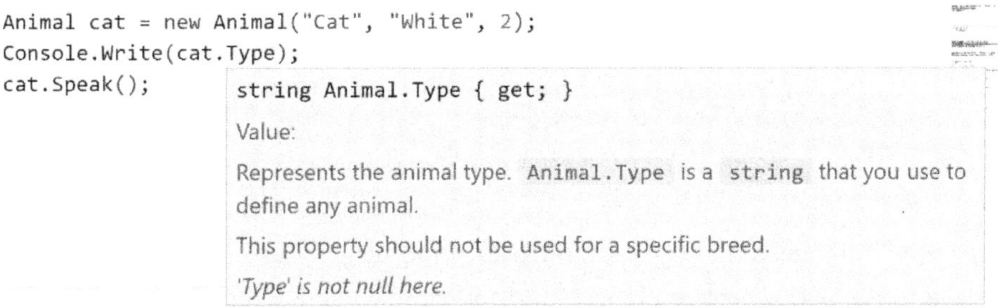

```
Animal cat = new Animal("Cat", "White", 2);
Console.Write(cat.Type);
cat.Speak();
```

> string Animal.Type { get; }
>
> Value:
>
> Represents the animal type. `Animal.Type` is a `string` that you use to define any animal.
>
> This property should not be used for a specific breed.
>
> 'Type' is not null here.

Figure 12.2 – Documentation of the Type parameter in the Animal class

Next is the `Speak` method, which has been documented to let whoever uses this class override it because it's empty. It also uses the `remarks` tag to display this message:

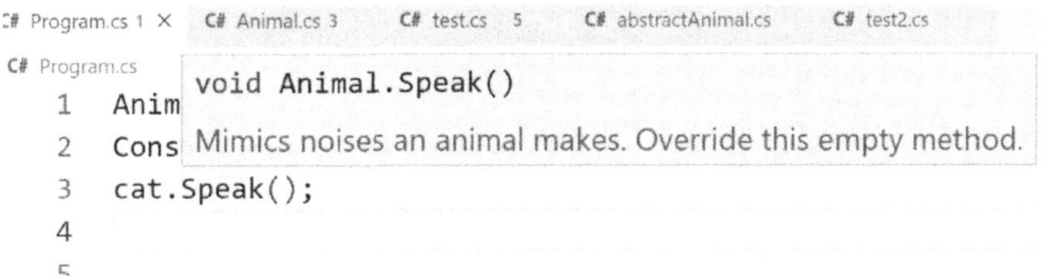

C# Program.cs 1 ✕   C# Animal.cs 3   C# test.cs   5   C# abstractAnimal.cs   C# test2.cs

C# Program.cs
```
1    Anim
2    Cons
3    cat.Speak();
4
5
```

> void Animal.Speak()
>
> Mimics noises an animal makes. Override this empty method.

Figure 12.3 – Documentation of the Speak method parameter in the Animal class

```
/// <summary>
/// This is the default constructor.
/// </summary>
/// <param name="animalType">
/// The type of animal.
/// </param>
/// <param name="animalColor">
```

```
/// The color of the fur or skin of animal.
/// </param>
/// <param name="animalAge">
/// The age of animal.
/// </param>
public Animal(string animalType,
               string animalColor,
               int animalAge)
{

    Type = animalType;
    Color = animalColor;
    Age = animalAge;

}
}
```

As you learned in *Chapter 10, Object-Oriented Programming,* constructors are basically special methods that run when a class is instantiated. This constructor contains information that this is the default constructor in the `summary` tag, because they can be overloaded within a class with various definitions. This is seen in the following screenshot:

```
Animal cat = new Animal("Cat", "White", 2);
Console.Write(cat Animal.Animal(string animalType, string animalColor, int
cat.Speak();          animalAge)

                      This is the default constructor.
```

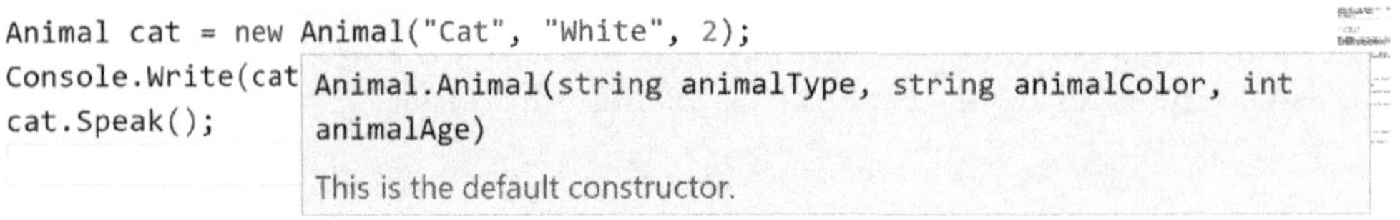

Figure 12.4 – Documentation of the Animal constructor in the Animal class

The parameters within a constructor or method can also be defined in the documentation with the `param` tag. The following screenshot displays the documentation when the cursor is in the `cat` object:

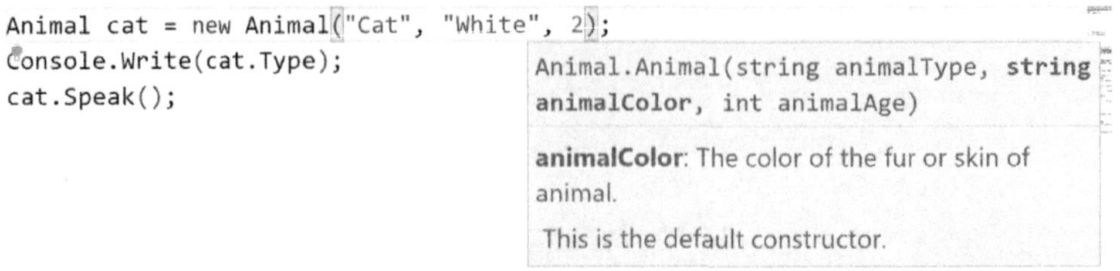

```
Animal cat = new Animal("Cat", "White", 2);
Console.Write(cat.Type);        Animal.Animal(string animalType, string
cat.Speak();                    animalColor, int animalAge)

                                animalColor: The color of the fur or skin of
                                animal.

                                This is the default constructor.
```

Figure 12.5 – Documentation of the Animal constructor in the Animal class

There are many tools, such as DocFX, that can generate code documentation based on these XML comments. You can learn more about this in the *Further reading* resources. This concludes the basic standards and practices within the C# language.

Summary

The best coding practices will be different between each team and each programmer. For example, you have seen examples in this book of camelCase being used for identifiers instead of only being used for parameters, as seen in the C# language guidelines documentation. Writing code in this manner may not be as consequential to a small team in comparison to a large software team implementing the same thing. However, a code base needs to be kept easy to read and the team's productivity maintained by making it easy to make fixes or add new features. Best practices in code can lead to many benefits, such as the following:

- Proper naming conventions make sure that everyone knows what the identifiers are for.
- Consistent syntax enables better readability.
- Reusable code makes it less likely to generate bugs.
- Extensible code allows software engineers to easily add or remove features.
- Documentation provides all software engineers and its users with best practice instructions on using the code. In C#, there are ways to generate documentation for the purpose of communicating to other programmers how the code should be used.

Writing unclear code that only you can decipher and understand does not ensure job security. First, most teams go through some sort of code review, where someone reviewing your code will ask you to make changes so that it's clearer. Second, another programmer will spend their time trying to understand what you did, and if it's not understandable, your code may be deemed so bad that it needs to be rewritten. Finally, this is bad teamwork. You should always think about what your team needs to be productive and successful, and this will usually be documented and communicated with the team to make sure everyone is aware.

The next and final chapter will delve deeper into the topic of professionalism in the software engineering industry.

Questions

1. What is an identifier?
2. What is the general guideline for naming methods?
3. What is implicit typing?
4. How can you separate the complexity in code?

5. Name a benefit of extensibility.

6. Name one guideline for using comments in code.

Further reading

- *Interfaces - define behavior for multiple types*: `https://learn.microsoft.com/en-us/dotnet/csharp/fundamentals/types/interfaces`

- *C# Coding Style*, authored by the .NET runtime team and widely adopted: `https://github.com/dotnet/runtime/blob/main/docs/coding-guidelines/coding-style.md`

- Documentation comments: `https://learn.microsoft.com/en-us/dotnet/csharp/language-reference/xmldoc/#tools-that-accept-xml-documentation-input`

13
Tips and Tricks to Kickstart Your Software Engineering Career

Now that you have learned about the software engineering process, coding, and algorithms, and have heard real accounts of software engineering from professionals, you must be wondering, "Where do I go from here?" A great place to start is to think about where you see yourself professionally in terms of what you have learned in this book.

To gain a position as a software engineer, especially for a first role, it's best to get prepared for what's to come. First, you'll need to decide what type of software development you'd like to do; then, you'll need to check the expected skills in those roles. After, you'll need to build up those skills and prepare to be able to solve different problems with them. Finally, you'll need to decide how you will show those same skills to your future employers.

This chapter will cover the following topics:

- Preparing to enter the job market
- Additional considerations that are beneficial for job preparation
- Preparing for the technical interview
- Searching for software engineering roles
- Understanding the interview process

By the end of this chapter, you will understand how to prepare for an entry-level software engineering role.

Technical requirements

There are no technical requirements for this chapter.

Preparing to enter the job market

Believe it or not, you started preparing for a role when you wrote your first line of code. Coding is one of the highly sought-after skills for a software engineering role, and engineers of all levels need to write code to maintain their skills. If you're entering the industry, you will need to spend a bit more time building up your skills in preparation for a role. As mentioned previously, reading this book alone will not be enough preparation for a job as a software engineer. You'll need to practice what you have learned and find new ways to apply your knowledge and continue to learn new things to build on the skills you already have. To be completely honest, it may be a long road of preparation, but keep in mind that many software engineers have gone through the same experience to get where they are today. You can do it too!

Strengthening your skills for a role

When it comes to preparation, you'll first need to think about how you want to continue your learning. You're probably now aware that you don't need to go to a university or college to become a software engineer; it's only a one path. There are many free tutorials and guides for software development that you can use to do self-guided learning to build your skills, or you can have guided learning through a school or boot camp at a price. Deciding what option is best for you is completely personal and it's up to what resources you have in terms of money and time – they're both proven successful options for entering the field.

You'll spend less time searching for the right resources to continue your learning in a guided environment, where the information will be up to date and usually you'll have instructors or mentors to help you with your questions. Finally, you'll be assessed through projects, which you can cite in your professional portfolio and resume. This option usually consists of institutions and boot camps that typically partner with companies that are looking for new developers and will hire new graduates. Finally, you will reach a point where you are technically "done" with your learning and are job-ready, though you may need to continue building on your skills while you're searching for a role.

You can decide to teach yourself and do self-guided learning where you can build your knowledge on your own time and schedule. However, to retain what you've learned, you must find a reasonable schedule that allows you to keep learning so that you're not forgetting what you did the last time you practiced. This path is for people who are generally self-starters and can set a routine around their learning. Self-guided learning can generally be much cheaper than guided learning, where the biggest resource for you will be the internet, where there are a lot of resources to learn from but you may also end up working with outdated information. If you end up learning something outdated, it may slow down your progress a bit. A great way to stay updated on current information is to look at when any written or video content was published, where anything older than 2 years may potentially contain outdated information.

So, how do you decide when you're ready to apply for a role? It first begins with where your learning has taken you. By the time you start applying, you should have a general idea of the type of programming you enjoy. For example, if you're deciding to stick with C# and discover that you enjoy web development, you'll want to search for jobs that have ASP.NET in them and compare your skills against what the position is looking for.

Getting prepared for an entry-level software engineering role

Here are some things that employers will generally look for in an entry-level or junior role of any type. If you are familiar with at least over 75% of the things that are in a posted role position and have built more than three projects with them, you're in pretty good shape to start applying:

- Some experience with source control, typically Git and GitHub
- Knowledge of a programming language
- Experience with a code editor tool

Keep in mind that this list does not cover specializations, such as web and mobile, but if your learning is leading you to a particular specialization, you'll most likely improve these three listed skills along the way. The next three sections will describe the level of knowledge you'll want to have for each of these skills for an entry-level role in software development.

Gaining experience with Git and GitHub

Source control is an important part of software development because software development is typically done in teams of software engineers, and source control allows them to all be able to work together on a code base and keep a record of past changes. Having a history of past changes can be helpful in a software engineering team, especially large ones – it can help them plan future features or track the history of a bug that was introduced.

A very popular form of source control is Git and GitHub is a popular website for storing code that you work with in Git. A great starting point to learning these two tools is understanding the difference between the two.

One of the great things about GitHub is that it's a free way to share your code, where employers will often look at the GitHub profile of a potential candidate to see what they are building or have built. It's also a way for you to continue building your skills by looking at what others are building out in the open, as well as opportunities for you to contribute your code to these open projects, which are called open source projects and allow collaboration with all developers to build tools that anyone can use.

This book does not go into details about these tools, but the GitHub website is a great starting point for learning more about Git and GitHub with guided tutorials and training. You can learn more by reading the documentation in the *Further reading* section to get started.

An entry-level developer who is skilled in Git and GitHub can do the following:

- Create a local Git repository
- Make branches in Git
- Commit their code to Git
- Push code to a remote repository, such as GitHub
- Make a pull request on GitHub
- C and update issues in GitHub

Building on your knowledge of a programming language

As you have learned, coding will be a vital part of your career as a software engineer. You've got a great start with the C# language, and the knowledge you have gained can be applied to other languages, though the syntax may differ. A large portion of this book has covered many aspects of coding, so those points don't need to be repeated here. However, you should be aware that preparation goes beyond just reading a book. You must pick a language you enjoy working with and continue to apply your skills through projects, research, and experimentation.

One aspect of learning programming is getting comfortable with trial and error, and learning how to search for programming help online. Engineers of all levels of experience have built code that didn't work the way they expected it to. This can be very frustrating when you are just getting started with learning. With practice, you will get used to working through a lot of errors and breaking your code, and eventually fixing it. You will find ways that work for you to build this skill. Here are some things to try when you get stuck while working with code:

- If your code doesn't have syntax errors, but you're getting unexpected output, use the debugger in your code editor to track down the problem. Information on debugging in Visual Studio Code can be found in the *Further reading* section.
- Comment out blocks of code and add them back in line by line.
- If you have an example or past project that looks similar to what you're trying to achieve, revisit it and compare the differences.
- Try to break down your problem with pseudocode.
- Take a break and come back to the problem.

Another common practice of working through problems in code is looking up errors on the web, where search results will often bring you to websites such as Stack Overflow, where many developers have faced the same issues that you have. There is no shame in searching to solve your problems as you will see that many others have faced similar challenges. Software engineers with many years of experience will sometimes need to search for basic information about coding to help them through a problem. It's nearly impossible to remember everything, and whether it's on the job or in practice, you will find yourself searching for help to get you through your issue. An important part of the search that can frustrate new programmers is understanding what to search for when they're having problems with their code. Here are some tips on how to search when you're stuck:

- If your code editor shows you an error in your code, try searching for the exact error. Sometimes, these errors provide an error code, which you can search for as well. For example, if you see an error stating `Use of unassigned local variable 'myBoolean' CS0165`, you can search for `Use of unassigned local variable` or `CS1065` to investigate it. Typically, you wouldn't add identifier names such as variable or class names when searching for these errors because it's unique to the program you are building. In this particular example, `myBoolean` would be omitted from a search.

- If your code editor shows you which code line the error is on, you may not get far if you put that line of code in to a search engine. Instead, try to describe what you were trying to accomplish. For example, if you are making a constructor but getting a syntax error, try looking up "`how to create a constructor`." The first answer you see may not always be the best solution. You may end up with a few open tabs during your search, which you should compare.

- If you find something that helps you solve your problem, be sure to take a moment to understand how the changes you made fixed it. Looking at others' code is an excellent way to get better at doing this yourself, but it's best when you understand how it works.

- Increasing your coding skills will take time and practice, and you will notice that the more you code, the more elaborate your projects will become. You may notice it happening over time, but if you stay consistent in your learning and building, you'll look back at your older work and realize how much you've improved.

An entry-level developer should be prepared to write code in the following ways:

- Knows how to work with various data types and know when they're appropriate to use.
- Is able to use various types of flow control covered in this book, including handling unexpected errors and preventing invalid user input.
- Can explain and apply object-oriented programming pillars.
- Has an understanding of basic data structures, such as arrays.
- Practices good coding standards that promote readable code.
- Basic knowledge of a unit testing framework. Refer to the *Further reading* section for information on xUnit, a popular testing framework for C#.

- Comfortable with figuring out problems in existing code. A common practice that software engineers will do when they first join a team is to fix small bugs to get a better understanding of the code base.

Gaining experience with a code editor tool

As you practice programming, you will also begin to get more comfortable with the code editor. When you first opened Visual Studio Code in *Chapter 5, Writing Your First C# Program*, you probably noticed there were a lot of options and features in it. Over time, you will find that using some of these features can be beneficial to you, starting with keyboard shortcuts. Getting comfortable with keyboard shortcuts is helpful because you spend a lot of your time typing instead of using your mouse. Shortcuts help you reduce the amount of time for which you need to reach for your mouse. This may seem minimal, but you probably use your mouse more than you realize. A great one to get comfortable with is copying, pasting, and cutting lines of code. Another great editor tool to get acquainted with is the debugger, which helps you track down issues in your code by stepping through its logic line by line, where you can "pause" the execution to explore the behavior and look at variable values in real time. Refer to the *Further reading* section for getting started with the Visual Studio Code debugger. Continue to read up on the documentation of your editor or IDE and be curious about its features and helpful extensions.

An entry-level developer should be prepared to work with their code editor in the following ways:

- Can navigate their editor to manage files and edit code

- Is comfortable with a few keyboard shortcuts

- Is familiar with the debugger

Putting your portfolio together

A great way to stand out and get noticed is to build a portfolio of projects that demonstrate what you have learned. These should be at least three projects that you have built yourself. Sometimes, thinking of projects can be harder than building them, so take some time to brainstorm some ideas. Use this opportunity to make these projects something special or unique about you. For example, if you enjoy swimming, you could build an app or website that logs your best laps. It doesn't need to be overly elaborate but should show everything that you have learned. The projects you build should be on your GitHub profile so that potential employers can see them. You can use GitHub's repository pinning feature to put them at the front and center of your profile. You can learn more about this GitHub feature by reading the respective documentation in the *Further reading* section.

You may also want to consider having an online presence through a website or social media that has a professional community. A website is a great way to represent yourself because you can customize it to your style, where it can be an extension of your resume, which only briefly describes your background and skills. You could even decide to put your resume on your website if you wanted to. You don't have to be a highly skilled web developer to have a website; there are many website-building platforms you can use to create one of your own in a few hours.

Preparing a resume

Your resume is the first impression that most employers will have of you – it's the first thing they'll typically see. Because of this, you'll want to grab the attention of anyone who sees it. For technical professions such as software engineering, it's important to show the skills you expect to be hired for, as this is what recruiters will be looking for initially in the resume. There are many resources for building a resume, so this chapter won't cover them here; they have been shared as resources in the *Further reading* section. Here are some important tips to consider when putting together a resume for a software engineering role:

- List out the skills that you have learned. These should be the languages, tools, and technologies you have actively used in three projects.

- Do not add any skills that you don't feel confident about answering if the employer were to ask you about them.

- Add your projects to your resume, including links to where they are, or at least where the code is. This could be on GitHub or a personal website. You should also consider adding a small description of what the project is and what languages and technologies you used to build them.

- Put any professional or academic experience on your resume, even if you've never had a software engineering role and your professional experience is unrelated.

Additional considerations beneficial for entering the job market

While the topics in the previous section are must-have items for your preparation, there are additional things you can do to increase your chances of finding your first role. You'll find that all these topics will involve other people, where you'll be working with someone else to build up your skills or sharing your learning with others. As you learned in *Chapter 2, The Software Engineering Life Cycle*, communication is a big part of software engineering. By no means do you need to be extremely social to gain a role, but having others to support you will help build your confidence as a software engineer. Sometimes, being in the right place at the right time with the right people can have surprising outcomes.

Seeking mentorship

You'll find that many technical professionals will have mentors who have helped them navigate their careers. Mentors are a great way to get honest feedback and guidance on your professional career, wherever you might be in it. A mentor, who is typically someone that has a few years of experience in the industry, can help you navigate choices on what specialties you consider, help clarify any questions you may have about the profession, as well as encourage you during challenging times. While it's not required to have one, it can be a great way to get inspired and motivated to learn new things and consider approaching problems through a different and more experienced perspective. There's a chance your mentor may have had the same questions and challenges in their career at some point and can share what they have learned along the way.

Building your professional networking

You have probably heard the phrase "It's not what you know, but who you know," which can be true for any role. In *Chapter 11*, *Stories from Prominent Job Roles in Software Development*, you learned that it's a common misconception that software engineers are not social. However, some of the personal stories in that chapter mentioned how networking shaped their careers. Strong communication is an important skill in the profession and networking is a great start to building this skill, as well as making connections in the industry, in addition to many other benefits. As mentioned earlier, you don't need to be extremely social to gain a role, but chance encounters through networking can have surprising outcomes.

Here are some benefits of networking:

- Being visible in professional circles of the industry enables you to be seen as a professional yourself. The more visible you are, the more you increase the chances that someone will remember you as a person who is active in the profession.

- Your professional network will expand because you're making connections, which can be beneficial for your career. Professional connections are people who are experiencing the same challenges and working toward similar goals as you are. You can share different perspectives about what you're facing in the profession. For example, you may adopt a new tool or software library by learning about how someone else is using it.

- Networking can be a source of inspiration, where you learn something new. Technology is always changing, so much to the point where it can be hard to keep up. You're almost guaranteed to learn something new at a networking event for software engineers. You may find mentors, friends, or even future employers and business partners.

- Your network can also be a source of career support, such as resume feedback and mock interviews.

There are many communities of technical professionals online and in person who have meetups and are great places for networking opportunities. There are also developer-focused conferences and events where many software engineers gather and special guests come to deliver talks on various technical topics. Conferences and meetups such as these can also be quite inspiring for software engineers of all levels. Some software engineers get so inspired that they decide to deliver a talk and share with the community what they've learned or new ideas and technologies.

The C# community is global, with many groups that connect virtually and in person. The .NET Foundation is a non-profit organization that supports community-led projects and social gatherings with a strong focus on technologies and languages using .NET from open source projects to events all around the world. It's a great starting place for connecting with communities that have developers of all kinds of experience levels. A link to the communities page of the .NET Foundation website can be found in the *Further reading* section.

Sharing your experiences

Aside from communities, you can take the opportunity to share your experiences and learnings. There's a common misconception that because someone else has shared how they learned something, nobody else can do it. Everyone has their way of expressing how they learned something, and it might just be the way someone else needs it explained to them. This is why you will see many books that cover the same programming language or technology. As an idea, you can consider blogging about what you are learning and sharing with others in your community. This can help keep you motivated and can be a great way for you to evaluate your progress along the way.

Preparing for the technical interview

One of the most daunting parts of the interview process is the technical interview, where you will be asked to demonstrate your skills. This can be an intimidating part of the process for any software developer because you're being evaluated on how you solve problems. The type of problem will vary, and the best guidance here is to study for what's to come. This is why a good understanding of algorithms will come in handy because, as you learned from professional software engineers in *Chapter 11, Stories from Prominent Job Roles in Software Development*, the algorithms you may have to write in the technical interview will not be ones you will often write on the job. Essentially, they are a way for an interviewer to see how you work through problems and whether it's a good fit for the team.

One of the first things you'll want to do is start studying, learning about a few more data structures and algorithms, and then learning how to approach programming challenges you may face. Data structures and algorithms will prepare you to solve those problems. Remember that at this point, you already have programming skills, so you're learning how to apply them to solve a problem. This means you could try working through some very easy programming problems, as you did with Fizz Buzz in *Chapter 8, Introduction to Data Structures, Algorithms, and Pseudocode*. The reality behind preparing for a technical interview is that it will take practice. Not only are you learning about different ways to approach a coding problem, but you also must deal with doing it in front of a future employer. Getting used to all of this will take practice.

As a start, try going through easy problems and working your way up from there. Getting through the first few problems will be challenging only because you haven't done it before, but as you continue to practice, you will find methods for getting through a problem. If you have decided to give up on the problem, it's okay to look at the solution, but you should return to it and try it again later to retain what you've learned. You could also try an easier one, or even take a break from it and come back. The key here is to keep practicing, even when you're not able to get through a particular problem.

There are many resources out there for preparing for a technical interview because it's a popular topic in software engineering; they are listed in the *Further reading* section. Now that you've learned a bit about getting prepared for an interview, you will learn how to search for software engineering roles.

Searching for software engineering roles

If you're ready to start applying and know what roles you'd like to pursue, then it's time to start looking for roles. Many sites will have open positions, but this is why you should have an idea of what languages and technologies you like to work with because this can help you find roles with those specific skills in them.

Roles can be found on any popular job site in your area. In the US, some popular job sites are Indeed and LinkedIn Jobs. Outside of regular job websites, you also might want to consider job openings on your local community website and in newspapers, as many local companies may be posting roles there. This is also a great time to start networking because you might end up speaking to a future employer or someone who knows a company that is looking for your skills. Sometimes, this opportunity can be presented to you through networking events that are hosted by companies who are looking to hire software engineers, or conferences that may be sponsored by companies who are seeking to hire as well. You should also take advantage of local career fairs in your area because even if the companies that are represented there are not specifically there for software engineers, it might be a good idea to network with recruiters who may be able to help you discover if they're hiring someone with your skillset. You can decide to share with your network that you are looking for roles within your skillset, which may return surprising results where someone who you didn't realize may be looking for someone like you.

When looking for roles, be sure it's a company that you want to work for. While this is a hard decision to make, especially if you're searching for your first role, you want to be somewhere where you will feel supported and productive, and motivated enough by the company's mission to do great work. Also, you should double-check the role's requirements: if you have at least 75% of the skills and have used them in 3 projects and are confident that you can talk to another software engineer about the skills without getting into too much detail, it should be a good match.

Keep in mind that this percentage will vary from role to role, where you might get automatically rejected if you don't match them 100%, and that's okay – there are some roles where the skills you lack will be something you can learn on the job, but some potential applicants will shy away from these roles because of this misconception. As an anecdote, I knew other types of source control, but not Git, which was and is still very popular. I was encouraged to apply for the role anyway and I successfully passed the interview. Another thing you may see in roles is that some require a bachelor's degree, though many companies don't make this a hard requirement and are looking for candidates who possess the required skills, so you should apply despite these requirements.

How do you decide on roles that are a good match for you? Use this small checklist to evaluate a position you're considering applying for:

- You have used 75% of the skills listed outside of a basic tutorial or book, where you have built projects that use these skills
- You're prepared to talk about the skills that are listed in the description and are prepared to let the interviewers know which skills you don't have experience in
- The skills that are in the description match what you have on your resume
- The skills that are in the description match projects you have done
- You can easily research the company to see what they do
- You'll be prepared to do a technical interview for the company within the next few weeks

There are many ways to get creative and playful with your search, but once you have a good list of positions to apply for, which should be as many as you can until you finally get an offer, you should start submitting applications as soon as possible.

Applying for a role

Most application processes will be straightforward, where you enter some basic information, upload your resume, and sometimes write a cover letter. For a first position, it's recommended to write a cover letter if there's space for one. While there's much debate on whether they will make a difference or whether someone will read them, you should do your best to stand out for your first position.

This is also a great time to reach out to your network. If someone you know is at the current company, you can ask whether they will refer you. This may help move your application along faster. Though the answer may be "no," you should not take this personally, as everyone has their reasons for not wanting to do a referral.

After you fill out all the required information, you should actively keep applying to roles until you receive an offer for a role.

What to do while waiting for an interview

Waiting for an interview will be a varied experience, where you may immediately get a rejection, a request for an interview after some time, or no response. This part of the process may be one of the longest, and you should use this time to keep preparing for an interview that may happen.

Here's a list of things to do while you wait:

- Continue working on any projects you may have or start a new one.
- Practice coding problems and try to go from easy to intermediate ones as a personal goal.

- Try to practice for technical interviews with someone; this would be a great place to tap into your network and local technical communities.

- Keep studying algorithms and data structures – there are many types to learn about and you should stick to the popular ones, which are most likely to be used in a technical interview.

- Continue searching for and applying to roles.

- Find open source projects to contribute to on GitHub – you can search for repositories by the language used to find ones that you know you can contribute to.

- Learn about a new technology and build something with it.

Be sure to keep building and refining your skills as you wait so that you're prepared. Just remember to be patient – this can be a long wait and remember that despite all the rejections, there is a role that is the perfect fit for you. Now, you'll learn about what happens when you have an interview.

Experiencing the interview process

Getting an interview is both an exciting and stressful time. Someone has noticed and acknowledged your skills as a fit for the team and company, and now you will have to prove why you're the top candidate by demonstrating what you put on your resume. While the hiring process will vary from team to team, you'll typically receive a call or email asking for you to schedule a time to talk with a recruiter or the hiring manager. From there, you will often do one or more "rounds" of interviews that focus on one or more of the following:

- **Technical screening**: Basic programming questions used to evaluate your skills.

- **Technical interview**: Programming questions that involve solving a problem with an algorithm you've created. Questions are slightly more advanced than screening questions.

- **Take-home assignment**: This is a task that requires you to build something based on a set of requirements. Typically, you're given a time limit. You may have to talk through your work in a follow-up interview. You may do an assignment instead of a technical interview, and sometimes, a combination of both.

- **General interview**: Members of the team get to know you and learn about your working style and how you work with others.

Something that's highly recommended, which you learned about in *Chapter 11, Stories from Prominent Job Roles in Software Development*, is that you should ask the recruiter or hiring manager about the interview process. You can be specific with your questions here and consider asking about what technical questions to expect. You will now learn more about one of the biggest parts of the interview process, which is the technical part of the interview.

Going through a tech screening

Technical screening is a way to quickly evaluate potential candidates on their technical skills. The questions are normally based on the technology listed in the position's skills.

Questions like this for the C# language may include the following:

- What is a class?

- What are objects?

- What kinds of classes can you make in C#?

- What's the difference between .NET Framework and .NET?

- What does the `private` access modifier do?

Technical screeners may be done over the phone, in person, or through a platform. They usually don't take too long and might require a little coding. After passing the screening process, you'll move on to another round of the interview.

Doing the technical interview

Depending on the team, the way that the hiring team will evaluate you in the technical interview will differ. Some may ask you to do pair programming with them, where the interviewer will give you a question and you will work with them to solve it. While this can look very intimidating, keep in mind that this is a way to show the team how you think and learn, and this is where you should show how confident you are in your skills. What interviewers will be looking for is how you understand the problem, what is reasoning is for solving it that certain way, and finding ways to make it better.

A take-home assignment is usually some starter code or a set of requirements you must follow to build something. You'll usually have a few days to finish it. In comparison to other technical interviews, this may be a little less daunting, but keep in mind that you may need to describe what you did in a follow-up interview.

Here are some tips for a successful technical interview:

- Repeat the problem back to the interviewer to make sure you understand the problem correctly.

- Ask any clarifying questions to better understand the problem at hand.

- You don't have to start coding right away. You can plan out what you'd like to do with some pseudocode or even drawing. This is especially important if you're having a hard time figuring out how to get started.

- While you're working through the solution, be sure to talk through what you're doing. Think about how you want to do this. Some find it hard to speak while coding, so be sure to find a style that fits you, where you can have a chance to comfortably speak about your work and progress through your solution.

- After you've built your solution, you should look at how you can make improvements to it. Where can you make things more readable or reduce complexity? Do you have code that would be better suited in a method or a value that should be stored in a variable? Try to do some basic refactoring to your code.

This is part of the technical interview that a lot of potential candidates worry about, but with some practice and attention to detail, you can be successful. Don't be too disappointed in yourself if you don't end up doing so well; many software engineers have had similar experiences. Remember that you have reached this far, so you certainly possess the skills to keep trying.

After all the parts of your interview have been completed, you will probably do a little more waiting before you get the results. Again, use this time to keep applying and studying. The time between applying and getting the results can also be a long wait.

Summary

Applying for a software engineering role requires some preparation, and you'll want to make sure you have the right skills for the right position that you want. First, you'll build on the skills you'd like to possess through self-guided or guided learning. Next, you'll keep working on those skills until you have enough personal experience through projects to be ready to apply for professional roles. Before and during applying, you'll want to prepare for the technical interview by studying programming problems and working on your projects. Finally, after some waiting, you'll have an interview where the technical part of it requires you to make the most of the skills and studying you have and apply them to a problem.

While this book does not cover everything you need to learn to be a software developer, you have learned enough programming basics to apply your knowledge to different programming languages or different platforms. If you're considering turning software engineering into a career, you're off to a great start! Now, you can experiment on your own and read other books about programming and deepen your knowledge.

Questions

1. How many skills should you know for an entry-level role to measure whether you have enough experience to start applying?

2. What skills should you put on your resume?

3. You can apply for software engineer roles even if you don't have a bachelor's degree in it. True or false?

4. Name something you should do while you're waiting for an interview.

5. What's the difference between a technical screening and a technical interview?

6. Name something you can do after you receive the problem you need to solve during your technical interview.

Further reading

To learn more about the topics that were covered in this chapter, take a look at the following resources:

- *How to write a killer Software Engineering résumé*: `https://www.freecodecamp.org/news/writing-a-killer-software-engineering-resume-b11c91ef699d/`

- *.NET Meetups*: `https://dotnetfoundation.org/community/.net-meetups`

- *Acing the technical interview: A complete guide*: `https://www.codecademy.com/resources/blog/technical-interview-guide/`

- *Git and GitHub learning resources*: `https://docs.github.com/en/get-started/quickstart/git-and-github-learning-resources`

- Leetcode learning platform: `https://leetcode.com/`

- Interview Cake studying and learning platform: `https://www.interviewcake.com/`

- *Getting started with xUnit*: `https://xunit.net/docs/getting-started/netcore/cmdline`

- *Debugging in Visual Studio Code*: `https://code.visualstudio.com/Docs/editor/debugging`

Assessments

Chapter 1 – Defining Software Engineering

1. The difference between computer science and software engineering is that computer science is the study of computation, while software engineering is the practice of building software.

2. The six phases of the software engineering process are planning, design, implementation, testing, deployment, and maintenance.

3. Three problems that could go wrong from skipping the planning phase are as follows:

   - The project takes much longer than expected

   - The software has many bugs

   - The software does not serve the purpose that it was intended for

4. One example of how the deployment stage of a software engineering project gets complicated is when the platform, such as mobile devices or laptops, that the software will be used on may need to be changed for the software to run properly. For example, a system or operating system update.

5. Software engineering is engineering because software, just like a bridge, requires careful planning and design with a number of experts working on different parts of the project to make it successful.

Chapter 2 – The Software Engineering Life Cycle

1. Project managers need to ask specific questions to confirm what the stakeholder needs to clarify requirements.

2. High-level design focuses on breaking up the requirements into large parts, while low-level design focuses on breaking down the parts into smaller parts and tasks.

3. They will test it and submit it to source control.

4. They can stop deployment from happening if there are serious bugs; they can also help software teams prioritize bugs.

5. The software life cycle ends when the software is no longer being maintained.

Chapter 3 – Roles in Software Engineering

1. PMs take the stakeholders' requirements and translate them into tasks for the software engineers.

2. Frontend engineers will primarily work with HTML, CSS, and JS.

3. A frontend engineer is normally a web developer who builds client-side code or code that runs in the browser. A backend engineer may or may not be a web developer and writes code that runs on the server.

4. One main reason a backend engineer will want to improve their code is to make the software run faster.

5. QA engineers write code that automates test cases so that they can focus on prioritizing other test cases that need more attention.

Chapter 4 – Programming Languages and Introduction to C#

1. A programming language will be converted by an interpreter or compiler so that a computer can understand the instructions.

2. A full stack web developer will usually use HTML, CSS, and JavaScript.

3. Three multi-purpose languages that were named in this chapter are C#, JavaScript, and Java.

4. Low-code and no-code platforms and tools can be used with programming languages.

5. The difference between .NET and C# is that .NET is a developer platform, while C# is a programming language that exists on the .NET platform.

Chapter 5 – Writing Your First C# Program

1. When faced with the choice to make software for different operating systems, software engineering teams can either make a cross-platform application, make a separate application for each operating system, or ignore the other operating system.

2. Software engineers use browsers to look up information on software problems they are working on.

3. Text editors do not install runtimes and SDKs, while IDEs do. You can write and edit code in both IDEs and text editors.

4. True.

5. The command to run a .NET application is dotnet run.

Chapter 6 – Data Types in C#

1. The benefit of a variable is that you can use the variable names for values without having to remember those values.

2. String concatenation is the process of combining two or more strings to create a new string.

3. An integer variable stores whole numbers, while a double variable stores floating-point numbers, or numbers with decimals.

4. Comparison operators should be read from left to right.

5. The index of the first item in an array is 0.

Chapter 7 – Flow Control in C#

1. A Boolean is the data type that's commonly used for flow control.

2. False – else statements are optional with if statements.

3. Loops stop when the loop's condition is false.

4. A method parameter is a variable value in a method definition, while an argument is an actual value.

5. You can create a method that begins with void when you don't want the method to return a value.

Chapter 8 – Introduction to Data Structures, Algorithms, and Pseudocode

1. The difference between a task and a construct in pseudocode is that tasks are what the computer will do, while constructs refer to common programming operations.

2. Software engineers want to reduce the number of steps in array data structure operations to save time.

3. In selection sort, the algorithm will begin with the value at index 0 in an array.

4. The two outcomes from the linear search algorithm are either the value is found, or the algorithm reaches the end of the array and the value is not found.

5. The difference between a binary search and a linear search is that the data structure in a binary search needs to be sorted. A binary search also eliminates indices to narrow down the possible location of the value.

Chapter 9 – Applying Algorithms in C#

1. A loop is needed to visit all the items in an array in the selection sort algorithm.

2. Nesting is the programming technique of inserting a programming statement into another.

3. If a loop reaches the end of the array in a linear search algorithm, it can be assumed that the value was not found.

4. The `break` statement will end a loop early.

5. False.

6. When the size of the input increases, the algorithm takes longer to run.

7. Refactored code makes the code easier to maintain.

Chapter 10 – Object-Oriented Programming

1. An object can be anything that can be represented as a noun.

2. Objects are created from classes.

3. False, a derived class inherits all members of a base class.

4. The `private` access modifier will keep member access within the class.

5. The difference between static polymorphism and dynamic polymorphism is that dynamic polymorphism happens at runtime while static polymorphism happens at compile time.

6. Virtual methods in a base class can optionally be overridden with the `override` keyword, but abstract methods in abstract base classes must be implemented and overridden with the `override` keyword.

Chapter 12 – Coding Best Practices

1. Identifiers are names that must be assigned to something in code.

2. The general guideline for a method is that it should include a verb that describes the action it takes.

3. Implicit typing is when a value can be inferred from the right side of an operator and it can be declared with the `var` keyword on the left side.

4. You can use methods to separate complex code.

5. Extensibility allows features to be added and removed and reduces the probability of introducing new bugs in existing code.

6. Comments should be on their own line.

Chapter 13 – Tips and Tricks to Kickstart Your Software Engineering Career

1. You should know at least 75% of the skills in a posted job position.

2. You should only put skills on your resume that you have worked on at least three projects.

3. True – you don't need a bachelor's degree to apply for software engineer roles.

4. While waiting for an interview, one thing you can do is keep working on projects.

5. A technical screening has smaller programming questions that are shorter to answer, while a technical interview will take longer to complete, and you will have to solve a problem within a certain amount of time.

6. Something you can do after you receive the problem in a technical interview is ask clarifying questions.

Index

‹packt›

www.packtpub.com

Subscribe to our online digital library for full access to over 7,000 books and videos, as well as industry leading tools to help you plan your personal development and advance your career. For more information, please visit our website.

Why subscribe?

- Spend less time learning and more time coding with practical eBooks and Videos from over 4,000 industry professionals

- Improve your learning with Skill Plans built especially for you

- Get a free eBook or video every month

- Fully searchable for easy access to vital information

- Copy and paste, print, and bookmark content

Did you know that Packt offers eBook versions of every book published, with PDF and ePub files available? You can upgrade to the eBook version at packtpub.com and as a print book customer, you are entitled to a discount on the eBook copy. Get in touch with us at customercare@packtpub.com for more details.

At www.packtpub.com, you can also read a collection of free technical articles, sign up for a range of free newsletters, and receive exclusive discounts and offers on Packt books and eBooks.

Other Books You May Enjoy

If you enjoyed this book, you may be interested in these other books by Packt:

The C# Workshop

Jason Hales, Almantas Karpavicius, Mateus Viegas

ISBN: 9781800566491

- Understand the fundamentals of programming with C# 10 and .NET 6
- Build your familiarity with .NET CLI and Visual Studio Code
- Master the fundamentals of object-oriented programming (OOP)
- Understand and implement concurrency to write more efficient code
- Create a database and handle data using C#, SQL, and Entity Framework
- Build web applications using the ASP.NET framework
- Run automated unit tests with NUnit to validate your code
- Use principles including SOLID, KISS, ACID, DRY, and design patterns

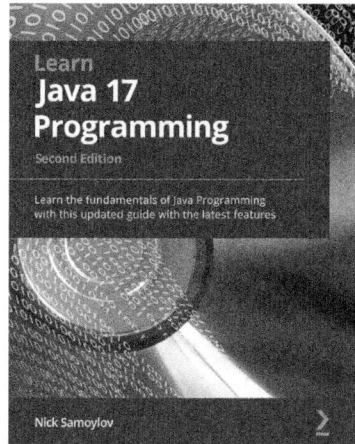

Learn Java 17 Programming - Second Edition

Nick Samoylov

ISBN: 9781803241432

- Understand and apply object-oriented principles in Java
- Explore Java design patterns and best practices to solve everyday problems
- Build user-friendly and attractive GUIs with ease
- Understand the usage of microservices with the help of practical examples
- Discover techniques and idioms for writing high-quality Java code
- Get to grips with the usage of data structures in Java

Packt is searching for authors like you

If you're interested in becoming an author for Packt, please visit `authors.packtpub.com` and apply today. We have worked with thousands of developers and tech professionals, just like you, to help them share their insight with the global tech community. You can make a general application, apply for a specific hot topic that we are recruiting an author for, or submit your own idea.

Share Your Thoughts

Now you've finished *Fundamentals for Self-Taught Programmers*, we'd love to hear your thoughts! Scan the QR code below to go straight to the Amazon review page for this book and share your feedback or leave a review on the site that you purchased it from.

https://packt.link/r/1-801-81211-X

Your review is important to us and the tech community and will help us make sure we're delivering excellent quality content.

Download a free PDF copy of this book

Thanks for purchasing this book!

Do you like to read on the go but are unable to carry your print books everywhere? Is your eBook purchase not compatible with the device of your choice?

Don't worry, now with every Packt book you get a DRM-free PDF version of that book at no cost.

Read anywhere, any place, on any device. Search, copy, and paste code from your favorite technical books directly into your application.

The perks don't stop there, you can get exclusive access to discounts, newsletters, and great free content in your inbox daily

Follow these simple steps to get the benefits:

1. Scan the QR code or visit the link below

`https://packt.link/free-ebook/9781801812115`

2. Submit your proof of purchase
3. That's it! We'll send your free PDF and other benefits to your email directly

Printed in Great Britain
by Amazon